Not your average TIDEWATER GIRL

MARY ANN KENNERLY CLINTON

PRAIRIE MUSE BOOKS INC
LINCOLN, NEBRASKA

This is a true account.
Names, characters, places, and incidents
are the product of the author's experience.
Any resemblance to other persons is entirely coincidental.

TIDEWATER GIRL
ISBN 978-1-952911-39-2

Lincoln, Nebraska

Dedication

To my dear parents who made my life so complete,
providing all the tools I needed in order to survive,
and cushioning each day with endless love.

To John who so completely loved me, and who
carried me up and down steps
throughout the world.

To Mark, who in his early life
thought that all mothers had wheelchairs.
Now, in my present precarious stage,
he begins to understand the battle that has been fought.

To the many characters who filled my life
with devotion, encouragement, and laughter,
and to all the friends who told me that
I had a story to tell, and who
encouraged me every step of the way.

To Fuzzy, who typed and typed relentlessly.
She made it look so easy and did it all so well.
To Marilyn, who proofed and proofed
while sharing a glass of wine.
They so willingly gave their time and
made the end result better.

Mary Ann age 2

Okay, world, here I am!

Prologue

WRITTEN APRIL 15, 2016

I am haunted by my memories. I still grieve for that little girl who was paralyzed from the neck down, not understanding the pain or why her mother couldn't be at her side. Or why the doctors asked her to walk across the floor, when they knew she couldn't.

She tried, really tried to make that first step, but instead she stumbled and fell. The last step.

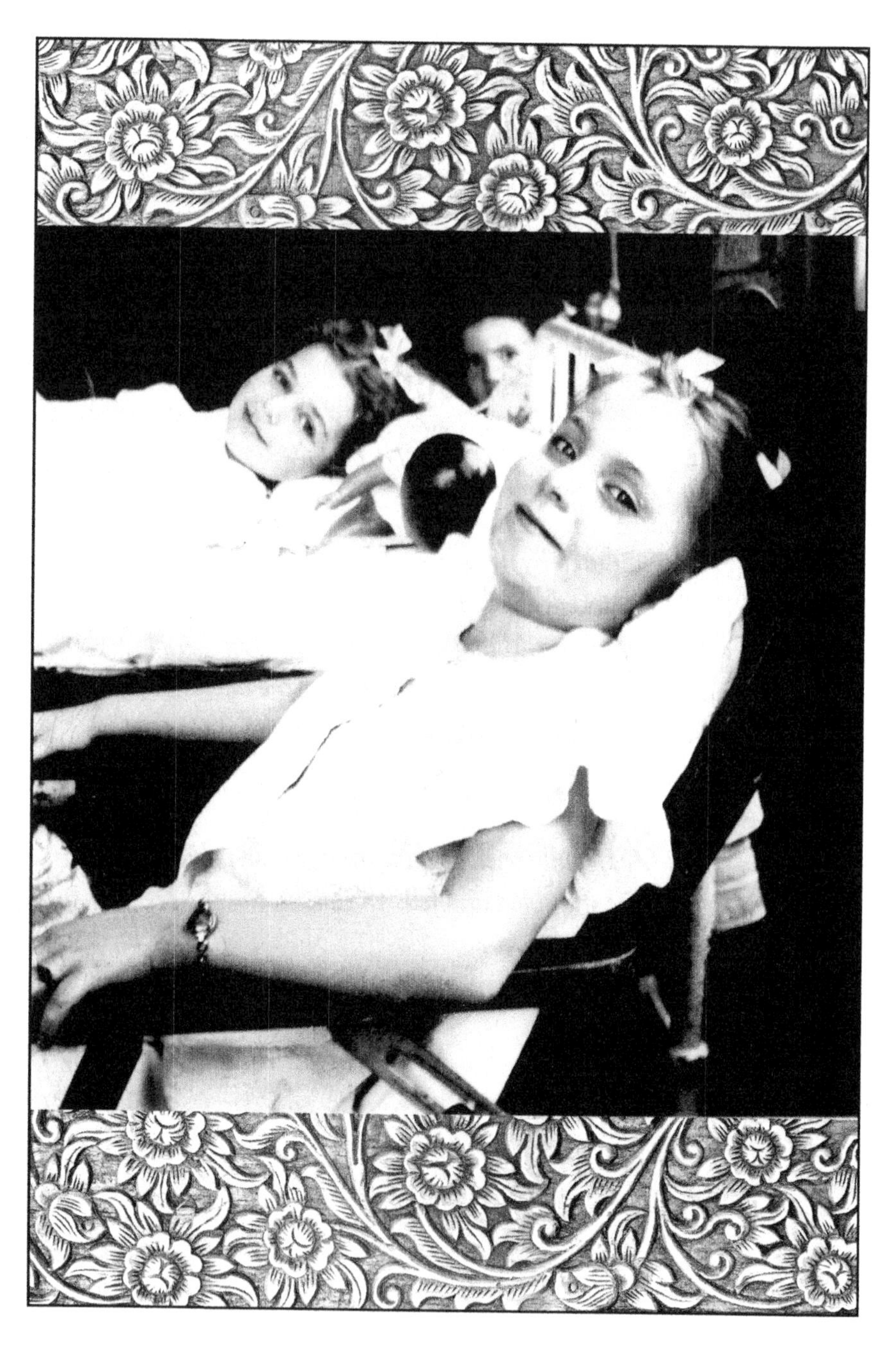

Mary Ann in hospital at age 6 ½

I'm still here

If I Could Walk

WRITTEN NOVEMBER 28, 2020

If I could walk, I'd first run, arms stretched wide
to embrace that freedom of movement.

If I could walk, I would playfully run with a
toddler, pausing to admire a leaf or a gnarly
tree bark or a colony of ants.

If I could walk, I would kneel to eye level
of a child and tell them how wonderfully
they are made.

If I could walk, I would once again walk
the lane to the river. Taking off my shoes, I
would step into the water, the waves lapping
at my ankles, sand between my toes. There is
something of eternity in that moment.

If I could walk, I would dance, dance the night
away. My body would respond to each change
of tempo like a tree responding to wind.

If I could walk, I would kneel at the altar of
God's House and give thanks for a life that,
though imperfect, was filled with endless
blessings from above.

A Better Life With Writing...

WRITTEN OCTOBER 24, 2019

IT HAS BEEN JUST OVER SIX YEARS since I first started writing. I'm not sure why I did start then. John had been urging me for years, even to the point of nagging me.

I read an article entitled "Life from a Wheelchair." I identified with much of what she wrote. Then, I started thinking, I was six years old when I was diagnosed with Infantile Paralysis. I had led a normal life up to that point in time.

But that diagnosis changed everything—my entire life and that of my parents. It is from that perspective that I started writing. Never did I think that I would learn so much. Somehow, putting words on paper, I came to know and understand myself better.

I could look at my reactions to situations and realize fear drove me to withdraw. After all, being completely paralyzed, what else could I do? I saw my parents bravely cope with every situation, smiling through their tears.

I cannot even imagine their terror when they received a phone call at 2:00 a.m. in the morning saying I probably would not be alive after their three-hour drive to the hospital.

Their intense love kept me alive. At that point, they were not allowed in my hospital room. They stood outside the building looking at me in rain, sleet, or snow.

Mother later asked me if I felt abandoned? I didn't. But when I was out of danger and they could enter my room, their touch was the most wonderful thing in the world. I can truthfully say I was never happier than when I was with them—right until they died.

I came to realize other defense mechanisms that I used to make myself acceptable in the normal world. My imagination knew no bounds, and often brought other children to me. So it has been one big accommodation on a daily basis, yet, I have been blessed beyond words.

Now, I turn the tables on myself. What will be *my* legacy? How have I made one life better?

Maybe it's not for me to know. I just know I'm glad that my written words made this life better.

~Mary Ann

A Story to Tell

MY HUSBAND, JOHN, IS RESPONSIBLE FOR THIS. He told me for many, many years, "Mary Ann, you have a story to tell." My response was always, "Who would want to read about me?"

But I guess constant repetition finally go through. About a year after we moved to Lincoln, I saw that there was a creative writing class. I dutifully purchased a red leather portfolio (thinking I surely would need something to prod me to take the time to write). It did! And I did!

The first sentence that I wrote is: "I still grieve for that little girl six years old and suddenly unable to move any part of her body." I distinctly remember holding onto my bed and protesting, "I'm not going to a hospital." Then I was in and out of consciousness when my fever reached 106 degrees.

The doctors wouldn't answer anymore questions from my parents. It was October 7, 1945. I was in isolation at the contagious disease hospital for six weeks. Mother and Daddy could only look at me through an outside window. As I regained consciousness, I would cry. I couldn't understand why they couldn't hold me.

The iron lung was rolled by my bed. The paralysis stopped when it got to my lungs. I was left with only being able to move my head about one-fourth inch. My bladder and digestive system were also paralyzed. It was a grim time.

My parents were called at 2:00 a.m. a few weeks later by the hospital saying I was dying. They lived a four-and-a-half hour drive from the hospital. My parents instinctively knew the right thing to do.

I was hospitalized for fifteen months. In that time, I forgot so much my home, my village, even some relatives. I had had only one month of first grade when polio struck.

At the hospital, a school teacher would come two days a week. My ward had children from nine months to twelve years old. It was certainly not the best learning environment. She tried to make me print, but I got so upset that my parents asked that the teacher not work with me.

The problem was my right arm was still up in a splint. My left arm was a little stronger, but I learned to print with my left hand.

I finally returned home in December of 1946. It was a whole new world. Mother had been shown how to give me physical therapy. I was home schooled, and quickly completed first and second grades. Who says that maturation doesn't help?

After completing first and second grade material, I was allowed to attend public school twice a week. I was an oddity for the other students. Yet to me it was so exciting. My first check-up after attending school for two days a week showed that I had gained so much muscle strength that doctors said, "Let her go to school full time."

So I was mainstreamed long before that term was ever used. Mother came at noon to bring my lunch, help me in the bathroom, and, by holding me under my arms and a volunteer child holding my legs, go down steps and outside for play.

There was one little girl, blond-colored hair and a sprinkling of freckles over her cute little nose, who always made sure she was first in line to carry my legs. I sometimes wondered if she even ate lunch, but just stood waiting for me to come out the door.

How wonderful—this child wanted to help. I love her for it. Children were curious about me, but it didn't take many weeks for their full acceptance. It probably helped that I became scorekeeper for volleyball and softball. As long as I was part of playground activity, I was happy.

Junior and Senior High brought completely new issues to the forefront. This age group is so active and this is when boy-girl relationships begin.

I couldn't dance or play sports. My disability was a glaring reality. Yet I always went to parties and dances, and I always had an escort.

In the middle of my return to a somewhat normal life, my doctors suggested that a muscle transplant be done over two summers. It might enable me to get rid of a brace.

He posed the question to me in front of my parents. My immediate response was, "What do I have to lose?"

So for two summers I was pretty much consumed by surgery, Plaster of Paris casts, and rehab. Alas, it was not successful. The muscles lost much of their strength in the transplant. But I like to think, "Nothing ventured, nothing gained!"

To me, a major event of my teen years was getting a brand new red and white Mercury car, fully equipped with hand controls. It was my ticket to further independence. I drove everywhere. And I could go or come as I wanted. I was overjoyed with my new freedom.

After high school graduation, I entered Drew University in September 1957. I was completely enthralled with life at college —loved the course work and my new life.

The freshman interview was unexpected and most startling. I arrived at the psychologist's office door at the appointed time and opened the door. The professor remained seated behind his desk. I was still walking with crutches then, and my first impression was, "How rude!"

He didn't stand when I entered, nor did he offer to take my crutches when I sat down. I was immediately in battle mode. His first words are imprinted on my brain. "You know I didn't vote for you to enter this university." My response flew out of my mouth, "Good, I don't want any sympathy."

I grew to love this man, and I think he cared for me. He was, after all, professor of my major! And guess who dashed across the stage at graduation to give me a big ole' bear hug!

My life really has been a journey of faith. From my earliest years, my favorite part of the week was going to Sunday School on Sunday. I said my prayers, with my Mother at my side, every night. So it is not so strange that when I was hospitalized at Children's Hospital in Baltimore, I resumed my nightly prayers.

One night the little girl in the bed next to me asked me what was I mumbling. I said, "I'm saying my prayers." Her response was in the question of "What are prayers?" I taught her to pray with me. She was discharged long before I was, but I have always wondered if she remembered her prayers. Prayer has been the constant in my life. The love of family and friends define my life.

Indications of Things to Come

WRITTEN SEPTEMBER 6, 2021

I DON'T KNOW WHEN THAT LITTLE GIRL first showed signs of her very own personality. But from all the stories often told about her, it was at a fairly young age. I do remember that when a lady from the neighborhood asked me my name, I just knew she very well knew who I was. So I told her my name was Susie Brown. Neither I, nor my parents, knew where I got that name. My father was so charmed with my inventiveness that he called me Susie Brown for years.

When I entered first grade, I was completely overwhelmed. It all was so strange. Mother had spent hours, all the time ironing, telling me to never use anybody else's comb and always be sure to go only to the girls' bathroom.

I remember her instructions, but if anybody could confuse matters, it was I. On one occasion, I asked permission to go to the bathroom. Permission granted. I followed all the rules. After completing my mission, I was ready to return to the classroom.

Alas, it would not be so easy. The bathroom door had blown shut and locked! What was a little girl to do? The bathroom window was open; hence, the wind blew the door closed.

And so with mounting terror that my teacher would come to find me, I decided to jump out of the window. It was about a six and a half foot drop to the ground. Punishment by the teacher carried more fear than jumping.

Once I landed, I ran to the front of the building to get back to the classroom. As I came in that front door, my teacher was exiting the classroom to search for me. "Mary Ann Kennerly, where have you been?" I stated my case, trying not to cry. "Well, come on back to the classroom."

That evening my teacher paid a visit to my parents and apologized. I never heard that part. And in the end, just a few weeks later, I was diagnosed with polio. I have often wondered if I had injured myself, would I have gotten polio? However, at the time I did what I thought was right to do. Now, looking back, I think many of my later decisions were made with just that philosophy.

My parents assumed that I would want to go to college. At a young age, yeah, that sounds good. But by the end of my junior year in high school, I was dating one young man, and it was serious. College didn't seem to be as enticing as it once was. And it became less enticing with each passing month. Then maturation came into play. Somehow, I realized I needed more than high school—and I wanted more.

That drive to seek more, to be all that I could be, led me on a path of life, sometimes of despair, that faded into joy beyond belief.

My Day of Infamy

WRITTEN OCTOBER 5, 2018

I HAVE COME FULL CIRCLE THIS WEEK. It was just a few years ago that I first wrote, "I still grieve for that little six-year-old-girl."

On Sunday it will be seventy-three years since polio came to me and completely changed my life. Not only my life, but that of my parents. I miss them terribly on this day. No matter where I lived, we were together on that fateful date—October 7, 1945.

Sometimes little was said about polio struggles. Yet, we were keenly aware of the importance of that day and time. We had waged war on this disease, and we emerged somewhat bloody but certainly unbowed.

I always dread this day because, try as I might, I play the "what if" game. Where might I be if polio had not come into my life? I am pretty sure whatever path I had chosen, it would have been an active one.

Be it dance or sports or whatever, I believe I am wired for motion, all of which has resulted in a huge dose of impatience.

A young child is often heard to say, "I can do it myself." That phrase must be imprinted on my brain, because that thought is a constant in my life each and every day.

Now, age adds another whole dimension. Shoulders complain mightily if I stand or transfer too many times in any given day. I can't be a candidate for surgery, so just grin and bear it.

Buttons. You'd think my fingers had never buttoned or unbuttoned a garment.

Fastening a necklace is an endurance test. And with each unsuccessful try, I become angrier. I use the word "idiot" a lot. I truly don't want to define myself this way, yet I tend to do just that.

There is always the "Oh, well, I don't really care" tactic, but that would be so contrary to who I am. I do care about my words, my self image, my meager accomplishments.

The one constant is that October 7th comes every year. This year, it falls on a Sunday, the very day it was in 1945. It will be a poignant time.

But I did survive, and have survived for a long time, contrary to what we were told.

You know, maybe there is something to that mantra, "I can do it myself."

My Day of Infamy
Part 2

WRITTEN OCTOBER 12, 2018

I SURVIVED MY SEVENTY-THIRD *Day of Infamy*. It was different from all the others. A new element of sadness was added. Most all who made this journey with me are gone—my parents, John, and most all of my family.

The exception being my sister of the heart. She made the comment only the day before that she knew that fateful day would be difficult. And it was. It was really strange.

John always brought me flowers and numerous, wordless hugs. Daddy seldom mentioned that fateful day. When he did, he would recount their frantic drive from Nanticoke to Baltimore.

There was no Bay Bridge then, only ferries. He checked the schedule and realized he would lose an hour waiting for the ferry, so he drove north from Nanticoke through Delaware, across the top of the Bay, back down to northern Baltimore (a five-hour drive). He did recount that I begged for water—I was burning up with fever.

Not many places were open for business on Sunday. Finally, he saw a small restaurant open, stopped and went in to ask for a paper cup of water. They said they didn't have any paper cups.

Daddy said he would pay for a glass with water—he had a very sick little girl in the car. The answer was the same.

When Daddy recounted this, I heard anger and some disbelief in his voice. It had to have been maddening. Somehow, he was able to put that anger aside and continue the trip to get me medical attention.

Mother, on the other hand, remembered each and every minute. And there was such anguish in her voice. It was a miracle that she survived. Even in advanced Alzheimer's, she would say, "If people knew what I know, they would run, not walk, to get their child the polio vaccine."

This journey was made by my parents, by me, and my Lord. Every step of the way, we were given strength and courage. Of course, there were bleak times, yet we came through them.

I am sure God gave me a double dose of feistyness that would explain my mantra "I can do it myself."

Commemoration

WRITTEN OCTOBER 6, 2017

IT'S THAT TIME OF YEAR AGAIN when I become nostalgic. It's such a strong feeling that it is difficult to verbalize. So many memories that I wonder how we survived. Tomorrow it will be seventy-two years ago that I was diagnosed with polio. A long time. A lifetime, really, since I only had six years of being a normal little girl.

Why did it happen? We will never know. There were no other cases in the county, and I'm pretty sure there were no other cases on the entire Eastern Shore. It just happened. Why do I always commemorate the day? Because I find it beneficial—not for what was lost, but that I survived and I have lived a good life despite the challenges.

I can remember standing with braces some nine months later, feeling like I was spinning like a top. That frightened me—I fully expected to start running. Then, I found out how laborious each step was. You had to retrain what muscle strength was left to do so much more than what it was first meant to do.

Isn't that amazing? How wonderfully we are made! The physical therapist called me the Eastern Shore faker. I was able to use a muscle for many purposes—the intended use and assist in other difficult moves for the therapist. I made it difficult to assess the strength of each muscle. It was a new normal for fifteen months.

Life revolved around other disabled children. When I finally was able to go home, I was shocked that I was the different one. It took some time to find a way to be a part of children's play. Then it became a contest as to who would push me in my chair.

Adults would tell me how special I was. It sure didn't feel special, but I soon learned to smile, and hopefully they would move on quickly. As an adult, I realize these adults meant well. How could they know that to me being special set me further apart? And all, *all* I wanted was to be a normal child.

I remember people coming to my parents and asking in hushed tones how was I doing. My hearing was and is quite good, so I heard conversation after conversation—and I learned to respond with my "fool the public" smile. All of this is, to say, these kinds of situations take a toll, particularly for a child with little or no defense mechanism.

Why am I different? Everyone thought it was so wonderful that I was front page news when I walked with braces and crutches across the stage to receive my high school diploma. I couldn't appreciate that at that time, all I wanted was to be a normal teenager. Alas, being a normal teenager was not in the cards for me.

After graduation, a group of girls invited me to go with them for four days to Ocean City where they had a rented apartment. I was sure it would be such fun. The operative word here is "teenager." They got up in the morning—juice and coffee, then to the beach.

First of all, we shared one bathroom. Ugh!!! I didn't like that at all! Then once at the beach, a short walk from the apartment, I would slide from my chair to a beach towel and they would pull me to their designated spot on the sand. So far, so good!

Then came the "chic magnet" games, which lasted until late evening. I was so out of place, so miserable, that I just wanted to go home. But I couldn't let my unhappiness show. What teenage boy is going to show any interest in me? Play frisbee? Nope. Race on the sand? Nope. Swim in the ocean? Nope. Make plans for the evening? Nope. Dancing? Nope.

Lesson learned? Never let yourself get in this helpless position again, no matter how well intentioned others are. AND I NEVER DID!!

It wasn't until college that I began to find the real me and not be ashamed of who I am, of not measuring up. It was liberating. I came to know what was impossible for me and if I had half a chance to accomplish an unknown, THEN GO FOR IT!

So, I am a survivor and this is what I commemorate—after seventy-two years, I am the victor. Oh, yes, there will still be battles to fight, but the victory is still mine!

The Good Life ... Then Comes Polio

WRITTEN APRIL 5, 2022

LIFE IS MUCH LIKE A GIANT PUZZLE. Each minute piece has its own significance. I tend to dwell in the moment. Yet, in my later years, I begin to see more clearly the importance of each phase.

My preschool years were wrapped in the love of parents and grandparents. Life was good. Then came polio, and my world was forever turned upside down.

I don't remember the pain as much as I remember the hotpacks. Strips of wool pulled from a cylinder of steam, wrapped around the body—one limb at a time.

I could not understand why they continued to hurt me. No one ever reassured me that the purpose of this was to make me better. I just thought their mission was to hurt me.

I truly think that my mind went to a neutral place—mind and body were floating somewhere in space. I am sure that I have used this many times throughout my life. I know for certain that I did with the two muscle transplant surgeries.

When I returned to public school, I was overjoyed, but I didn't take into account that I was physically quite different. Inside, I was the same little girl.

Recess was the worst. Everyone ran outside, jumped on the merry-go-round or swings, chased each other, played tag or ball—all required physical movement.

Being an audience of one was just no fun. I needed to interact with my classmates. At some point, I became the scorekeeper.

The teen years were brutal. The only times teens are still is when they sleep. They are thoroughly involved in ball games—softball, baseball, football, volleyball—and the rest of their days are spent dancing.

Bless them, those were, for the most part, happy days. But a little part of me died each time I was a part of that activity. My dear parents seemed to know this, though nothing was ever said.

I am sure they investigated every possibility before giving me a car. Interestingly, only about ten years earlier we had visited F.D.R.'s Hyde Park. Daddy spent a lot of time looking at F.D.R.'s car with hand controls.

I couldn't grasp what took him so long at that exhibit. My eight-year-old self could not think that I would ever drive a car. That was for normal people, not me.

It took college to show me that I had something to offer the world, that I was adaptable, and college studies were fascinating, and I wanted more. College was the best key to the rest of my life.

I was about eight years old when first I acted out my anguish. It was a weekday and I guess I had reached the limit of my frustration level. I threw myself on the floor, wishing that it all would end, sobbing uncontrollably. I didn't want to be touched.

Mother immediately called Daddy who was there in minutes. He sat down on the floor beside me and said, "You don't want to hurt your mother, do you?"

He meant well, but that wasn't what this was about. It was the anguish of a child who had reached the limits of being disabled.

I never did this again. I internalized those feelings. It was the first time, but certainly not the last.

No wonder that many years later as a psychology student in college did I allow myself to see the hurt I dealt with on a daily basis and know that I never gave up or gave in.

So, accommodating Shakespeare, *let the music of life play on*!

Oh, Woe is Me!

WRITTEN MARCH 2021

IS THAT MARY ANN SITTING UNDER A TREE? And just look, she is writing in a book. What will she say? Tears streaming down her face. Is this the time or place to tell of all the wars she has had to face? The six-year-old who could not understand why those she loved most could not hold her hand. No one came to take the pain away or explain my plight.

Should I give up? A still small voice said, "Fight." And I did by just accepting, all the while believing all of this would be rejected. A return to my former life was all that I requested. Little did I know the fight had just begun. There were dark days ahead and too little sun. The long days in hospital when I forgot my friends and home.

My past was just a blot. After fifteen months, I was set free. You would think I would be excited. But, no, not me. It was a very different me who came home that day. Actually, I had few thoughts or words to say. It was all vaguely familiar, but somehow I just didn't fit in.

Where was that little girl who had been ready for life to begin?

Change Changes and Changing

WRITTEN JUNE 8, 2018

I have never been a big fan of change. I like the "steady as you go" approach. Nor am I so naive that I can't see some changes as beneficial. Yet, I do feel more secure in routine, and that feeling is stronger with each passing year.

Pre polio, I really didn't want to be too far from my family. My little world seemed perfect. And I guess it really was. Then came polio.

For months, I was too sick to realize what was really happening. I didn't understand why Mother and Daddy couldn't come into my room. Yet, within a few weeks, I guess I just accepted that that's how it was.

I don't even remember wondering why I couldn't move. I was in this bubble. No one but nurses and doctors could come into my bubble. And when they came, I was so frightened, thinking, "how will they hurt me this time"?

For a few months, this was all I knew. And in my own way, I accepted it. From my vantage point now, what choice did I have but accept my life as it was then.

From Sydenham, I was moved across town to Children's Hospital. Now my parents could come in my room and actually touch me. I thought they came to take me home. So when visiting hours were over and they left me, I was hysterical.

I don't think that the realization of my being paralyzed had ever entered my mind. That little brain that had been so traumatized had gone in neutral gear. It was a safety valve.

Within weeks, I was taken to the big ward where other female patients were, the theory being that the stimulation from being with other children might help me find my place in a totally different world.

Again, I adapted to the change.

You were awakened at 7:00 a.m.; breakfast by 8:30; lunch at twelve noon; dinner at 5:00 p.m.; and lights out at 8:00 p.m. Day after day for a year.

I had physical therapy three times a week. Visiting hours were Thursdays and Sundays, 2:00 to 4:00 p.m.

Again, blessedly, I accepted this routine and I was comfortable with it. Shortly before I was discharged, my parents were given permission to take me in their car to ride through the Baltimore Zoo. I could glimpse what animals were there.

When I was finally discharged to go home, as good as it was, I had forgotten people, their homes, and even my own home seemed strange to me. Once more, I was confronted with change. When people would say, "Aren't you so glad to be home?" I would answer in the perfunctory affirmative.

But, in truth, I didn't know. You see, the hospital routine had become my reality. Once again, I had to find my new normal.

I was home schooled, and every three months had to return to the hospital for a check up and a visit with the doctor. I went through the torments of the damned, absolutely petrified that my doctor would say, "Miss Mary Ann, maybe you should come back to the hospital for additional treatment."

You see, I was once again comfortable with my routine and wanted no part of returning to that old routine.

Eventually, I did return to that same hospital for surgeries two consecutive summers. But I was thirteen and fourteen then. I could be me, because everyone else was in a wheelchair.

I would ask Mother to bring home-baked goodies on visiting days and after visiting hours everybody knew to come to my room.

Maturation changed everything. I wasn't even sure I wanted to go home. Change often comes fast; acceptance comes slowly.

My whole life, it seems, has been adapting to change. Because of my supporting cast, I have been able to survive.

Not only that, I have experienced love, joy, and lots of laughter.

Changes

WRITTEN JUNE 14, 2018

IT NEVER STOPS—CHANGES. If we don't somehow adapt to change, we become lost in an uncertain whirl.

I have had a fair amount of changes; but, blessedly, I have been able to accommodate most of them.

After fifteen months of being in the hospital, I went home. There was a twin bed in the dining room where I was "supposed" to rest a few hours each day. I hated a bed in the dining room. It was so out of place. It was not the proper order of things.

My mother surely felt a twinge of regret when the entire house was somewhat rearranged. Daddy had to carry me up and down the stairs in order for me to get to the bathroom and my bedroom.

Within a three month period, he had an elevator installed, a bathroom on the first floor, and a big playroom on the second floor. Major changes for us all. But it made my world a little more normal.

A neighbor child came to play, and returned home to tell her Mother that "Mary Ann had an 'alligator.'"

After I was deemed strong enough, I was allowed to attend public school three days a week. What an astronomical change it was. I was used to having my friends in wheelchairs just like me. Now I was the different one.

At recess, they would all run, swing on the swings, go on the merry-go-round or see-saw. For some reason, adults thought they were doing me a big favor by letting me watch the activities.

Eau contraire. I didn't want to watch; I wanted to participate! Somehow, I realized if I wanted to be involved, I had to make up games where I could participate. I became a leader of the pack. And thus it remained until I completed the seventh grade.

At which point I became hysterical to know that I would no longer be going to that little country school where I was so accepted. There were only five or six in my class. In the high school, there were three hundred in my class.

It is one thing to stand out in a total school population of eighty students in the entire school; then go to a school where you had three hundred kids in one class. I felt like a fish out of water. Oh, and I refused to use my wheelchair. I walked on crutches.

Still, someone had to carry my books from one class to another. And there were three floors, lots of stairs and, of course, no elevator.

One of the guys from the football team carried me up and down the stairs. Everyone thought I was lucky—I didn't quite see it that way!

At that tender age, beginning your teen years, you are so self conscious —am I too fat? Will he see my pimples? Do I have bad breath? It was such a tense time. I can truthfully say that there was not a lot of joy in my mind then. This was my life for two years.

Then a senior high school was built, campus style. There were four or five buildings connected by an open breezeway in between them. So you were inside and out throughout the day. I walked those halls and breezeway on crutches. I probably clocked a mile each and every day. I had boils under my arms the size of golf balls. "It certainly wasn't the best of times, and certainly not the worst," but close.

When I got my first car, for a brief moment I was just like everyone else. This was the age of drive-ins. So I could load the car with girlfriends, go to the drive in, and see how many boys we knew were there. Interesting! But at least I felt more normal than ever before.

I began dating, and at one point it was serious. But even that only made me more aware of my limitations. Just when I began to get comfortable, it was time to leave for college.

I "did" and "didn't" want to go. I felt I was going to such strange territory where I didn't know anyone and that I could never measure up. I was allowed to keep my car on campus.

My first roommate presented me with a different way of thinking, but we managed. And suddenly life was good again. Independence was good.

John Clinton was chosen to take me to classes, and up and down the numerous steps. I foolishly wrote home and said, "If I ever had a brother, he should be like John." Has that ever come back to haunt me!!!

Every step of the way there have been changes, some handled fairly well, others I have fought until all that was left was to come to terms with it.

My parents certainly—in every way—made the pathways of my journey accessible as possible.

I was given the chance to succeed in life and, even more importantly, my place in life.

Some Family History

WRITTEN AUGUST 17, 2021

The tidewater area of Maryland is my home territory. It is in my blood. I long for the sound of the river washing the shore; the pounding of the waves in a storm. They looked like they were topped with whipped cream as they crashed on the shore.

The weekend before September 15th, watermen were busy at the harbor repairing boats, checking engines; then on September 15th, by 6:00 a.m. there was a steady stream of traffic to the harbor and their boats.

I never heard this sound, but the sound of boat motors starting in the harbor to begin oyster season must have been similar to heralding a king's appearance. It had to be a beautiful sight!

There were two ways to harvest the oysters—tonging or dredging. Tongs were used, much like the tongs we used to place salad ingredients into bowls. The oyster grounds were called beds, some privately owned, some by the state.

My grandfather started the oyster shucking plant in the mid 1930's. After college, Daddy joined him in the oyster business. Dupont—yes, Dupont, wanted to hire him, but he chose going in business with his father.

In the meantime, Daddy had a cousin—Rollinson by name—who lost both parents. They lived just down the lane from my grandparents. Rollinson, as I understand it, was charming, loving, and sensible.

Like many families at that time, the males thought that letting him work on a boat would make him a good man. Rollinson wrote my grandmother—who was like a mother to him—that he, Rollinson, had decided to come home and find some other kind of work.

Alas, this was not to be. Rollinson was stabbed to death in a bar fight in Baltimore before he could come home. My grandmother was bereft. She blamed herself for not stopping Rollinson's decision to go to sea. I know she carried that regret to her grave.

In the fall of 1954, Mother and Daddy and I, plus my best girlfriend and her parents, drove to New York City for a weekend of fun. Ann and I chatted throughout the drive. After arriving at the hotel, we had dinner and planned our next day's activities. By ten o'clock, we were ready for bed.

The best of laid plans! At 4:00 a.m., the phone rang and it was my grandfather Kennerly calling to say that one of the warehouses was on fire. By 4:01 a.m., we were on our way back to Maryland. The scene was grim. Little of the warehouse was left. Thankfully, no other building was burned.

What was so impactful to me was the response of the people in the surrounding villages. They came to the harbor, offered help in any way that was needed. They stopped at the house and expressed their concern. At the time, I think Daddy had the most employees in the county. Yet, each and every one wanted to offer their help. Small town living is at its best in difficult times.

These people of my little villages were special. For example, one man watching me struggle to walk with braces and crutches—pointed to a spot on the ground and said, "You put your feets right there and you'll be on your way." I wanted to hug him, it showed such pure human kindness.

Never will I forget all the phone calls to my parents asking if they could stand outside the church windows and watch me get married. And they came and stood outside in 90 degrees heat and humidity!

These dear ones showered me with so many kindnesses from tons of greeting cards whenever I was hospitalized, for birthdays, holidays, to handmade items or baked treats or books they thought I might enjoy.

I was wrapped in their loving care. No wonder I feel so very blessed!

Precious Moments

WRITTEN JANUARY 18, 2022

THERE ARE MOMENTS IN TIME throughout my life that are like treasures—they cause me to smile, cry, or outright laugh.

One such early memory was riding my tricycle behind my mother riding her bicycle. This was big time! We didn't get very far because I insisted on trailing my mother so close that I would hit her bike.

She would have to stop, caution me not to get so close to her bicycle. I would quickly promise that I would do just that. And, just as quickly, I would bump into her again.

Now, dear reader, two-and-a-half years later, I wanted to race my wheelchair against another, only to crash into a radiator, catapult to the floor, break my leg and chip an ankle!

Fast forward again about twelve years. Some guys from the neighborhood challenged me to a drag race. I had my car and driver's license.

What red-blooded American girl would turn down these teenage boys' challenge? I accepted the challenge and left them in my dust!

From my college in New Jersey, I would drive by myself back to Maryland for the holidays. I quickly learned where the state police would try to conceal their car and pick up speeders.

Of course, I whizzed by a spot and he had me dead to right. So I did what comes naturally to me I gave a slight wave, big smile, and slowed down.

This all goes to show I have always had a special relationship to wheels—I pushed the limits on all my wheels!

When the late Jack Moors asked me why I went so fast in my scooter, I quickly responded, "I love the wind in my hair."

He never let me forget it!

Precious Moments
Part 2

WRITTEN FEBRUARY 1, 2022

WHEN OUR SON MARK WAS NEARLY A YEAR OLD, I began working in the office of my father's seafood business. I did the bookkeeping, or it might be better said I learned how to do the bookkeeping for all three of the businesses.

I never had a great love affair with numbers, but I somehow managed to balance all three sets of books and earned the respect of the tax collector.

On my way to work, I would leave Mark with my mother and pick him up on the way home. On one occasion, she carried Mark in his snow suit to the car and gave him a graham cracker. Big mistake!

Mark had only a few teeth at the time, consequently he mushed the graham cracker, then would pat me and say "nice mommy." I loved the sentiment, but wet graham cracker crumbs not so much.

By the time I had driven the twenty-five miles home, I looked like a huge graham cracker crust. I had crumbs on my glasses, in my hair, on my coat. I thanked Mother, but asked that she not do that again.

Turn the clock back several—maybe many—decades. My parents and I were in New York City. Daddy really didn't like to shop. Mother and I, on the other hand, liked nothing more than an all day shopping spree.

Daddy knew that Mother couldn't push me in the wheelchair through the streets of New York City, so Daddy said he would push me to Gimbel's or Macy's since it wasn't far from our hotel.

Of course, the streets were packed with people. Daddy started the journey well enough. From my point of view, it was a belt buckle moving picture.

All of a sudden, this very slight young woman veered in front of us. There was no way to stop from hitting her. She lurched to one side, turned, and picked up the high heel of her shoe and continued her journey, walking with one good shoe and long nails protruding from the heel area of her other shoe.

Of course, I thought it was funny and was laughing uproariously. My father failed to see any humor at all and sternly asked me to stop laughing which only made it funnier to me.

More precious moments—my husband John and I took a driving tour of the L.B.J. area in Texas. As we passed the ranch, Mrs. Johnson was seated on a chaise lounge. Our driver tooted the horn, and Mrs. Johnson gave us a big wave.

Somehow, that fit the image I had of Mrs. Johnson, a most gracious woman. I had hoped to see an offspring of Little Beagle Johnson, but my luck ran out.

In the early '50's, my parents and I were touring the White House. Dear reader, you must know, at that time not many wheelchair disabled people were seen in public places. Quite simply, people didn't know what to do with us.

The White House was a prime example. How could you accommodate wheelchairs? There was one elevator, of course, for F.D.R. They allowed me to use the President's elevator. When the elevator opened, out walked Harry S. Truman! I mainly saw his back, but I had seen the President!

Reminiscent of that time, only some sixty years later we went to England. Everyone would ask me what I wanted to see. My reply was always the same—the Queen, of course. And I did just that!

We had toured Windsor Castle, and were in the gift shop when this dear little lady said, "If you want to see the Queen, go over there," pointing to a spot where the castle wasn't far away.

Mark pushed me through a quickly gathering crowd to the very front.

AND THERE SHE WAS! Walking like a young woman, the Queen had been at Windsor for a luncheon.

What did I do? I cried. It was unbelievable!

The Greatest of These is Love

WRITTEN JUNE 24, 2016

I have always said that God knew what He was doing when He gave me to my mother. I think she literally lived and breathed for me—and there were times she almost did.

Mother was a pretty woman who dressed with such flair. Daddy said he fell in love with her because of her coal black hair with blue highlights. They dated in high school. Then Daddy went to college and Mother went to Baltimore for nurse's training. She came home after eighteen months. It has always been a mystery to me as to what caused her to leave. When I asked both my parents about this, they were always vague about what happened. But those very nursing skills served me well.

Mother and Daddy married in 1935. She became in charge of the payroll for both the oyster business and the farm. She became my mother when I was born in 1939. In my adult years, she was not only mother, but my best friend. I am told she loved dressing me in pretty little dresses and white hightop shoes that were polished each nap time. She knelt with me each night as I said my prayers.

As good a mother as she was, I always managed to keep life interesting—I loved to run away! She thought I was sleeping, when she was called to the neighbors next door. She could see my bedroom window which was open, so it was with utter disbelief that she heard a man's voice say, "Ma'am, is this your little girl?" I had climbed out of the crib, came down the steps from the second floor, out the back door, and headed down the lane to the river.

Fortunately, carpenters were there building a log cabin for a doctor. I found their lunch boxes and began eating from them when I was discovered. It was just the first of my many escapes. Mother tried everything to stop these frightening escapes. She tied me to the clothes line. I quickly took care of that by winding myself in the rope. Mother decided she would take her chances while being even more diligent in checking on me. In later years, she told me she wished that she had let those little legs run as far as they could!

While in the hospital, I eventually was able to sit in a wheelchair. I needed clothes, so Mother went shopping. It had been seven months since I had had real clothes on my body. The department store, like Dillards, had a large selection of children's clothes. Mother selected eight or nine dresses, all being able to slide over my head easily.

She was questioned by the clerk as to why so many dresses. The clerk must have called the front office, and one of the owners, Albert Hutzler by name, came to the children's department. Mother explained that she had a daughter who had had polio and that now that I could be out of bed, I needed dresses.

Mr. Hutzler said, "Mrs. Kennerly, you take all the dresses you want and take your time returning any she can't use." I have been blessed so many times by the sheer goodness of humanity.

There is more to the story. Mother left a supply of dresses for me, and when she returned the following visiting day, she was more than surprised, maybe a little angry, to see all the little girls in the ward dressed in my dresses. Mother corrected that situation in a hurry!

Mother was taught by the physical therapist at the hospital the exercises I would need to do daily when I got home. She was a natural, thanks to her nurses' training. It had been so long since I had seen home that I had forgotten so much. Home looked familiar, but different. It was I who was different. It took some getting used to before hospital routine faded.

As I gained strength, I was tutored at home twice a week. In a short time I was, class wise, right where I should be. Mother made sure that other children came to play. The number of treats she served over time is astounding. We had ice cream floats, fresh limeade, fresh lemonade, pretzels, or homemade apple sauce, and cookies. She made it all seem so effortless. Her love knew no limits.

In high school, Mother made sure I would be a part of any of the current fads—a silver disc with initials on a chain, a charcoal blazer just like all my friends. When I was in college, she brought a seamstress with a portable sewing machine, plus my two grandmothers, so that a beautiful cocktail dress could be fitted properly for Spring Weekend, a major social time in the life of college students. Nothing was too much for mother. Mother paved over so many rough spots for me. She truly was extraordinary.

In my married life, she would say, "You look so weary, you are going home with me." Then I would spend three or four days at the Kennerly spa! I would sleep late, have lunch on a tray, and Mother and I would have a gin and tonic at four o'clock in front of the fireplace where we would talk and talk and talk!

In 1997, Mother was diagnosed with Alzheimer's disease. For a few more years, life with her was mostly normal. She gradually became blind, but her love for me was ever abundant. She thought I was the prettiest, the smartest, and did the nicest things for her. What I did was just try to make her life as pleasant as possible.

In January of 2009, everything went wrong. She entered the hospital, but they soon said they could do nothing for her; she should go to Hospice. Daddy was strongly against the move. I think he couldn't admit the end was near. Somehow I convinced him that it was best, and it was one of the few times he didn't fight me.

A week later, the pastor at the Hospice unit asked to speak with me. She told me that my father kept telling her to tell my mother to "keep up the good fight so she could come home."

The pastor said, "She is fighting, but it's futile."

So I spent the night with her and told her how much I loved her and thanked her for making my life so wonderful. Then I said to her, "Mother, it's time to go with God." I kissed her at 7:15 a.m. and told her once more, "I'll always love you; go with God." She died an hour later. She was a remarkable woman, a mother that filled my life with love.

The October before mother died, I was once again reminded by her enduring love. Daddy called that Sunday afternoon, and said, "Mary Ann, I probably shouldn't tell you this, but all day yesterday your Mother kept asking, "What day is it?" And he would respond, "Dorothy, it's Saturday." She asked the same thing four or five times more that day. I'm sure he became frustrated, and I can hear him say, "Now, Dorothy, I've told you many times, and this is the last time, 'it's Saturday.'"

He picked up the Sunday paper early the next morning, when it hit him—Saturday was October 7th, that infamous day 64 years ago that I had been stricken with polio. Somehow, in that terrible haze which is Alzheimer's, love proved stronger—that dear soul remembered. I cried and thanked Daddy for telling me. You see, it was her last gift of love. Indeed, yes, "The greatest of these is Love."

The Art of Falling

WRITTEN MARCH 14, 2022

ANYONE WHO HAS INJURED A LEG OR TWO knows the consequences of a fall can run the gamut from "get up quickly before anyone sees you" or, in my case, "I learned to look for the biggest football player!"

I innately knew how to fall because, for the most part when I fell, I really wasn't seriously injured.

One of my early notorious falls occurred when I pulled myself up from the toilet using the sink in front of me like a handle bar. I didn't move, but the sink did! I pulled it out of the wall.

The plumber, when he reattached the sink, said, "She'll have to use dynamite to move it now." As far as I know, it still stands.

Another time in high school, students were led outside for the May Day celebration. Before the program had started, I came out of that door and was so engrossed with all the pretty girls, I missed a step and down I went!

My guardian angel must have been on duty. I was bruised and shaken, but more embarrassed than anything!

In college, I was going into my favorite professor's classroom. It had been raining, and a leaf or two had come in on someone's shoe.

Naturally, my crutch came into contact with the leaf, down I went, hitting my head on the professor's platform. It nearly knocked me out, but all I could say to John was "get me up before the professor comes."

Even today, I could give you the exact date because my class notes looked like hieroglyphics.

The view from the floor leaves a lot to be desired. The altitude of standing is much preferred.

Still, my personal view is belt buckle level!

Dennis

WRITTEN MAY 27, 2021

DENNIS WAS A BIG PART OF MY GROWING UP and right up to our marriage. He could read. He had a good mind. He really didn't speak the local Negro dialect. No wonder he passed as a white man in Philadelphia where he worked for Sears during the depression years. His was a responsible job, but he wanted to return home to Maryland after the depression.

I loved riding in the car with him as he took me to and from school. Then I would pelt him with questions as what it was like when he was a little boy. He told me he started working when he was three years old.

Of course, I said that it wasn't possible. His job was to fan the babies in the cradles on the porch. Read 'white man's babies'. He had to keep flies off of the little ones. Lest you think it was whenever, it wasn't. It was seven days a week.

My mother, in one of her reminiscing moods, said she remembered Dennis' mother who smoked a corncob pipe and drove a team of oxen. They called her Aunt Mary Wash, and she was born a slave. It is difficult to know her real name or much more of her hard life, but I would be interested in her story.

Dennis would recite poems, such as:

> "When I was a boy, I lived by myself.
> All the bread and cheese I got, I put on the shelf."

There was more, but my memory fails me. There was a second poem he would often recite:

> "There was a girl from Pocomoke.
> She ate oysters 'til she choked.
> She loved them stewed, she loved them fried.
> She ate those oysters 'til she died."

This could have been early rap music. History shows that Negroes documented and entertained by that oral tradition. It is sad that so much of that tradition is lost forever.

Early in Dennis' employment at my father's seafood business, he heard the office phone ring. Knowing the secretaries were not there, he answered the phone. The man calling asked to speak to my father. Now, when Dennis got excited, he stuttered. So Dennis tried to answer, but all he could manage was: "I, I, I tell, tell him." The man on the other end stuttered a response.

Dennis nervously waited for my father and when he arrived, Dennis said, "Captain June," (a nickname for my father used by many), "I think, I, I made someone mad."

Daddy went into the office, saw the telephone number Dennis had left, and called. The caller was an engineer who was working with Daddy on adding two industrial freezers. It wasn't many minutes before Daddy started laughing. You see, the engineer stuttered and thought Dennis was mocking him!

Julius was another man from the Negro community. He had a

weather beaten house, a mule, some hogs, and chickens. Whenever anyone needed their garden tilled, Julius was the man. Julius may have had half of his teeth, certainly no more, but he had the nicest smile, a genuine smile that lit up his face.

You knew exactly when Julius was at work—you heard the jingle of the mules' harness, then "yee haw." "Yee haw" was "right" and "left" in mule language. I remember being impressed that Julius—who had so little—was content, dare I say, happy!

Custis was another notable man from the Negro community. I don't think he had a house. He stayed with whomever would offer him shelter. He was available for "odd jobs" throughout the neighborhood.

My maternal grandmother insisted on calling him "Cursis." I could not convince her otherwise.

She would go find Custis to crank a freezer of homemade ice cream and there were many freezers of ice cream! As soon as his pay hit his hand, Custis was off to find as many bottles of whiskey as he could. Finding whiskey was never a problem for Custis. Then he was happy. And when he was happy, he would walk out on a rugged stone jetty that embraced the harbor, sit down and sing.

I can remember hearing him singing on a foggy night, completely obscured, and after each hymn came a "Praise the Lord"!

These people and many more like them are part of the fabric of my life. I value their lives. They showed me patience and that you can be content with very little. And, yes, every life is meaningful.

New York City

WRITTEN MAY 13, 2021

IT'S BEEN A GOOD SPRING DAY. The doctor said I could attend public school full time. It was joy unbound. My school mates always wanted to push my chair, making me feel a part of their world again. Miss Travers, my teacher, had to scold me today—I felt as if I had won the

Medal of Honor.

It all started when we had to choose a continent to trace and color. I had a big box of crayons which I gladly shared. Shared meant sliding the crayon box on the old oil floors back and forth. I admit it was a bit noisy and even more distracting.

So Miss Travers said, in her "I mean business" voice, "Why don't you just pass the box." I did and they did. Then I was teased unmercifully about the color I chose for Australia—pink, no matter! I thought it was beautiful.

So there I am in bed, after a nice hot bath, under my princess comforter (pink and blue), replaying the events of a great day. Then I hear them, the peepers (tree frogs) loud like a chorus welcoming spring. My eyes close. Looking forward to another great day at school.

My first big trip with my parents was to New York City. We drove from Maryland to Wilmington, Delaware, and took the train to New York. I was so excited and was traveling with my brand new luggage marked with my initials. When the porter blithely tossed my suitcase on the cart, my mouth opened, my father jiggled my chair as a cautionary warning. So, I was reduced to giving him a very dirty look. How dare he throw my suitcase like that! I was surely a country mouse.

We went to the Empire State building. I was first impressed by having to take two elevators to reach the top. The view was breathtaking. I thought I surely could touch the clouds.

Our next stop was a visit to Gimbels. As we managed the crowds, a young woman stepped in front of us. There was no way Daddy could avoid hitting her. She lurched to one side, stopped to pick up the heel of her shoe as she tried to balance herself on the nails of her heel-less shoe. I laughed; couldn't stop laughing, further embarrassing my father. He really didn't appreciate my humor.

We did the carriage ride in Central Park and went to the Barnum and Bailey circus. Sitting between my parents, one would say "Look at the tigers" while the other would say "Look at the elephants." Finally, I said, "I can't look at two things at once."

Emmet Kelley was my favorite. His face was so sad until he saw a pretty girl, then a red heart on his chest lit up and pulsed. I feel so fortunate that I saw his most famous sweeping act. From the center ring, he would sweep the spotlight into smaller and smaller circles. Then everything went black. Amazing, he never said a word. He didn't have to. His actions said it all.

Reflecting on this journey, I am truly touched and understand that this trip was symbolic—their daughter may be disabled, but she would see and experience as much as possible. And that's how it was for all of my life.

Loraine
My Sister of the Heart

WRITTEN DECEMBER 20, 2019

AND SO IT IS—INTO EACH LIFE SOME RAIN MUST FALL. Thanksgiving and Christmas have come and gone. The glow of these holidays were somewhat subdued.

My sister of the heart, Loraine, left this earth two days before Christmas. She had been in and out of the hospital all fall until finally her heart could no longer function.

I knew it was imminent, yet really couldn't accept that fact. I called her on a Saturday, and she said she wasn't feeling well and couldn't talk. I said, "We will talk tomorrow." When I called, no answer. I called five more times, with the same result.

Finally, heart pounding, I phoned one of her sons, who told me she was back in the hospital and things didn't look so good, but she had asked for her cell phone.

I called Monday and left a message, telling her I was holding her hand on this final journey. I don't know if she ever heard the message, but so hope so. She died early December 23rd.

I felt as if the state of my early life was erased. Loraine was the last in my family who had shared so much of my early life. I think God gently reminded me of how fortunate I was.

In the summers, Loraine and I would spend weeks together—first at her house, then at mine. She would go with my parents and me on vacation. One of the earliest trips was to Boston, Massachusetts. It was at least a ten hour drive from our home in Maryland, and it was very hot, and the car did not have air conditioning then.

My parents were exhausted, but not Loraine and me. My parents wanted an early bed time. We dutifully took our baths and got in bed. In the adjoining bedroom, my parents did the same.

And what to our wondering eyes should appear when the lights were turned off, a neon sign outside across the street that read "Typewriters, Watts Typewriters, Typewriters, Watts, Watts Typewriters."

Loraine and I took turns reading the sign over and over, laughing every few words. It almost goes without saying that our sign reading and laughter did not endear us to my parents.

Finally, we heard the decree. "If you two don't stop talking and close your eyes, we'll leave for home tomorrow morning." Of course, there was a bit of muffled laughter, and then silence. Loraine and I had many shared times like this.

Loraine had a bubbly personality. She laughed a lot growing up. Loraine was my matron of honor when John and I were married.

A few years later, I was just pregnant, and we were living down the street from Loraine's parents. The pastor of the church that we had started to attend had come to visit. It was summertime.

And suddenly I heard Loraine on the sidewalk singing, "Show me the way to go home," with a jug of apple cider slung over her shoulder. She popped in the door, and I said, "Hi, come meet our pastor."

She stopped dead in her tracks, probably hoping the floor would open and she could fall through! Our pastor, never at a loss for words, said, "I love apple cider. John, let's have some."

All's well that ends well!

I got most of Loraine's clothes when she outgrew them. I was known to say, "I hope you grow fast 'cause I really like that dress!" Anything that belonged to Loraine was special to me.

We often reminded each other of those special times.

I still listen for her daily call or start to phone her. How very blessed I am to have such a sister of the heart.

Cheating

WRITTEN AUGUST 16, 2019

I STARTED READING A NEW BOOK THIS WEEK, intrigued by the title, "Anonymous Woman." The main character was taking a personality test for a psychiatrist. One of the first questions on the survey was, "Have you ever cheated?" The subject answered in the affirmative.

It made me think how I would have answered the question. My initial reaction was "I don't think so." Then I had to do some soul searching.

I certainly am no "goody two shoes," but try as I might I could not think of any time that I had actually cheated.

What I do remember is trying to get rid of the instrument of punishment—my father's wooden hairbrush! He would tap my bottom with it twice, and I would howl with humiliation. It really didn't hurt, but the brush became the object of hate.

To me, it was obvious what I must do—get rid of that hateful brush! So, when no one was in the two rooms (den and kitchen), I put the brush in with the trash, carefully hiding it in all the discarded papers.

I felt rather proud of myself—until I heard daddy ask, "Has anybody seen my hairbrush"? I pretended not to hear the question. Then as he looked st me very sternly, and still trying to maintain my innocence, I suggested that "maybe it fell into the trash container"!

Not only did I not cheat, I couldn't lie very well either.

And that is how I have always been. I think growing up I must have had every board game known to mankind. So in the summertime, our house was party central.

My sister of the heart was visiting me for the week and, as usual, neighborhood kids came for an afternoon of fun.

Monopoly was the game of the day. I was so close to winning, until Loraine pulled off a deal that allowed her to win. I can't say I was especially upset. I just loved the fact that kids were there to play.

After we were in bed that night, Loraine started to cry, and she told me she had cheated in order to win, and apologized. I said it was okay. I think this says more about me. Just to interact with other children was so important. It didn't matter—win, lose, or draw.

When I got my car and driver's license, daddy warned me not to go into certain areas of the county. I respected his proclamation—until I didn't! I went into that restricted area and turned the car around immediately and left.

Now, I knew someone there probably saw my car and would gleefully tell all who would listen. So, home I went, and found my father, and said, "Before you hear this from someone else, yes, I went there. It was disgusting, and you don't have to worry about me ever returning there!"

So, I don't think I have ever cheated, but it's for sure I'm no angel. Yet, my code of behavior is as natural as breathing. I can't say why. It's just who I am.

One Halloween I went trick or treating with a group of my friends. We were all elementary school age. And, of course, we had to go to our teacher's home. I really loved this teacher. While we were talking, a few of the group disappeared only to return minutes later and we all continued our trick or treating.

The next day the teacher angrily said, "Mary Ann Kennerly, did you keep me talking while the others went to my rather secluded clotheslline, remove all pieces of clothing, and wrap them in mud?"

"No." I guess I played the stooge. I had no idea what they did. And I felt that they had in a way taken advantage of my situation—which, indeed, they had. I hated their actions and never did see what pleasure they got from doing such.

Lemons to Lemonade

WRITTEN MAY 6, 2021

SOMEONE ONCE ASKED ME, "How would you like to be remembered?" My response, then and now, "A woman of faith." For, indeed, it has been faith that carried me through those dark times.

As a very little girl, Mother would say prayers with me each night—on our knees, of course. When I was first stricken with polio, I spent the first two months in a Contagious Disease Hospital. No one was allowed in my ward. My parents would stand outside of my window and wave and mouth their love for me.

When released from there, I was sent to Children's Hospital in another part of Baltimore. It was there that I was reintroduced to faith by a visiting Sunday School teacher who appeared each week.

The ward had at least twenty-five beds, all filled with children from around the world—Chile, South Africa, India, Mexico, and from all over the United States.

At one point, I had a young girl from far western Maryland in the bed next to me. We became good friends and listened to radio programs together and played tag with mirrors reflecting on the ceiling. Twila had the advantage—she could use both arms, while I could use only one. But the fun was in the challenge.

One night after lights out, I was saying my prayers when Twila asked, "Whatever are you mumbling?" She didn't know what prayer was? So from that time on, we said prayers together each night.

I always wondered what she remembered when she got home. I am convinced that children are the very best at making lemonade out of lemons!

In the summers of 1953 and '54, I returned to the hospital for muscle transplant surgeries. This was somewhat experimental. But when my doctor said, "Miss Mary Ann, what do you think about the surgeries?" my reply was, "What do I have to lose?" If successful, I would get rid of one half of my braces; if not, things would remain the same.

The first surgery went well—until I went into shock from blood loss. However, after that, recovery was good, and life was even better. My parents and friends always came with homemade candy, cookies, cake, and fruit. So after visiting hours, the other young people (ages 13 to 17) dashed into my room for a party, and party we did! Or, as today's generation says,"hang out."

It was the age of rock and roll and transistor radios. It was fun. Therapy was incidental. I enjoyed myself to the point that when I was discharged, I was reluctant to go home. Lemons into lemonade!

The second summer, the situation was the same. Except for Leo, 16 years old and a new polio. He lived on a farm and loved driving a tractor and square dancing on Saturday night.

When he saw his leg braces like mine, he fell into a pit of despair. At first he refused to see anyone, but I went in anyway. We talked about our dreams and wondered if any of them would come true. At that point, I had been disabled much longer and perhaps saw the bigger picture.

He returned to his home much later, got a convertible with hand controls, and a part time job. Then he went off my radar. We had written to each other up to that time. I later learned that he had committed suicide.

From an adult perspective, I think the "young" polios adapted much easier. The "older" polios realized how great their loss, and how difficult it was to fit into the normal world. Their lemonade was barely bittersweet.

More Village Love

WRITTEN OCTOBER 13, 2021

AS A CHILD, I FOUND MRS. ADDIA ENORMOUSLY INTERESTING. She would drive to the post office every afternoon to get her mail.

Her car was a 1926 to 1928 Chevrolet Coupe comprised of a front seat and a trunk. I supposed you could place a small package in back of the front seat, but that certainly was the limit.

To me, the most interesting thing was how she drove. Head was turned to the left, leaving only one eye looking forward!

Thinking this was an enviable way to drive, I started riding my tricycle in the same manner. My mother couldn't understand my new driving technique. I had to explain to her that I was driving like Mrs. Addia. This was quite the topic of conversation in the neighborhood for a few days!

Looking back, I can see that Mrs. Addia's life had some real low times. She had worked in the little bank that served the three small communities, until funds were discovered missing and it was found that Mrs. Addia had misappropriated these funds. Of course, she lost her job, and the bank closed its doors.

I am unsure if she served any prison time. I think some men in the three neighborhoods paid back her debt.

Mrs. Addie was married, but did not have children; yet, she bought toys that little girls would love. She had the five Dionne Quintuplets. And when I first came home from the hospital, she gave me one of the quintuplets—Ceceil, I believe.

Never again was she part of the community. She was there, but she wasn't. Her husband was the first to die and it wasn't much later that she died, also.

Her house was found to be filled with valuable antiques crystal, china, and more toys. It was a sad life I always wondered if she was ever happy or content. She sold eggs and anything else home grown.

She worked hard and, yet, she had little contact with anyone. Hers was a sad life, indeed. I just wish I knew more about her in her early years.

Boys to Men

WRITTEN NOVEMBER 10, 2016

IN JUNIOR AND SENIOR HIGH SCHOOL, I always seemed to have an escort to most of the dances and parties. It was time, however, even before that, I found a friend or he found me. We shared stories of our lives. I think you could call it *simpatico*. Alas, Kenny moved away. We corresponded for a few years and then we each became busy with our own lives.

Interestingly enough, Kenny found me again as a college freshman. We met and talked of old times, old acquaintances. At some point, I realized he wanted to tell me he had found the girl for him. I congratulated him. But as he got out of the car, he said, "You are a beautiful young woman." He was always sweet like that, and I count this period of my life as the best introduction to the male/female relationship.

Then there was the unwanted suitor. He pedaled twenty-five miles on his bicycle to visit me in Nanticoke. No warning; he just showed up. As fate would have it, I was visiting my grandmother four houses away. When Mother phoned to ask if she could send him to Gram's, I replied loudly and clearly, "No. Send him back to Salisbury."

Gram was not happy with me. She wanted to invite him to dinner!! That was the end to even a probable friendship! Tommy went to many events with me throughout senior high school. He had a brilliant mind and wry sense of humor. I don't think he ever forgot a word that he read. He was in the group that Daddy took out on the boat one summer. Of course, Tommy dropped something overboard and he always said, "Oh, fudge says the judge; oh, fury says the jury." Small doses of his humor was enough for me.

Then came David. I had gone through school with him. It was when I was sixteen that we started dating. We really had some good times. There were about four other couples in the area and so the cars would park in a circle, turn on rock and roll, sit on the hood of the car, and just enjoy. So many laughs and exchanges of viewpoints. It ran the gamut. There was an occasional movie trip to the drive-in. The fifties movies replicated our time perfectly. It was fun.

College changed everything. I wanted to go, but didn't want to leave David. I wore his class ring on a chain around my neck. We agreed we would write and see each other on vacations, and somehow things would work out. I was so very conflicted. And it was worse when guys asked me out to college events. At first, I refused invitations. Then I realized I really wanted to accept these invitations. I didn't want to miss anything!

So, unexpectedly, I drove home to Maryland and arranged to see David. I explained that I thought we both should have social lives—we were young and had some living to do. It wasn't easy, but I felt I had done the right thing.

Back at Drew, I jumped in the social whirl totally. One evening I had three different dates: one for dinner; one to study in the library; and at 10:30 p.m. I was paged and accepted the invite to go for apple pie and coffee! This was a crash course in socialization like no other. I quickly identified the Casanova, but enjoyed it all. It was truly a learning experience that I wouldn't trade for anything.

Now John, whom I saw every day, was becoming more and more interesting. John was a scholarship student and worked at various jobs for spending money. We both liked theatre and music; and because we were not that far from N.Y.C., and I had a car, we could take advantage of Broadway offerings. We saw *Music Man, Bye Bye Birdie, Flower Drum Song, Gypsy,* and ate at trendy restaurants.

John soon became aware of how much I loved flowers and would bring me a long stem rose each week. Those were the days! By the way, I did study. I have Jimminy Cricket permanently on my shoulder, but

I'm sure I could have studied more!

Life is interesting. My disability sheltered me from much give and take of my peer group, so I was a novice player at best. But when circumstances occurred, I was able to separate the wheat from the chaff. As always, God was there to guide me.

Advanced Freedom

WRITTEN MAY 12, 2021

Each year at school, the fifth, sixth and seventh graders got to go on a day trip. My first trip was to Annapolis, the state capital of Maryland. The capitol building is the oldest state capitol building still in use. George Washington resigned his military commission here. This was a big deal. More importantly to me, I got to ride on the bus with my classmates!

Dennis, who was employed by my father and took me to and from school each day, went with us to lift me on and off the bus and push my chair. Surprise, surprise, there were no elevators to the visitors gallery and the law said that no one could sit on the main floor. So the delegate from our county had a bill of exception just for that day for Dennis and me to sit on the floor. The floor recognized me and Dennis. I was so impressed!

Revisiting this memory, I find some thing else much more important. Dennis was a Negro who easily passed for White. However, Negroes were not allowed on the floor and probably not in the gallery either. No one knew! And the building didn't collapse! It was just a normal day except that it wasn't! In the following years, we went to Philadelphia and Washington, D.C., but the trip to Annapolis stood out from all the rest.

A sixteenth birthday is always special. To me, it felt like the little girl time was over. New and exciting times were on the horizon. I celebrated with a party for twelve or fourteen friends. Daddy took us for a boat ride. Then we came back for ice cream and cake—both homemade.

But my seventeenth birthday was the game changer. Mother instructed me to dress for a party with my grandparents. My paternal grandfather had passed away the preceding January, so it was a bitter sweet time. At 7:00 p.m., a knock was heard at the front door. A man that I slightly knew gave me an envelope and asked me to read it. His son was one of the football players who carried me up and down steps at school.

My grandfather, who was deceased, had left instructions that he wanted to give me my first car. In the driveway was this beautiful red and white Mercury Montclair with hand controls. I didn't know whether to cry or laugh—I did both, I think. Here was my ticket to advanced freedom. For the first time since 1945, I was able to leave the house on my own! It was exhilarating!

A state police officer taught me to drive and all the rules of the road. By the time I took my driver's test, I had all the rules and regulations in my head.

At nine o'clock on a Wednesday morning, my parents and I arrived at the police station. I took the written test, no problem. Then came the driving test. Always trying to do the polite thing, I asked the policeman if he was familiar with hand controls. He assured me he was. The way he answered, I knew he had no idea how hand controls operated, so I showed him, anyway.

I drove around the block, up and down some other streets to his satisfaction. As we approached the station, which was on a steep hill, he asked me to parallel park on said steep hill. I read him like a book. If he really knew about hand controls, he would know that to park on a hill with one lever pushed down to slow the car and the self same lever pushed another way to advance or reverse the car, is no mean feat.

My determination meter reached high in seconds. I parked the car in three turns of the wheel. The officer got out of the car, saying nothing. That is when I heard applause. On the sidewalk across the street were about 30 to 35 people who worked in the area. How they knew I was trying for my license that day, I will never know. But it was a great acknowledgment!

College Days

WRITTEN MAY 19, 2021

College was a life learning experience, not just book learning. My first roommate freshman year (who was selected on the advice of the dean) was to assist me in any way I needed. She was helped financially by my parents.

Looking at these words brings new meaning to "million dollar baby." I am in awe of my parent's love for me and the extent to which they were willing to go to ensure a good life for me.

Ellen was nice, sarcastic and opinionated; she thought she was religious and her housekeeping skills left a lot to be desired. I was the one who scrubbed the wooden floor and did most of the cleaning. She soon had a boyfriend, so she was out of the room a lot.

At some point, I discovered a growth on my eye that irritated the whole eye. The school nurse looked at the growth and told me that it would have to be removed. She made the appointment, and I asked Ellen to drive me—she refused! A man that I had been casually dating agreed to drive me to and from the appointment.

Ellen was even more determined when she heard who was taking me. "I won't get in the car with him." She had a strange sense of humor: she short-sheeted my bed; put a snowball under the covers; and anything she deemed hilarious.

I made the decision to change roommates in my sophomore year. My new roommate couldn't have been better. We laughed a lot, studied much, and had great conversations.

Often Sam would push me in my chair to the guardrail where the classroom buildings were located. John would meet me there and carry me up five or six steps. If he was unable to meet me there, there always were young men who gladly helped. Today nobody was around (my guess is we were late). Sam left me at the bottom of the steps, walked up them, turned, and said, "Well, come on, Mary Ann."

I started laughing, but stopped when I saw the stricken look on her face. She kept saying, "I'm sorry, I'm so sorry." I stopped laughing and hastened to tell her that she had paid me a supreme compliment. "You saw *me*—not the braces, not the wheelchair, not the crutches—just *me*. That is a wonderful gift."

Sam's name was Carol Magee. Why did I call her Sam? From this:

> *Now, Sam Magee from Tennessee,*
> *where the cotton blooms and grows,*
> *why he left his home in the south to roam,*
> *God only knows!*

She is still Sam today!

Lest you think college was no fun, let me offer proof it was otherwise. My roommate was pushing me in my chair to the classroom building when she hit a bump. She tried to tilt the wheelchair back so as to roll over said bump.

The next thing I knew, my chair was tilted back as far as it would go, leaving me still in a sitting position. The trash truck happened to be going by, saw my dilemma, and one of the crew rushed over, looked down at me and asked, "Is there anything wrong?"

Before I could think, the words came out of my mouth, "No, I always sit this way." And he turned around and left me still in this weird position. I deserved that, really, and when I related the story to my parents, I was glad I was ten hours away! My father was ready to disown me.

I tried to explain, "Look at it from my point of view, Daddy." I was angry and frustrated to be in this strange position. That fell on deaf ears. His daughter was supposed to be a lady at all times!

I was the only freshman allowed to keep a car on campus. As such, I tried to be very circumspect—and I managed that for four years. It was in the fall of my sophomore year, and Sam and I had been studying all afternoon. About four o'clock, I said I was thirsty for cider and we could drive north a short distance and buy some cider from a roadside stand.

In short order, we had a jug of cider in the car—which we thoroughly enjoyed!

Then the question arose: Where to store it? If we put it in the dorm refrigerator, it would be gone in a few hours. So, I had the brilliant idea of hanging the jug from our window. It was only fifty degrees outside. We did, and then one day we forgot to put it outside,and set it by the radiator. In another few days, we decided to finish off the cider.

When John came to take us to dinner, Sam and I were very happy. Sitting at the table, we would giggle and hiccup.

Finally, John said, "What is wrong with you?"

We giggled some more and hiccuped some more and told him we had the best cider ever. We elaborated more by saying we had to finish it off because there were "little white things" floating in the cider. I seem to remember him saying, "You dummies, that cider is fermenting." Who knew? We just laughed even more. I learned all sorts of things in college!

An Unwanted Interlude

WRITTEN AUGUST 10, 2021

IT WAS SO EASY TO SLIDE INTO A NEUTRAL STATE OF MIND. Living by rote comes almost naturally—get out of bed, turn the coffee on, get dressed, have scones, waffles or toast, read the local paper. Remind myself there is a desktop full of things needing attention, but my current book is calling.

Next thing I know, it's lunch time—a piece of fruit, yogurt, and a cookie takes care of that. Then I have the feeling of a deadline—not to clean my desk, but to finish my book! I admit, this is my escape. And escape I have to the tune of forty or so books.

I also have had much time to contemplate moments of the past good, bad or otherwise! I found a picture of me seven years old, lying on a bed with my mother. I'm not at my home, I'm probably at one of my grandparents.

And as I was not long out of the hospital (I had been hospitalized for fifteen months) and Mother was told that I should have an hour and a half rest time each day, so wherever we were she made sure I rested. But her body, snuggled up to mine, radiates love in every fiber of her being.

What a rich life I have had, largely due to my parents. Their loving care created a world in which I could participate. They hired a man to take me to and from elementary school. Mother came at lunchtime with my sandwich and take me to the bathroom. She did this for ten years—day in and day out.

She made sure my girlfriends were treated royally when they came to visit. I had one of the earliest collapsible wheelchairs, and many children would fight as to who would push me.

I didn't recognize these blessings until later, much later; yet, in so many ways, they allowed me to be Mary Ann—not the crippled girl in a wheelchair. Can you imagine the good that did to that little girl's psyche?

By the time I got to high school, I mainly walked with crutches and I walked well over a mile each day. Blisters under my arms were the size of golf balls, but I refused to use my wheelchair. In my mind, as it was in many instances, I would not give up or give in.

I'm sure this wasn't easy for my parents, yet they so wisely knew that I had to prove MYSELF to ME. My sense of self was oh so important to that teenager. I'm sure they consulted with my polio doctor, and I can almost hear him say, "Let her go"!

Expectations

WRITTEN MAY 20, 2021

WHEN IT BECAME QUITE EVIDENT THAT I WAS THRIVING in a school situation, my parents began thinking that I would have a real future in life. My little elementary school only had classes through the seventh grade. High school (eight through twelve) was twenty-five miles away.

A fifty-mile daily trip was thought to be too much of a drain, so my father bought a lot down the street from one of Mother's sisters and built a house—step free. Mother and I stayed there Monday 'til Friday, returning to my "real" home for the weekend.

I wasn't thrilled with this arrangement. I wanted things to stay as they were, but eventually I accepted the change. I never even thought of the sacrifice my mother and father were making, which, as an adult, I find amazing. I made friends and they would come to the house "to study" or projects of the week.

I joined Rainbow Girls, an organization sponsored by the Eastern Star. Life was good again. Oh, the high school building was three floors of classrooms. It was arranged that a football player would meet me at the steps and carry me to the level where my next class was located. This was a bit intimidating at first, but only at first. Those guys were not only handsome, but so gentle and fun. I would sneak cookies from Home Economics to these young men.

So many expectations were fully realized in the eighth and ninth grades. In the tenth grade, we moved to a new campus-style high school. That meant a tremendous amount of walking on crutches. I could have used a wheelchair to change classes, but that was too easy. Some days I walked over a mile. I had boils under my arms where the crutches rubbed. But no matter, I was upright!

It was that tenth grade year that I realized greater expectations were ahead. College was more and more brought into the conversation. I think I saw this as sheer fantasy. Surely, I couldn't manage living on my own.

As always, Daddy, with Mother at his side, started to investigate. I would require few steps and a temperate climate. Mother actually saw an advertisement in a magazine for "a college search made according to your requirements" the Lovejoy Agency in New York City. My parents made the appointment and sent a list of requirements. The agency assured us that our requirements were very manageable. We received over seventy catalogs.

Through interview after interview, Drew University in Madison,

New Jersey, became our first choice. It changed my life forever. All of a sudden, I had to make decisions on my own. I was allowed to keep my car on campus, the only freshman with that privilege. Not only that I had to have the oil changed, run my car through the car wash, all things done for me in a former life. I loved it!

Then came the interview with the University psychologist. I arrived at the appointed time, knocked on the door, pushed it open on the command "come in." He sat at his desk and just stared at me. My first thought was, "What a rude man." A gentleman always stands when a lady enters the room. Shades of Scarlet O'Hara!

He indicated where I was to sit, which I did, but took my time laying my crutches on the floor and unlocking my two leg braces.

His first words were, "You know, I don't feel sorry for you at all." My instant reply was, "Good! I don't want your sympathy." It was a rather testy interview, but we shook hands at the conclusion of the interview.

That evening my parents called and I related "The Interview." My Mother was in instant Mama Bear mode. She was ready to take on the psychologist! But Daddy hastened to say, "Dorothy, he was just testing her," which did nothing to appease Mother.

This same psychologist became a real influence in my college career and life. I became a psychology major, and actually adored the man. When I walked across the stage to receive my diploma, Dr. McClintock broke rank and rushed to hug and congratulate me. We kept in touch until he died.

Musings ad Nauseum

WRITTEN MARCH 23, 2018

I WAS, I THINK, A VERY SERIOUS CHILD. From my childhood photos, my smile seemed to have a haunted look. Something in my eyes reflects a sadness. This in no way means that I was unhappy. I do remember happy times.

I loved physical activity. I ruined a pair of shoes in six months riding my scooter. Then A.P. (after polio), I see in that same face confusion and fear. It is hard for the able bodied population to truly understand physical disability.

I went back to public school completely unaware how different I was from all the other students. No wonder they stared. And, yes, sometimes their words hurt. I hate, and hated then, the word "cripple." It was like a big negative sign hanging over me, but I tried to change their perceptions.

I learned very quickly that I did not have the strength to serve a volleyball, and I could only hit one out of twenty softballs from my wheelchair. So I became scorekeeper. At least I was a part of play.

In the classroom, there was less of a problem, but there was always the unspoken challenge, "You have got to prove yourself."

High school was really, really difficult. How could I compete with all those perfectly formed young girls who could easily participate in any sport and dance the evening away at all parties while I sat on the sidelines with a date trying to make some kind of conversation?

I can't say I enjoyed one minute of it, so the best part was when it was over. I would return home trying to relay the feeling that I had a wonderful time to my parents. It was even better to get in bed, cry, feel my way through the grief and anger.

The most daunting part was that it only reinforced the fact that it would never be any better.

The local newspaper tried to make me a heroine—I didn't want or need that. I wonder, if I could have expressed my turmoil, what they would have printed. Probably "young polio victim further impacted by psychological problems"!

Then came college. It was here that I first saw the benefit of laughter. It was funny to think of me still seated in a wheelchair, my back on the ground level, and my legs still bent in a sitting position. There came to be more humor in my life.

My major in psychology revealed humor is a way of protesting and protecting your emotions. I laughed more than I ever had. It was a freeing experience.

Now that I am a widow, I am once again feeling the burden of my disability. Transportation is a big problem. On weekends, it doesn't even exist.

Life is lived in fear. A fall could easily put me in a bed for an extended time, at the end of which I would have lost so much muscle strength that I might barely be able to sit.

But I refuse to be frozen in fear. I am extremely careful. But that, too, is draining.

And don't even get me started on doctors! There may be ten (count on your fingers) doctors in the United States that still know how to treat polio survivors.

This means a lot of us could further do damage to our bodies. A normal physician would immediately recommend an exercise regimen. No! No! No! That's why, in part, we have trouble now.

We have had to rewire our nervous system to the extent that more exercise would annihilate that, too. We would be reduced to total disability.

I read a quote this week that sums up my present outlook:

"In communion with the beauty of nature, I feel an affirmation of all that is, including me."

Stormy Weather

WRITTEN SEPTEMBER 14, 2018

I CONFESS TO BEING SUPER NOSTALGIC THIS WEEK. I have been watching reports of Hurricane Florence by the hour. It makes me tearful as I watch people trying in every way possible to protect their property. This is all too familiar to me.

Hurricane Hazel was probably the biggest and most destructive storm I remember.

Daddy, having lived by the water all of his life, had gauges and all kinds of equipment to tell him the pressure reading, wind velocity, and always the storm surge.

There was an excitement that came over the whole community. You saw a steady stream of cars heading to the harbor to secure their boats. That all sounds logical.

However, if you saw all those men tightening the ropes to secure their boat from escaping or hitting another boat, you would have recognized it as a form of art. Slip knots here, another there, until their boat was secure.

The boats had to have enough space to move with the water, but not enough to hit the boat next to them. It was an art form passed from one generation to the next.

Everyone filled their bathtubs and buckets with water so you could flush the toilets. If you had a gas stove and/or a fireplace, you could cook and have a source of heat.

Television antennas were always the first to fall. After Hazel, Daddy had our antenna put on a creosote telephone pole—which is still standing today!

You couldn't open the refrigerator door too frequently or what food was in there would spoil.

Daddy put Mother's car in the garage at a diagonal angle. It must have taken him a half hour to maneuver that big car (a Cadillac) in such a confined space.

Of course, I had to know why he did this (I excelled with "why" questions). He figured the wind direction and strength, that should the garage door be blown in, it would do the least damage to the car.

The aftermath of the storm was no electricity for two or three days, a few barns blown over, and many homes with roof damage. Anything left outside was gone, most likely never to be seen again.

I would have liked to be on the beach on the day before and the day after the storm. On any given day in the summer, the ocean rolls to shore and laps the sand—a soothing sound.

BUT...just before and just after the storm, waves thrash onto the beach, pounding it like a jackhammer. Wave after wave hitting each other, sending a spray of water in the air. I think it is one of the most magnificent sights. A real *tour de force* by Mother Nature.

That ocean and river is such a part of me. I long to see it again. It is a visceral need. It was always a part of my life. I can't count the number of times in my life that I would drive to the ocean or river and let that energy fill me with calm, excitement, or awe at their sheer beauty.

My John

WRITTEN SEPTEMBER 22, 2017

I first met this man in 1957 at Drew University while at camp for the first All Freshmen Week in the hills of New Jersey. John seemed to gravitate towards me to assist me in getting around—up to a dining hall or else at a nightly campfire. The terrain was uneven, at best; otherwise, washboard ready.

One of the counselors took me at night back to bathrooms, then to the cabin. To say the least, I wasn't prepared for this! When we returned to campus, the powers that be decided that John was the one to assist me to classes and the dining hall. The dye was cast.

My first impression of John was "a relative of Opie or his dad in Mayberry." John emphatically stated that he was a religion major and hoped to become a Methodist minister. That was nice and didn't bother me at all. After all, there was the man of my dreams back in Maryland!

But we did eat dinner together every night, and our table was always filled. Lots of "serious" discussion, teasing (mostly me), and laughter! I was seen as the Southerner! This arrangement worked very well. We both dated other people. I wrote to my parents saying, "If I had a brother, I'd want him to be John." I heard that phrase for many years hence.

Then the fall of 1958, things changed. John invited me to be his date at our big "Fall Weekend." Friday night was cocktail dress, dinner, and a program. Saturday night was the formal dance. I think I still have the crumbling corsage dried in my zoology book! From then on, it became an exclusive relationship. I got a beautiful rose bud each Friday!

John went home with me on the occasional weekend. I visited his home once or twice in the ensuing years. His youngest brother did not take too kindly to my visits. He felt I was invading his territory. At the banquet the night before our wedding, he was asked what song most likely characterized this event. Philip never missed a beat. "When Johnny comes marching home!" We were married anyway.

John had spent enough time with me already that he understood my basic needs. He loved me. I worked to support us while he got his Masters. When he graduated, he got a high school teaching job in my hometown where I had gone to high school. We had a house waiting for us that had been built for me back in my high school days.

At this time, I was just pregnant and did not explore any job possibilities. I had been away from Salisbury four or five years and my school classmates had scattered. So, life as a married couple was new, and now we had to find our way in the community.

We had attended a church for a few weeks and thought we might join. The evening the minister visited, I happened to be on the sofa with my Bermudas unbuttoned to accommodate my bulging waistline. I quickly cradled a pillow to my waist.

Conversation was going well, when what to my wondering ears I hear someone singing "Show me the way to go home." It was my Sister of the Heart bringing me a jug of apple cider!

John and I were somewhat flustered, to put it mildly. Loraine wasn't fazed, but didn't stay long. We resumed the conversation and almost immediately the minister said, "John, let's try some of that cider. You know, I love apple cider." So, we all had some. Then, we heard hiccups! The pastor said, "You know, cider always makes me do this." We still laugh, and teased him for years.

My first job after we were married was at Washington Hospital

Center in Medical Records. No two ways about it, I hated it. The Medical Records area of this fairly new hospital was in the middle of the hospital—that meant no windows. In the wintertime, I never saw the sun. I went to work shortly after 8:00 and left at 5:00.

For me it was like living in a tunnel I prefer lots of glass. But I stuck it out for a year when I went to work for the State of Maryland.

We were so young and, like many couples, we thought the world was our oyster!

Marriage

WRITTEN MAY 26, 2021

BY OUR SENIOR YEAR IN COLLEGE, JOHN AND I KNEW we wanted to spend our lives together. So the Christmas of 1960, John proposed and I accepted. One likes to think of a marriage proposal in a romantic setting. However, we had a third party to deal with: the family cat, formally known as "Alexander" but mostly called "Sandy."

Sandy wanted my attention, and "no" was not acceptable to him. He purred, patted me on the arm, jumped in my lap—he was not to be ignored. When Sandy had exhausted all of his tricks, he went to sleep. Let's just say it was not a classic moment!

We were graduated from college on June 5th and married on June 10th. What was I thinking? My poor parents! But they came through with flying colors, as they always did. When I told them months earlier that we wanted to marry after graduation, they asked: What type of wedding did I want? My reply was: In our village church with all the fuss and feathers that go with weddings.

And that is exactly what I had. It was a beautiful day, June 10, 1961—sunny, lush green manicured lawns and my little village church right in the center of it all. The church interior was decorated with mostly ferns, interspersed with white flowers. The ferns were provided by a neighbor who, as long as I can remember, called me young'un even on my wedding day.

I cringe to think of all the planning that went into this perfect day. Mother and her two sisters addressed more than three hundred invitations. Then there was a reception, the food and the flowers—no little job.

I wanted a rainbow wedding with five attendants, dressed in luscious shades of blue, yellow, pink, lavender, and green, carrying matching bouquets.

I was showered with parties. I think there were seven or eight. Corningware was popular at the time. Considering that my culinary skills were limited to peanut butter and jelly sandwiches, I had a lot of learning to do. I marvel how I finished college exams. Somehow, it all came together.

The day of the wedding, there were no "no shows." People had called begging to be allowed to come and they were willing to stand outside and look in the windows! My parents couldn't refuse them and made sure they came to the reception. The church would only hold three hundred max, but the reception hall could accommodate many more.

When I came out our front door to go to church, tears filled my eyes, the only time that day. There were cars on each side of the road as far as you could see.

It was simply overwhelming to think so many people wanted to share my day.

Now, by 2:00 o'clock the church was packed, swarms of people at each window. I remember thinking what a blessing these people had been to me—these people who had watched me grow, struggle and achieve. I was in the church where I had worshipped since childhood.

My great grandfather's name was in the cornerstone; the organist had played every Sunday for forty years (without pay); and the soloist who warbled her best. Ordinary human beings showing a full measure of devotion. I always knew that little congregation was the salt of the earth.

When Daddy and I started down the aisle, Mother dutifully stood up—and never sat down through the entire ceremony. It was probably ninety degrees or more. She never lived it down and her anniversary cards always read "still standing."

At the rehearsal dinner the night before, we had a rollicking good time. Somehow, we started thinking of songs to fit members of the wedding party. John's youngest brother was the winner, hands down. He proposed the song for John would be "When Johnnie Comes Marching Home." He wasn't sold on this marriage—it was upsetting the natural order of things in his life!

Dennis and his wife, Ruth, were guests at our wedding. It was so very fitting. This man, who had shown me so much, was there for another major event in my life. John and I, quite naturally, had been a part of many of our friends' weddings and we had participated in "decorating their cars." So, now it was time to be on the receiving end.

Thinking we would outsmart our friends, we hid our car at Dennis' house. No one would ever think to look there. Someone brought the car back to the house while John and I were changing from our wedding clothes. When we came out of the house, our car was filled with crumbled newspaper. We couldn't even get in the front seat! Eventually, we were able to get in the car and roared away. It was a beautiful day surrounded by many we loved.

Escapades of Mary Ann

WRITTEN APRIL 16, 2021

I AM KNOWN TO HAVE GOTTEN INTO RATHER ODD SITUATIONS from time to time and, fortunately, I have lived to tell of them! Having been disabled at a young age, I had to use my brain due to my lack of brawn.

One of the earliest instances happened in grade school. There were always lots of children who wanted to push my wheelchair. This particular day, Patty was pushing me. Many of our classmates headed to a field overgrown with weeds. It was a rough, uneven surface. Patty would have to stop, pull the chair out of a rut, and start on an alternate route.

Suddenly, we heard the school bell. Kids ran everywhere. Patty and I started a new path back to the school house. All of a sudden, this silver and black snake arose from the weeds. Patty started to leave the scene. Oh, no! And, very calmly, I coached her to pull me backwards, said snake still looking eye to eye with me. When we got a few feet away, I strongly encouraged her to run, all the while pushing me. There were no losers that day!

Not too many years later, a few days before Halloween, Mother helped me carve a Jack O'Lantern. We always set the Jack O'Lantern on the front steps. But every year some trick or treaters would take my Jack O'Lantern, put it in the middle of the road and wait for a car to smash it.

This particular year I wasn't going to let that happen. I enlisted my father to help me. Actually, I think he really admired my plan! I would sit on the screened in porch, and when the tricksters arrived and started to take the Jack O'Lantern, I would signal Daddy to turn on the hose and, "voila," the Jack O'Lantern would be saved!

But it wasn't over yet. The tricksters started a water fight. Before you could blink, the yard was suddenly full of kids, plus my father. All were soon drenched, that is, except me, still on the porch. I scored big time that year!

Years later, as a high school student and driving my car, my friend Betty and I stopped at the house in Salisbury. It was summer and the house was essentially closed until school started again. I retrieved whatever I had come to get and was backing out of the driveway when, suddenly, there was a gosh awful sound, like a piece of equipment knocking down trees.

Truthfully, it was just a hedge.

But that hedge was twined around my back bumper like it had been growing there for five years! Betty tried and tried to separate hedge from car. No luck.

Go to Plan B. I drove car and hedge down the street to my aunt's and uncle's.

The noise made from that hedge dragging on the street brought neighbors to use their pruners and a saw to free the bumper.

College gave me a brand new canvas to provide further smiles, if not laughter. My roommate and I decided we would take a night off from studying and go to the movies. The movie of choice was in Morristown, only nine or ten miles from campus. It was almost sold out when we arrived. I had parked close to the theater in a gated parking lot.

We enjoyed the movie and returned to the parking lot. The gate was locked. Panic! I rattled the gate like a monkey, and all the time shouting. Finally, a watchman came out of his hut and pointed to the sign. I hastily explained, "I didn't know it would be locked; and, furthermore, I couldn't have walked from another parking lot down the street." He scratched his head and said, "Let me get my keys."

These times were silly, but each time is treasured. It reminds me of the saying "Nothing ventured, nothing gained."

Wedding

WRITTEN JUNE 10, 2016

IT WAS A BEAUTIFUL DAY, JUNE 10TH, 1961; sunny, lush green manicured lawns throughout the community, the church in the center. The church was decorated with assorted ferns and baskets of white flowers. The ferns were mostly from a neighbor's greenhouse. She wanted to be a part of my special day. I was always "young'un" to her, even on my wedding day!

My mother and her two sisters addressed over three hundred invitations, arranged for the reception, food, and flowers, lodging for out of town guests, and kept a running tally of the accepts and the declines. I had always dreamed of a rainbow wedding, so my attendants had dresses of blue, yellow, pink, lavender and green, and carried matching bouquets.

I was showered with parties—I think there were six. Corningware was the gift of choice, considering that my culinary skills were limited to peanut butter and jelly sandwiches! I had a lot of learning to do. I marvel that I even finished my college studies, particularly all the comprehensive exams. Somehow, it all came together.

The day of the wedding, there were not any "no shows." People had to stand outside in 90 degree temperatures and look in the windows. People had called and begged to attend—even to stand outside! So, when I came out the door leaving for the church, tears filled my eyes (the only time that day)! There were cars as far as I could see on both sides of the road. It was overwhelming to think so many wanted to share my day.

By two o'clock, the church was packed, as was the lawn outside. At 90 degrees plus and no air conditioning, the people outside may well have been cooler. As Daddy escorted me down the aisle, I remember thinking, what a gift their presence was, these people who had watched me grow, struggle, and achieve. I was in the church where I had worshipped since childhood.

My great grandfather's name was in the cornerstone; the organist played every Sunday for over forty years without pay; and the soloist, while conservatory trained, warbled her best. Ordinary human beings giving their full measure of devotion. I always knew that little congregation was the "salt of the earth."

When I started down the aisle, Mother dutifully stood and never sat down through the entire ceremony. Her anniversary cards in the years to come always read "still standing."

At the rehearsal dinner the night before, we had a rollicking good time. Somehow, we all started thinking of song titles that might fit the bride or the groom. John's youngest brother was the winner, hands down! He proposed the song title of "When Johnny Comes Marching Home." He wasn't sold on this marriage. It was upsetting the natural order of things in his life!

It was a beautiful sunny day that June 10, 1961. We started a wondrous journey, full of love and ready to face the world.

Church and Pastor

WRITTEN OCTOBER 13, 2017

PASTORS FROM THE CHURCHES WHERE I/WE LIVED, throughout our lives, have influenced and blessed us. The earliest time that I remember a pastor was early 1945. Mr. Romans preached at the Sunday evening service at our little country church. Mother would put me to bed and then leave for church.

When the windows were open, I could hear Mr. Romans shouting to the congregation. I didn't think it was very friendly. Shouting meant anger to me. Consequently, when Mr. Romans spoke to me at Sunday School, I was scared. Mother would explain, "Well, he does get wound up."

In the hospital, we would have a lady who came intermittently on Sundays and try to tell us Bible stories. She was at a great disadvantage. There were no microphones at that time and she had to walk up and down the center aisle between beds to speak. There was no way to keep the attention of the children who only heard every other sentence, let alone the range of ages (four to fifteen years). That is probably why, after a few months, she no longer came.

My little village church was one of three served by a pastor. So, when it was time to send a new pastor, our charge was at the bottom of the list. Not many ministers wanted to preach three sermons every Sunday. Every once in a while a new young man would be sent to us. He would have to have the wisdom of Solomon not to interject too much new material.

Going to a university on a campus with a Methodist seminary, I learned a lot. Ministers are human—they like to laugh and play pranks on each other, much like the college students! Wonder of wonders! When they did a chapel talk, I became aware of a more substantive sermon.

John and I were married by a Methodist minister who taught

psychology at my high school. Come to find out, he had been in college with my father. I liked his casual approach to a wedding. The minister's wife, who was serving our church at the time, wanted all the attendants to do a three step down the aisle. I thought it would look like ducks bobbing in the water! And gently (I hope) suggested that I would prefer they just walk down the aisle.

When we lived in Radford, Virginia, we quickly joined a church, after visiting some three other churches. It was a young church, vivacious and outgoing.

They would have a game night. Everyone brought their favorite game and EVERYONE came!

This pastor visited us, and his first question was, "Do you have a cat"? I answered in the affirmative, and he requested the newspaper, which he promptly rolled into a cat swatting defense. Of course, Miss Sniff made a bee line for the pastor. His horror was so obvious, you would have thought he saw a thousand pound gorilla! I don't think he visited us very often after this.

Our next home was in Bowie, Maryland. Our first Sunday there, we attended a Methodist church not far from where we were living. It had a new sanctuary and still had some finishing touches that needed to be done. As John was helping me into my chair, a church member came to us and said, "If there is anything we can do to make it more comfortable to worship here, tell me after church." That was impressive! And, "Yes, we said, "A curb cut would be nice." Monday morning, work was started on a curb cut!

We worshipped there for twenty-two years. John started an adult Sunday School class that grew to have fifty-five or sixty members.

And, yes, we had parties! How we fit everyone in our living room, dining room, and down the hall, I don't know. But no one complained.

One of our Christmas parties will always be remembered. By that time, our son Mark had his seven foot Steinway, so there was lots of singing. Then the two pastors started recounting church humor. One story, after another. My neighbor said she heard us laughing!

The funniest tale I have heard came from the associate pastor, who had been in the military. He was asked to conduct a military burial service out on Long Island, New York. The day arrived, rainy and messy. The tent was put up for the family and friends, with grandmother, parents and siblings on the front row.

The grandmother was elderly, and no one had warned her or the children of the gun salute. So, when the guns fired, grandmother fell from her chair, and the grandson next to her shouted, "Jesus Christ, they shot Grandma!"

That story brought the house down! And it was so easy to visualize.

It was hard to leave this church—so many memories of good times and bad. The evening we heard of the hostages being released from Iran, we found ourselves heading to church just like twenty or so other families. And we rang the church bells. Never did freedom sound so good.

I will forever miss the life-size wooden cross that was placed close to a stained glass window. The shadow of that cross is still with me.

Expecting

WRITTEN MAY 6, 2016

I WAS EXPECTING, NO DOUBT ABOUT IT. Morning sickness made it very clear, and certainly no respecter of time or place. The doctor confirmed what I already knew. We decided to keep this news secret for a few months, just to see how things would progress.

In the meantime, we traveled with my parents to Illinois for John's brother Paul's wedding. Always the history buff, I insisted on stopping in Springfield, Illinois, to visit Abraham Lincoln's home. At breakfast that morning, my father (knowing how I loved coffee!) kept refilling my coffee cup. By that time, I could barely stand the smell of coffee, let alone drink it!

Somehow I drank and soldiered on.

We arrived at the historic home. I was a little shaky. But just as we got inside the house and purchased our tickets, morning sickness struck. "Please, John, get me out of here," and he did. I promptly marked Abraham Lincoln's front yard. From that time on, the baby was called Abe or Abby! My Mother was in shock mode. She asked, "Whatever is wrong with you, Mary Ann?" No need to mince words. "I'm pregnant," I replied. I knew they both would worry, yet I had no doubt I could carry this precious baby.

Years later, I learned that my parents had consulted with my orthopedic doctor in Baltimore. The doctor said I could not carry a baby beyond five months. Learning this, I realized why there had been no baby showers. That was hurtful. However, my church circle had a shower for me. It meant more than they will ever know. My pregnancy was validated and I could express the joy in having this baby.

When I was newly pregnant, I realized that life would never be the same. Sleeping through the night was the norm for me. Now, having to get up at 2:00 a.m. to use the bathroom, was a major inconvenience. More so, because my wheelchair would not fit through the bathroom door in our brand new apartment, so I would have to awaken John, who would carry me into the bathroom. Early on, I nudged him as a wake up call! I thought he was awake, his eyes were open, and he asked, "What flight are you taking?" It's funny now, but then the humor was lost to me.

Pregnancy was not really problematic for me. I did have to wear a corset in the fifth month which eliminated my ability to lean over from the left or right. Of course, bending from the waist was no longer an option either. These facts were driven home the day I dropped an open carton of eggs on the floor. Twelve eggs, some scrambled, some sunny side up! What to do? I slid down on my bottom, and with a wet dish cloth drug the eggs in a circle and picked them up with wet paper towels. I used all of my daily supply of energy in one activity!

On December the 9th, labor pains started. Except I didn't know they were labor pains! I thought it was the stuffed pepper at dinner that disagreed with me. And I wasn't supposed to go into labor. My C Section was scheduled for January 10th, but at midnight I was at the hospital. A high school friend, a nurse, met us there. Ann waved the Admissions nurse aside and, as we got on the elevator, she was still saying, "But she must—"

Can you believe it? The elevator got stuck! After pushing every button and jiggling the gate, we slowly rose to the third floor. My obstetrician was waiting. My plea was: "Do whatever you have to do, but just save this baby."

I was wheeled into the operating room at 1:00 a.m. One thinks of the darnedest things when in a crisis. My thought was: "I'm glad I shampooed my hair today!" Mark was born at 1:10 a.m. at five pounds, ten ounces. I thought then that he was a gift from God. And I still think so!

Mark

WRITTEN FEBRUARY 27, 2020

I HAVE SAID MANY, MANY TIMES THAT I THOUGHT Mark was sent right from heaven. His first seven months were a little rocky—he had colic and never slept more than three or four hours.

John and I took care of him in shifts. John had him from 3:00 a.m. on, I did the earlier shift. We both were zombies! The doctors said, "Just let him cry." We couldn't do that.

So, he was seven months old before he slept through the night. That first time he slept through the night, I awakened in the morning, startled, sure he had died. Why had it taken so long for this to happen? My diagnosis was that being born a month early, his body lacked the maturation of other full term babies.

He probably shouldn't have gotten the milk formula that he did. But after seven months, it was the best of times. I enjoyed this baby. It was a joy watching him adapt to life.

When I would have a jigsaw puzzle on the card table, he wanted one also. So, I cleared the coffee table and he had his own puzzles!

He loved books, and I read a lot. We also watched cartoons, and still laugh at Bugs Bunny and Elmer Fudd.

Mark went to kindergarten and loved the time there. One day I had suggested he bring a little friend home for lunch. I admit I was nervous—would it frighten his friend to see me in my Franklin chair?

To Keith's credit, he never made a comment until he was leaving. I followed the boys out the door, to make sure Keith's mother was there to pick him up, and I heard Keith ask Mark, "Why is your mother in that chair?" Mark nonchalantly said, "Oh, her legs don't work and she has to use the wheelchair."

That was all that Keith needed to answer his question. Sometimes children can make a difficult situation so easy!

From an early age, it was obvious Mark was pretty sharp. So when an elementary school principal wanted to practice giving an I.Q. test to a young child, she asked if Mark could be her subject.

John and I could see no problem with this; however, I did caution if he became restless, maybe we should end the test. Margaret agreed.

Well, Mark loved it. He thought this was such fun. And Margaret got a big laugh when she asked Mark if he knew the definition of Brunet. Mark replied, "Oh, you mean Carol Brunet."

Needless to say, his test scores were extremely high, and the laughter quotient as well!

Mark always had questions. When I picked him up after working for my father, he would comment on a storm, or lightning, whatever was going on. I gave the simple answer, but we would look it up in my Old World Book Encyclopedia when we got home.

That first year of kindergarten I had the lady, who helped me with house work, walk Mark from school. Years later, she told me Mark would see her coming and shout, "Go back, Chris, go back."

Chris always wore a white uniform, and the children thought it was a nurse coming for him. But he negotiated nicely—Chris walked in front, Mark followed with his friends a half block behind.

It's scary and amazing how your child trusts you. Mark saw death up close and personal at a fairly young age. Our neighbor was cutting his grass early one evening when he fell to the ground dying from a heart attack.

We lived in an older neighborhood and all the women told us to get Mark back in the house. I uttered an emphatic "NO"! This was a teaching moment.

When we returned to the house, I spoke with Mark that this was a part of life. It was nothing to fear. Mr. Taylor had gone to live with God.

I tried not to make it too dramatic, and I was rewarded when, after Mark was in bed, he called to me, "Mommy, it really is all right, isn't it?" "Yes, Mark, it really is all right."

My only regrets were that I couldn't show and share the world with Mark. I started with taking him out in a carriage or stroller. It just wasn't possible. I longed to take him exploring on the beach and riverside that I loved so much.

Thankfully, my father did a lot of that, as he loved the river and beach as much as I did. Daddy bought a yacht which, of course, was named Captain Mark. Mark, in the early stages of piloting the boat, gunned the engine and lost the "bimini" top. It was a sort of family joke.

Mark went for many years to Cody, Wyoming with my parents in the summer. They became good friends with Bill Cody, Buffalo Bill's grandson—and an exact replica of Buffalo Bill.

Mark rode horses, which pleased me no end, and went camping in the mountains with Bill, which did not entice me in the least. But, again, I loved it that he got to see such beauty.

I always thought it was a privilege to work. So when Mark announced one summer vacation that he was bored, I said that I could remedy that and put him to work weeding and mulching around all the shrubbery. We had a rather large yard and, funny enough, he wasn't bored the rest of the summer! TO BE CONTINUED!

Motherhood was a special gift to me. I delighted in seeing Mark grow and seeing things through a child's eyes. And that motherhood gene is still alive and well.

Guess who called her son and asked if any of his Asian students went home for Christmas? "Mother, they've been back since January 6th." It was my duty to check!

Mark
Part 2

WRITTEN JULY 8, 2016

FROM THE DAY HE WAS BORN, I considered myself the luckiest mother in the world. It is true, love for a child is love at its purest. No matter how many sleepless nights there are, your only concern is for the well being of that baby. Mark was a difficult baby until he was seven months old, when he finally slept through the night.

Looking back, I think I should have challenged that little mind more. But what did I know? I was an only child and had never been around babies. No wonder my first thought when Mark was put in my arms was, "Oh, Dear God, what have I done?"

But my philosophy was always: I may not do it like everyone else, but I can do it my way with the same results. I would hold him against me with one arm while wheeling my old Franklin Roosevelt-type chair with the other arm. It worked.

When Mark started to walk, there was a different challenge. Somehow, I instinctively knew that I must find a way to make him respond to me immediately. Of course, he had to test this process. It is as vivid in my mind as if it were yesterday. Mark had done something naughty and ran away from me when I called.

I could see the wheels of that little brain turning; he paused, ran in back of the sofa, half way to the middle. "She can't get me here." In that instant, I grabbed the yard stick, reached behind the sofa and tapped him. "Old buddy, one day you will be smarter than I am, but not today." The look on his face was priceless. He never tried that again. Lesson learned!

Mark talked in full sentences shortly after he was a year old. I thoroughly enjoyed him at this age. I was working part time, so I would leave him with my mother or one of my two grandmothers. Mark and I had delightful conversations as he munched his graham crackers, then patted me with the same mush—not a pretty sight by the time we got home.

At age three, he discovered his all time favorite toy—a phonograph. Slide the disc in, close the door, and let the music begin. He wore it out. It wasn't long after that he was with a neighbor child whose mother had taken both boys to a church where she was arranging a meeting. Mark saw a piano. He didn't strike the keys randomly, but played a tune.

The organist there happened to hear him and inquired as to who he was. A few weeks later, Homer (by name) called, identified himself and said, "I think you have a very gifted son. I would like to meet him and see just what he can do."

We didn't respond immediately. How could we expect this little boy to submit to the routine of learning to play the piano and practice? Surely, it was too much. We reclaimed my old Spinet piano from my parents to see what Mark would do. Sure enough, he loved sitting at the keyboard. He would play the *Star Spangled Banner*, then play it in different keys. It was then we decided to revisit Homer.

Homer was by no means an ordinary organist. He had numerous degrees and was an extraordinary organist and pianist. We took Mark on a Sunday afternoon to be tested by Homer. He gave Mark a college level audition test for over an hour.

Afterwards, Homer privately told us that Mark's musical gift was beyond anything he had ever seen. "I couldn't fool him when I played a note on the piano—he could go play the same note every time." Homer said he would be honored to have Mark in his music studio. Mark studied with Homer for two years until we moved to Radford, Virginia. And so our musical journey began.

Ups and Downs

WRITTEN DECEMBER 1, 2016

Every life has its history of good times and bad. My life is no different. My hope is that I have learned from the bad times, even found some benefits, and then fully and gloriously enjoyed the good times.

We lived in Bowie, Maryland, for twenty-two years, moving from Radford, Virginia in 1972. John had a teaching position at Montgomery College in Rockville—the other side of the beltway from Bowie. We made the move so that Mark could study at Peabody Conservatory under the tutelage of Julian Martin, a top student of Leon Fleisher who arranged for this to happen.

Bowie was a Levitt community. Levitt built his first community on Long Island, N.Y., for returning World War II soldiers. Other communities soon followed. Housing was a big problem then. There were five models of houses from which to choose. Bowie was built to be a bedroom community for Washington, D.C. It was a massive production, unlike anything yet seen.

Levitt bought huge acreages near Route 50, cleared the land, marked lots, laid concrete slabs, and proceeded to build the two versions—Colonial and Cape Cod—and two versions of a ranch. The joke was there wasn't a square corner to be found. Once the houses were framed, it became routine—two weeks of roofing, two or three weeks for shingles.

The supplies came by train. And Levitt, the good businessman, had found deals on Belgian shingles, G.E. appliances, air conditioners and gas furnaces. This may sound ticky tacky, but the truth was that these homes were basically nice. The traffic flow pattern in all models was exceptional.

There were stories of a stove backed up to a wall where there was no electrical outlet or tools or papers left under or around, but the end product was more than adequate and affordable. It was Nirvana for us! When we began house hunting in our price range, we were shown bungalows, laundry in the basement, bedrooms and bath on the second floor, and several steps to enter.

To say we were discouraged doesn't even get close to how frightened we felt. We had sold our house in Radford and would have no place to live! We got a call on a Saturday morning that there was a rancher in Bowie just on the market. It became our home. Our belief that Mark deserved that chance at Peabody drove us, and it finally came together.

A few years later, I had fixed breakfast for Mark (who was getting ready for school), when I poured my coffee in an Exon freebie cup. It was supposed to be insulated, yet the bottom dropped off as I was holding it between my knees, carrying it to the table. I had on wool slacks. Between the leather of the braces and the wool slacks, that hot coffee scalded me. I yelled for Mark and begged him to pull my slacks down. I don't remember how, but I got on the sofa.

Mark called his dad and a neighbor. John was driving this little Volkswagen, foot to the floorboard, around the beltway. Mother, some two hours away, was hanging clothes on the clothesline when Daddy flew in the driveway, opened the car door, and said, "Get in, Dorothy. Mary Ann has been hurt." She didn't even have her pocketbook and wasn't wearing lipstick (which was a cardinal sin!) They got there in an hour and a half.

By that time, John had taken me to the doctors who wanted to hospitalize me. I had first and second degree burns on my leg and buttock. I said, "No." And he said, "Okay, but you must stay in bed with clean sheets for three days, sterile conditions as much as possible, then come back to me."

It was a month before the sac of water broke and I could sit properly, six weeks before I could put braces on. I was so grateful to be able to, once again, stand at the sink—never mind the dirty dishes! It was a powerful reminder: "Never take anything for granted." True, my movements were not normal, but I had put together a pattern of moving that worked for me, and any loss was a great inconvenience.

I am convinced that the bonds of love far surpass any other human tie. We were living in Salisbury. Mark was about three years old, when my father dropped a bombshell announcement. He and Mother were going to Pittsburgh to seek treatment for what he thought was a heart problem. He was a very private man and didn't want anybody to know he wasn't well.

He had a family friend who was a doctor at a large hospital in Pittsburgh. I remember he came to say goodbye to Mark and he was very unlike himself—it was a strained conversation.

He went through a week's testing from head to toe and found that it was his gall bladder causing the problem. Surgery was scheduled. He had made it very clear that I wasn't to leave Mark, but my heart told me differently. I called my two grandmothers and asked if they both could come to take care of Mark, and they were willing.

Mother's two sisters lived in our neighborhood and agreed to keep tabs on our household. We drove in our little white Comet through the mountains to Pittsburgh. We arrived about 4:00 a.m. and were able to go to the hospital with Mother for the 8:00 a.m. surgery. I couldn't have stayed away if I had tried—that bond gave me no other choice.

On his way home from Pittsburgh, Daddy stopped at our house and tearfully said, "Boy, we are going to have many more years together." It was the best benediction!

Another family catastrophe occurred in the late '70's. John, Mark, and I were in Baltimore at Peabody for Mark's lesson. We did something we rarely did, and that was to go out to dinner before driving home. This was a special treat!

When we arrived home, it was after 9:00 p.m. The phone was ringing. John answered—there had been a robbery at my parent's home and Mother had gone in shock. The doctor had been called and sedated her. Her two sisters and spouses were all there.

I said, "We'll be there by midnight."

We threw some clothes together and headed to Salisbury. John drove as fast as he possibly could, but just on the outskirts of Salisbury a State policeman stopped us. We heard the all too familiar phrase, "You know you were driving over the speed limit!" John explained we were on our way to the Kennerlys' who had been robbed. The policeman said, "It's been all over the airways. Be careful, but go on."

Mother and Daddy had been to a meeting at our little village church twenty-five miles from Salisbury. When they came back, the front door was open—then the horrible shock. Mother's complete silver service coffee pot, tea pot, sugar bowl and creamer on a large matching silver tray were gone as well as some silver flatware pieces, silver candy dishes, and trays.

Mother had left her dress watch, a Peugeot, on her desk, and that was gone, plus a few other pieces on her dresser. It was the time when silver prices were high.

Mother was sleeping when we got there. The next morning she was puzzled why I was there. Then the questions: Why? What happened? Did the police catch them? Over and over. Mother never got over this event.

Even when Daddy told her that with insurance they could replace it, she wasn't pleased. It wasn't her silver. She didn't want new or anything else. She wanted her silver returned. By then I'm sure it had been melted and sold.

When I dismantled my parent's home in 2012, I found a sugar bowl of Mother's silver pattern high on a shelf. Daddy had bought it for her but it wasn't hers. I am glad I found it, because Mark was supposed to inherit her silver.

We carefully wrapped it to send to Mark, only to find we had to insure it for $15,000. I could have easily missed it and Mother discarded it—not because she didn't appreciate the gesture, but she felt violated by the loss of her treasure.

When we built our dream house in 1994, we thought we would be there until the end of our lives. There were the dreaded community covenants, but they did grant us an exception to build a shed for storage in our back yard. We had a one-car garage which allowed me to go from the car into the house.

We were not supposed to have an outside clothes line unless it was collapsible. We had a collapsible clothes line—we just left it up all the time. Trying to reduce any chance of dissension, I put a trellis around three sides and planted climbing roses. So I was very surprised by a visit from the Covenant Association. He told me that my clothes line was against the rules. I countered with, "the only way you can see said clothesline is from the second floor of my neighbors."

Furthermore, I thought there were far more important things to do. "May I suggest reading for the blind, driving senior citizens to appointments or mentoring needy children." By this time, the man's face was flushed, he stammered and stuttered, and left.

We never heard anything more from the Covenant's Association, but I did wonder what that poor man reported back to the Covenant Association. I don't know whether this is an up or down, but it seemed just common sense to me.

Halloween

WRITTEN SEPTEMBER 29, 2017

THE FALL SEASON HAS BEEN ROYALLY INTRODUCED. The Lincoln Symphony played an outstanding program this week. The audience was so glad to see the musicians, they gave them a standing ovation before a note was played! And what a program it was. The players seemed to be inspired. My heart soared with the music. Now I know what I have been missing. Their music carried me to the heights, then to a lilting serenity. I felt rejuvenated.

If I were back in Maryland, the first cool days would signal the beginning of window washing, followed by changing clothes from one season to the next. The dry cleaners bill looked like the national debt, never mind the "umpty umpt" loads of items I laundered.

The squirrels worked right along with me—gathering acorns and building nests. Their autumn carried the same meaning as mine. The lethargy of hot, humid summer days was a thing of the past. Although, these days, I tend to carry lethargy from one season to the next!

The build up to Halloween in October seems to be the main focus of fall. Merchants have been displaying Halloween items since August.

Mark's first Halloween that he went trick or treating, we dressed him as Casper, the friendly Ghost, and he carried an artificial pumpkin in which he could put his treats.

The first stop was at my parents'. We parked across the street and cautioned him to knock on the door and say "trick or treat." He didn't quite get the message. When mother opened the door, this little boy's first words were, "Don't be afraid, Mama Dear, it's me."

Halloween for little ones is always cute. For older trick or treaters, it has become more about the tricks. One year, some older kids pulled a widowed lady's wooden steps away from the door. Fortunately, some adult rode by and corrected what could have been catastrophic.

I was with some of my schoolmates when we stopped at our teacher's house. I was, unknowingly, the decoy. So, while I was talking with the teacher, they proceeded into the darkness, found clothes on the clothesline, and wrapped each piece in mud. They were gone so long I thought they had gone on to another house. I apologized to the teacher the next day. Old soul that I was, then and now, I can't understand what pleasure you would get from such actions.

Another trick often used was called "tick/tacking." You would place a stick underneath a piece of siding and saw back and forth causing an eerie sound within the house.

Another Halloween, one of the young men in the community put on a white sheet (were there even colored sheets then?) over his head, hid in a ditch bank with lots of willow trees on the side, and waited for groups of trick or treaters. When my group approached, he floated (on his very long legs!) across the road. The ringleader almost left me sitting in the road! All scattered like falling leaves—which just proves "those who scare can be scared"!

The first Halloween that I was home from the hospital, Mother explained the concept of trick or treating. I had forgotten? There was a knock at the door, Mother let this person into the house. I knew immediately it was a woman dressed in a man's suit.

But, who was it? My first and only guess was the church organist. She had a sheet covering her head, with cutouts for eyes, nose and mouth. I didn't have a clue until she came over and kissed me. "Grandmother!" I exclaimed. Her sweet nature gave her away.

For many years our little community would have a Halloween party at the Fireman's Hall. All who came were in costume. The top four costumed folks were put on stage and the audience had to identify them.

Miss Annie was always one of the four and she always was identified because she had very skinny legs and ankles. Sitting up on the stage, her legs and ankles were a dead giveaway!

Such simple times, but they were filled with laughter and much camaraderie. Who can forget good times such as these? It brings to my mind "it takes a village to build the world!"

John
Part 2

WRITTEN NOVEMBER 3, 2017

I THINK JOHN COULD BE CHARACTERIZED BEST AS AN "ENIGMA wrapped in a conundrum." When I first met him, he really wanted to be in the midst of things—some things never change! All night jam sessions, he was there! Volunteer for most anything, he was there!

He thought he would be a religion major and he would hang with the chaplain and his group. He was a part of that outreach group that would spend a weekend with young people who had been in jail or were on probation.

He convinced me to go with him on one such event. Most likely, it was because I had a car and more students could go! We stayed in private homes. Belatedly, I found out the females were to be lodged on the third floor of an old house. There was no heat, and limited hot water. It was November in New Jersey. If I could have, I would have left the same day we arrived. I talked with several of the young men. I'm sure I was a real curiosity. "Why was she here?" Guess what? I was thinking the same thing!

Even with all of that, it was a learning experience. These young boys knew only to live in the moment—if they wanted a Coke, steal it! Thank heavens this was long before the drug epidemic. But, suffice it to say, this was the first and last outreach program I participated in. John's invitation to future outreach events fell on deaf ears.

John had a great love of music. He played the baritone horn in the high school band and sang in several choruses. Then at the beginning of his senior year, his parents enrolled him in a private boys' school in New Hampshire. That year translated into a scholarship at Drew.

As our dating became more serious, I began to ponder the problem of being a minister's wife. In the Methodist system, ministers are appointed where needed. That meant you lived where the conference dictated—in houses with steps, both into the house and to the second floor and down to the basement, let alone into the church itself. How could we ever make that work?

We talked and talked and talked. Finally, I said that I just couldn't do this. Plus, ministers' wives are expected to do many things—serve on committees, teach Sunday school classes, take care of refreshments.

Steps were and are my nemesis. The able bodied community has no idea how limiting this is. And this time was the dark ages of pre A.D.A. John, bless him, said, "I'll switch majors to political science," which hopefully could open many doors for employment. Did I feel guilty?

You bet I did! I carried that guilt for a long time.

In the end, John found his niche in life to be teaching. He started out teaching in a public high school. The students loved him. They showed up at our house on numerous Friday or Saturday nights. This resulted in our buying cases of Coke and many tins of Charles Chips—pretzels and potato chips. It was always interesting to listen to them.

John still hears from many of those former students.

He has gotten beautiful letters thanking him for his teaching. It is gratifying to see the impact he made on all of those young people.

His teaching ability was also translated to teaching Sunday School classes for probably thirty years. He is very innovative and always had a "filled to the brim" class. John also substituted preaching for vacationing ministers. Maybe this reduced my guilt somewhat. Maybe.

Those early years were very fulfilling. Those high school students adopted a needy family for Christmas—and delivered gifts like you could not imagine. They, and we, learned it is always important to give to those in need. John has done this wherever we have lived.

He is still a man of good heart.

John
Part 3

WRITTEN MAY 28, 2018

It almost goes without saying that I loved John and I knew he loved me.

Early on in my life, the handicapped were kept in the shadows. Thankfully, my parents did not subscribe to that way of thinking. And John. John made sure that I missed out on nothing.

There was the time, while we were in college, that for Valentine's Day John got front row tickets on the second or third level at Madison Square Garden, New York City, for the Ice Follies. Another couple went with us.

My car made life easier, not only for me but many. John was undaunted by driving the first time in New York City. We found parking, entered the building, and were directed to our seats. Front row seats, remember?

Now, the steps to the seats were at a seventy degree angle. John picked me up and started down. Oh, did I mention that John was scared of heights? He managed ten steps and stopped. He was white as a ghost. He really looked and acted like he was going to faint, with me in his arms!

The usher approached; John had already figured out Plan B. He told the usher to offer someone in an aisle seat our front row tickets for their tickets. Bingo! Problem solved. And a wonderful night followed!

John did not like to drive over the St. George's bridge in Delaware. It was quite high, giving you a magnificent view of the Atlantic ocean and Delaware farmland. At first, I always drove that part of the journey. Later, he would drive—white knuckled all the way!

John was a lot of things, but a handyman was not one of them. I had bought a new toilet seat, and asked him to install it. While he was working, I was outside pulling weeds. I heard my name being called, so came to the back door and saw John with a most sheepish look on his face.

He said, "I think we should call a plumber." My silly question was "Why?" Apparently, the old seat was somewhat difficult to remove, and in John's logic, a hammer was needed. Need I say more? He cracked the porcelain, so now a whole new toilet was needed!

At some point in our early marriage, we had to buy a new lawn mower. We looked at the ads in the newspaper and went shopping. We came home with a Toro. Of course, John was eager to try this new machine.

Two thirds of our back yard sloped down at a thirty degree angle, so it had to be mowed across the lawn, not the length. A hedge separated these two sections of the yard.

Mark and I heard the motor start, then we saw John's head over the hedges going by rather fast. One more swipe and the motor stopped. Mark and I waited and waited!

Finally, John trudged back to the house and announced he couldn't use this mower—it went too fast! Mark got out the directions and reduced the speed somewhat.

But, as long as Mark lived at home, he cut the grass! Cutting the grass was always a distasteful chore for John.

I think in many ways John should have become a Methodist minister. That's where he was headed when he went to Drew. I was the reason he didn't follow that path. I could never have been a successful minister's wife. Pure and simple!

Methodist ministers are assigned to a church and a parsonage. You probably could count on one hand the parsonages handicapped accessible in 1961.

John would always deny that he changed because of me, but in my heart of hearts I know differently; yet, I am convinced that God opened other pathways.

In Bowie, Maryland at St. Matthews U.M.C., he started an adult Sunday School class—the first adult class to ever exist there.

When we left Bowie twenty years later, there were sixty-five members every week. One of the early classes, when he asked someone to read a Bible passage, she said, "I've never had a Bible." She did the next Sunday!

Every year on that date, long after we left Bowie, she would call and thank him for the Bible and his messages. She called just last week, and we cried together.

John's preparation was throughout the week, not just Saturday night. At that point in time, John was taking Mark to Peabody Conservatory every Saturday. John would take books and papers to put the finishing touches on his Sunday message. He touched countless lives.

Then, when we moved to Millersville, we found a Methodist church close to us and immediately knew we had found a new church home. After a few months, I said, "I miss Sunday School class."

John talked with the pastors, who said, "You can try, but know it has always failed here."

At our first class, there were twelve people. A significant number, wouldn't you think? By the time we left, we had sixty-five or seventy dedicated members.

With both classes, I was the entertainment chairman. I loved to plan parties, and we always had crowds of people!

God works in mysterious ways, I have always heard. One of the last Sundays that we were in church, two men (whose families we support from the Sudan) spoke to the congregation about the need for clothing back in their village.

John was truly moved by their plea. You see, we had had direct contact with a young boy from the Sudan who was given a home by Philip and Debby when they were living in Egypt about fifty years ago.

Ephron had shared, reluctantly, the terrible times in Sudan. As a teenager, he found a way to escape to Egypt before being slaughtered.

Debby's home church in Lockport, New York, sent Ephron to college, where he was graduated, then went on to get a Masters and Doctorate, and was hired by Johns Hopkins as a public health officer.

This is all to say that, for us, a plea from the Sudanese is personal. And John got up from his seat as the last hymn started, interrupted the organist, and asked the congregation to show their support by coming to the altar and shaking their hands.

Everyone in the church came forward. It was electric, it was real. I have come to see this as John's last testimony of faith. He truly was a man of faith.

Pets I Have Known and Loved

WRITTEN JULY 15, 2016

BROWNIE WAS THE FIRST DOG I HAD EVER ENCOUNTERED. He was a Chesapeake Bay Retriever and acted as if he would chew your leg off, if given the chance. His reputation was well known.

There was a pile of sticks by the telephone pole at the corner of his yard. You see, the bus stopped here, and people didn't feel safe waiting for, or departing from, the bus. Brownie belonged to the village's self appointed mayor. Brownie was the model of doggie decorum when the mayor was around, but left on his own, he could terrorize the neighborhood.

One evening Brownie was sitting in the front seat of the mayor's car with the car windows rolled down just a few inches. In his little doggy brain, he must have been thinking, "It's time for action."

Brownie was comfortable with all the men sitting on the bench, as it was the nightly routine. Just then a somewhat older, somewhat heavy woman walked by the mayor's car. Brownie stuck his nose out of the window and gave one very loud bark, right in her ear. She screeched, she cried, and all but fainted. And, Brownie, he was so pleased with himself!

My encounter with Brownie showed his true nature—a bully. I was walking with my crutches across a vacant lot, between my home and a neighbor's, when Brownie charged out of nowhere. He and the mayor were visiting the neighbor. I quickly realized that Brownie saw my crutches as weapons. So I said, "Oh, Brownie, go home."

Tail between his legs, he ran away whimpering.

When I was first home from the hospital in 1946, a family friend brought me a Persian kitten—black, yellow, and white. With Mother's help, we decided to name her Tabitha, but she soon came to be Kitty Tab. She had a wonderful disposition and allowed me to dress her in doll's clothes and put her in my doll carriage where she would nap. That cat endured so much! When she reached her limit, she just ran away. For some unknown reason, my Mother would not agree to having Kitty Tab spayed. Consequently, she became a kitty machine! I can't remember how many litters she had, but there were many. She was killed by a car.

One of her many kittens, Black Boy by name, was such a love as well as smart. This was at the time Mother and I left Nanticoke on Monday morning only to return after school on Friday. While we were away,

Black Boy would go four houses down the road to my grandmother's, where she would feed him until Friday when Mother and I would be back. How did he know to do this? That was his routine for years, until he just disappeared.

Our next and last cat was Miss Sniff, straight from a Golden Book. Someone dropped her in our front yard and Mark found her. He brought her into the house with the time worn question, "Can we keep her?" I told him we must wait until we could check with his Dad. By the time Dad got home, we had fed her and given her a saucer of milk. Sniff had already made up her mind!

She lived with us for fifteen years, all the time thinking Mark was her human. When John scolded Mark and tapped him on his bottom, Sniff bit John on his ankle!

When Mark was home recovering from Chicken Pox, he became bored. Reading, TV, fooling at the piano, just wasn't enough. So, he devised a game involving Sniff. First, he tied a string from one bedroom door to another. Then he tied the other end to Sniff's tail. All the bedroom doors were open, so when he said, "Sniffy, run," you heard three doors slam. It was creative, and Sniff would only have allowed Mark to do this.

Sniff loved her family, and when John drove in the driveway in his Volkswagen Bug, he would pause, and Sniff would jump on the hood and ride into the garage. Sniff was a hunter. She killed a rabbit, brought it to our front door, and stretched it out perfectly. She spent two hours pushing a turtle up the driveway. She caught a bird, brought it into the just cleaned family room, shook it as hard as she could. Feathers and down floated like snow. She was giving us gifts and was so pleased with herself!

Cats probably teach us more than we teach them. But there is a bond there that gives us joy. Stroking a cat and hearing it purr is so satisfying. And when it's gone, the days are often silent and sterile.

Dogs

WRITTEN JULY 21, 2016

I ALWAYS WANTED A DOG. DADDY WAS FINE WITH IT, but Mother was adamantly against it. Looking back, I can understand Mother's position. She would have been its major caregiver and she certainly didn't need anything more to care for.

So, it wasn't until I was an adult that I got a dog. She arrived Christmas day in a toilet tissue box on the kitchen floor. Her name was Allegro because she made me happy. Now, I knew how to care for a dog about as much as I knew how to care for a baby.

But Allegro and I soon understood each other—with the exception of house breaking! She would signal me to go out; I'd put the leash on her and take her out. Then, the process began; nose to the ground she would sniff the whole area, turn and look at me with those precious eyes, as if to say, "What else do you want?"

She used this same tactic when she thought Mark was going to give her a bath. I can hear him say, "Now, cut it out, Allegro." As a silver miniature Schnauzer, she didn't get groomed until she was three months old. Until that time, she was a cuddly ball of fur.

Mark went with me to get her from her first grooming appointment, and when he brought her back to the car, I immediately burst into tears. This wasn't my dog! Allegro looked at me so sorrowfully as if to say, "Why don't you know me?" I came to terms with it, but she sure wasn't a puppy anymore.

Allegro loved her family, particularly Mark. She would sit by him as he did his school work. It never failed that when he played any Brahms piece on the piano, Allegro had to sit under the piano. I have no idea what attracted her to Brahms. Having said this, Allegro grew up hearing the piano played all the time.

One day Mark was rehearsing with a singer from church. When she hit high C, Allegro (nose in the air!) just howled. I was mortified. I grabbed her, held her in my lap, headed outside where we stayed until the rehearsal was over. It was cold, but, thank heavens, it wasn't raining!

Allegro loved our fenced in yard. At some point she started digging and found a very muddy beanie baby, no doubt left by the children of the previous owners. Allegro was determined to bring said muddy toy into the house. I quickly realized she wasn't going to give it up, so I grabbed the mud ball and washed it in the sink. Lo and behold, it was a cute red bear. Next, I hung it from the clothes line where Allegro sat until I took it down. She promptly grabbed it, ran and hid her toy in the house behind the ceiling to floor drapes. Years later, I realized she thought this was her puppy. She guarded this puppy until the beans started to spill out!

Allegro would eat anything that didn't eat her first. She loved her Puppy Chow and would gobble every morsel in a matter of minutes. Then she would give the loudest burp. It was as if she was saying, "Thank the Lord for that meal."

One day she was out in the back yard a little longer than I had planned, and when I went outside I discovered she had eaten green apples that had fallen from our tree. That evening John and Mark went to an Oriole's ball game, so it was just Allegro and me. She usually stayed by my side, so when I missed her I started looking, only to find her in her bed. She raised her head and moaned most pitifully. She had a tummy ache and it was bad. She got little sympathy from me, but I did rake around the tree every day.

When Mark left to attend Rice University, Allegro was depressed. She sat on his bed, looking out the front window waiting for his car to come in the driveway. She worried herself to death, I think.

After just ten years, Allegro died of pancreatic cancer. I sat in church the following Sunday with tears rolling down my face—I couldn't stop crying. She had been my daily companion and given me so much love and joy.

Three weeks later I said I must have another dog, so we adopted

Pepper, another miniature Schnauzer, three years old. She came from a family, one of whom had developed severe allergies. Pepper was a man's dog. She automatically went to the male in the room. She knew I loved her, but in her previous life she had been cared for by the father.

Pepper sat at our front door for months, waiting for Harry to come get her. It broke my heart. She wouldn't eat, and drank little. Finally, we hand fed her and gave her more attention, if that is possible, and she started to settle in.

I think, of our three schnauzers, Daddy liked Pepper best. He took her riding in the car, and when we visited, she stayed by his side. Mother never became a dog lover. She couldn't understand why dogs didn't pick up their toys!

Pepper was very protective of me. One day I went out the front door to speak to some men who were to do some landscaping. I failed to close the front door behind me, so when one of the men approached me, Pepper dashed out the front door like a cannon ball, barking as if she would eat the man for dinner. The man backed up slowly, then turned and ran to his truck. My little fifteen-pound defender had saved the day!

Pepper, a true Schnauzer, ate most anything. While we were away for an evening, Pepper found the trick or treat Halloween candy and helped herself. She smelled something good in my pocketbook, sitting on the floor, and pulled out the chewing gum. You haven't lived until you try to get gum out of a Schnauzer beard at 11:00 p.m.

While visiting my parents, Pepper found and ate one of my father's partially smoked cigars. On another visit, she ate a candy bar. Contrary to what is written, Pepper never got sick after these indulgences.

These two dogs gave me far more than I could ever put in words. Unconditional love is such a gift and all three of our dogs showed such patience with me as I went through all the maneuvers in order to fill their food dish. I ran over a few paws, but they never complained.

Magnolia D. Clinton

WRITTEN AUGUST 26, 2016

WHEN PEPPER DIED, I THOUGHT I COULD NOT LOVE another dog. These dogs filled my life—I was alone quite often, so having a dog made me responsible for her welfare—to feed, play with and, most of all, to love. I needed those dogs. I needed something living, breathing to love. The house was not complete without a dog—that clink, clink of her tags as she followed me, lying on the floor, her head between her paws, watching everything I did.

Magnolia D. Clinton was the *pièce de résistance.* I decided a white Schnauzer was just what I needed. White is not the usual color of a Schnauzer, but from time to time one is born in a litter. It took a few months to find one advertised in the Washington Post. The breeder lived in northern Virginia, so we arranged a visit.

She had two white puppies that she brought to the car for me to see. One was very timid, cowering against the front tire; the other one was busy investigating everything—the car, the grass, and even tried to climb in the car. "That is the one," I said. She had spunk—she was ready for everything!

I looked at John who immediately knew what I was thinking! "Don't even go there," he admonished. I wondered if we could work a deal to buy both dogs! Instead, we drove home with Magnolia a/k/a Maggie.

Maggie lived up to my first impression in every way.

She quickly learned how to get away from my scooter. At first she followed me so closely that I would run over her paws. That was lesson number one!

We were still in the housebreaking stage and I was still trying to learn her routine. John and friends had gone to an Orioles baseball game, so it was just Maggie and me. I decided to take my bath, so I gave Maggie a chance to go out. She knew exactly what I wanted, so she went through the doggie routine—nose to the ground, sniff, sniff, looking up to see if she was being watched, repeat procedure as many times as needed. OK, here's the deal, you stay in the crate until I get my bath. Maggie was not happy with that, but did settle down.

So, I stripped, put my shower cap on, and was ready to transfer to my bath lift, when Maggie started howling. I paused. Was she barking that she didn't want to be confined? Or was she saying, "I really have to go?"

I wrapped myself in a bath sheet, got Maggie from the crate, and took her outside. Once outside, it came to me what are you doing? Suppose one of my neighbors came out on their deck? Here I am looking like a giant mushroom with a dog on a leash! Maggie was still going around in circles and I am praying, "Please, God, don't let anyone see me like this."

Then the thought hit me: if the kitchen door closed, it would be locked. I sent up another prayer. Finally, I interrupted the circling and dragged Maggie back to the crate, all the time admonishing her that she would be confined in the crate until I decided otherwise. How could you not love her—a dog who was such a con artist!

We were living in our dream home when we brought Maggie to live with us. We had not yet put a storm door on our front door when Maggie discovered it was partially open. Always up for adventure, Maggie left. I had not missed her, and when the doorbell rang and the little neighbor child told me Maggie was in their backyard, I went into panic mode. I yelled for Ruth (my helper) and started on my search.

Now, we were living in a new neighborhood and everyone was trying for the best lawn. To make matters worse, it was rainy and really chilly. So, here I go plowing through yards in my scooter calling for Maggie. I wondered if we would be thrown out of the neighborhood association.

Then I saw her. She had crossed the main artery of the development. Cars were backed up and all I saw were brake lights. Ruth picked her up and she was trembling like she would never stop. I put her in my lap and returned home.

I think Maggie and I both learned a lesson. She never attempted that again. Good thing, too. My heart could not take too many incidents like that.

Sunshine and Shadows

WRITTEN FEBRUARY 16, 2018

EDWARD A. GUEST ONCE WROTE, "It takes a heap of living to make a house a home; a heap of sun and shadows, and you sometimes have to roam."

John and I have done a fair amount of roaming from our first apartment as newly weds, to a newly built apartment in Hyattsville, to the ranches in Salisbury, to the ranches in Radford, Virginia, back to Maryland in Bowie, then Millersville, and finally Lincoln. We left part of us in each place.

That first apartment was bleak and small. I remember cleaning the stove for the first time. It took me five buckets of water to finally get the oven nearly clean. Not spotless, but usable.

Parquet flooring—we never got the dirt completely out between the squares. But we were happy and played a lot of card games with another young couple.

I truly disliked my job in Medical Records at a local hospital in Washington, D.C. In the winter I went to work in the dark and returned home in the dark! I craved sun. I truly don't know how people live without sun. Shadows are only tolerable for a short time.

John was in graduate school, but life was great. Then we moved to Salisbury in the house that had been built for me. The operative words here are "built for me" to live in, not to take care of.

We had to find a way to put the stove on a level that I could reach from my chair. The washing machine had to be a front loader for me to use it. It worked well until a certain toddler opened it while it was washing. This was after my Mother had just told me that "said toddler could never open that door." It was a new learning experience each and every day!

Mark started kindergarten here and found a kitten in the front yard which, of course, we kept. There were a lot of sunshine moments!

Our next home in Radford, Virginia was really perfect for me—a rancher, no steps, garage adjoining the house, in a young neighborhood.

School for Mark wasn't far away (Mark was registered at Radford College as a music student!) We settled in quickly, got really involved in a wonderful church. Life was full.

Then I lost my Gram. She was the first person that I had lost who was so very dear to me. Mark also had spent many hours with her. It was a shadow-filled time.

Mark played for Leon Fleisher at the Peabody Conservatory in Baltimore. Mr. Fleisher offered him a chance to study with his top student under his supervision—all with the understanding that at some point Mark would have the opportunity to study with Mr. Fleisher. It was a chance of a lifetime.

So we returned to Radford, put our house on the market, sold it rather quickly, and found a one-floor home in Bowie about forty-five minutes from the Conservatory. A time of lots of sun and shadows.

It didn't take long before we made our house into a home and once again became super involved with our new church.

Shortly after moving to Bowie, I lost my maternal grandmother. For my Mother, it meant no parents at all.

For me, my role changed. I was no longer a granddaughter. The structure of my family had completely changed. I was an adult. That was emotionally frightening.

We lived in Bowie twenty-two years. With prodding from my father, we started looking, once again, for a new home with live-in capabilities. He always planned with the future in mind.

John and I found a builder in a community about thirty minutes from Baltimore, and in 1994 we moved to Millersville. We did a lot of living in that house. I loved every inch of it.

Unfortunately, I lost both parents while living there. The family dynamic drastically changed. It seemed so sudden that we were the older generation.

Shadows became more sharply defined, and the sun became even more needed. The ebb and flow of life, sunshine and shadows.

Mr. Guest puts it quite nicely, "It isn't home to you, though it be the palace of a king, until somehow your very soul is wrapped around everything."

Help
Domestic

WRITTEN AUGUST 5, 2016

I HAVE ALWAYS HAD TO EMPLOY HOUSEHOLD HELP. Early in my married life, I would have someone work for me just a few days a week. Then when Mark was born, I needed full-time help. Chris was a loving soul and looked at Mark as if he were her own. If Mark wanted a bologna sandwich every day for lunch, that's what he got.

Chris would walk Mark to and from school each day.

As Mark got older and wiser, by which I mean, he had passed from kindergarten to first grade. He would insist Chris follow him several paces behind, so that no one would know they were together.

Years later Chris would tell me Mark would repeat over and over "Stay back, Chris, stay back." Chris was with us until we moved to Radford, Virginia, in 1970.

In Radford, I was fortunate enough to find Carlotta. She was about my age, with two young boys. I always felt she had so much more to offer. And when we left Radford two years later, Carlotta took courses at the community college and was hired in a very responsible secretarial job. This pleased me so greatly.

Carlotta and I loved humor. At the time, Burt Reynolds was the reigning "most handsome male in Hollywood." I made the remark that our postman looked a lot like Burt Reynolds and he could deliver a package to me every day! We laughed and joked about this for weeks. Then I saw the nude photograph of Burt in Cosmopolitan magazine. I carefully cut the two-page picture from the magazine and draped it over the washer and dryer and closed the door.

The next day, I waited for Carlotta to arrive, and when she opened the laundry room door, I heard this very loud squeal. We laughed for days!

When we moved back to Maryland, I had to start all over. No little task! We found a perfect rancher in Bowie, halfway between D.C. and Annapolis. First, there was Rosalie, who was perfect. All I had to do was say, "I'd like this or that done today," show her the cleaning products I used and the vacuum cleaner, and it was taken care of. She was the lucky one who had just finished cleaning our family room when Miss Sniff, our cat, bird in her mouth, shook the dead bird, and feathers covered the rug. But Rosalie got pregnant, and that was the end of that!

I next hired an English woman with a delightful accent. She arrived on Monday morning, and to make conversation, I asked if she had had a nice weekend. "No," she replied, "the dog et my boonies." Now, I had no idea what she meant. So, I kept repeating it in my head. Finally, I gave up and just asked what "boonies" were. She looked at me as if I came from another planet. Then she said, "I raise boonies, a/k/a rabbits." To this day, we will often refer to boonies!

After a few weeks, my English lady left because she wanted only day work. Thinking that much of housework is rather routine, I thought that perhaps someone marginally mentally challenged could be helpful to both of us, so I phoned the appropriate office and they agreed to send someone.

She drove her car to the interview, which I thought was a good sign. We set time limits and pay, and then talked about what I needed done. The last chore of the day was to be to scrub my kitchen floor. I was expecting John's mother to arrive any minute.

Gwen was well into the job when I heard her call me. I dashed to the kitchen only to find she had backed herself into a corner and couldn't get out without walking on a very wet floor. I suggested she remove her shoes and carry them and the cleaning supplies to one of the three doors in the kitchen. This wasn't going to work either.

Next came the Japanese lady. She was very thorough in her cleaning and, for the most part, seemed to know what she was doing. Except when I saw her starting to dust mahogany furniture with a wet cloth. I did notice she coughed constantly, and when I saw blood on the tissues, it was all over. So, once again, back to the drawing board.

Most churches know a lot about their community. So, maybe a pastor would know of someone who needed a job and would do housework. Enter my very special lady—she was with me for over thirty years. Rhonda was scared of dogs, but soon came to love all three of our miniature Schnauzers. She had three grown children, so we quickly became family.

Rhonda was a product of the fifties—still segregation in southern Maryland. Her mother had ten children. They all lived in a tiny house.

Rhonda had somehow acquired an old trailer that was on family property, and a car. She had worked in the tobacco fields and knew everyone in the county. But that was seasonal and she wanted full-time employment.

A pastor of her church brought Rhonda to our house. Like many of the black population at that time, she was suspicious of white people. What was my ulterior motive?

It wasn't long before she realized I was harmless! We had to work out a few kinks, but I saw it as a work in progress.

She just would not show up for work one day; then appear the following day. Her excuse was that she had something to do! Fine, but you must call and tell me that you won't be here.

Her car was always needing repair, which we bankrolled. Finally, it just died. So, we bought her a car. I cautioned her to take care of this car. In fact, if you take it to our service center, we will take care of regular oil changes. No, she would do that herself!

Shortly before we moved, she came to work saying a red light was showing in her car. I asked how long it had been on; answer: for a few months! We got it repaired. How long it lasted, I don't know. I do know she hasn't a car now.

Spring and Fall, we would take a trip to a large nursery, some thirty minutes away. Those times we labeled the car as the "plant mobile"; we would load the car with all sorts of seasonal plants and supplies. I loved those trips. This nursery grew plants and shrubs for the White House. So, you can imagine how beautiful it was.

Rhonda did not share my love of all nature. I fed the birds, squirrels, and humming birds. We also had chipmunks—Alvin, Theodore, and Simon. One day I discovered this gigantic mound of dirt under my kitchen window. I had no idea who constructed this condominium. The answer soon became evident the chipmunks were having a family. Rhonda immediately offered to get the hoe and take care of things. "No," I shouted, "there might be babies in there." A few weeks later, we could tell the mound was no longer occupied.

We had a turtle come on the sidewalk almost to our front door. She went into an area and started digging. She dug for hours. Then she laid her eggs over another few hours. When she was finished, she covered the eggs with the surrounding dirt. I find this amazing. She spent most of a day finding a spot to lay her eggs, digging the hole, depositing the eggs, covering them with dirt, then leaving.

My next thought was that Alvin, Theodore, and Simon may consider this gourmet dining, so at 11:00 p.m. at night, I placed nylon netting over the egg site and staked the netting with plant spikes. I don't know how many turtles actually hatched. I saw three, and like their mother they were Boxer turtles, an already endangered species.

Rhonda had to have knee surgery and couldn't work for two months. What can I do? Finding someone at this point was almost impossible. Daddy suggested that I look for a live-in. After all, that is why we had our home built. We already had a bedroom, sitting area, closet, and bathroom just for a live-in.

But where do you look? John happened to read an article about a local lawyer who brought nannies to the States for works. Maybe she could find someone for us. A young woman from the Ukraine agreed to our terms and came to the U.S. We met her at Dulles airport way out in Virginia.

Demolition Derbies...Sort Of

WRITTEN MARCH 2, 2018

I CAN BE, AND OFTEN AM, A ONE WOMAN WRECKING CREW. It is all done incidentally. Heaven forbid I truly tried to destroy something!

Like most young children, I would try to take the eyes out of a stuffed bunny. My mother removed bunny from my clenched little hands and put him on the fireplace mantle.

I responded, "I can get bunny. All I have to do is pull a chair to the brick hearth and bunny would be mine!" Bunny or Mother won—no more demolition here.

When I first came home from the hospital, I soon learned to use the toilet by myself. It was a major victory for me—until I tried to pull myself up from the toilet by using the sink right in front of me.

Lo and behold, I pulled the sink from the wall! It actually could have been disastrous, but I escaped unscathed.

Then I decided to side step around the outside of the house. Things were going well. Nobody knew where I was or what I was doing. When I got to the first corner, I lost my balance and, quite naturally, I grabbed the two story gutter and pulled it completely away from the house. From flat on my back, that gutter looked mighty tall.

I was not hurt, and Daddy sent someone to put the gutter back in place. All's well that ends well!

This was only the beginning of my demolition career. I have been known to trim door frames, one small sliver at a time.

I pulled a door from its hinges. Well, actually, I pulled the door and hinges from the door frame. It took some work to fill the hole.

Then there was the worst incident. Mark was coming home from Rice University for his spring vacation. We had had all the interior walls of our home freshly painted. I was so pleased how fresh everything looked.

Then I got from my chair, outside the tiny bathroom, to use the toilet. When I got back to sit in my scooter, I started to lose my balance and, in a panic, I grabbed the tiller and drove into, and partially through, the wall!

The phone rang. Mark was calling from Houston Airport saying he was ready to board the plane for Baltimore. I was crying.

Mark asked what was wrong. I answered that "I had put a hole in the wall."

To be of comfort, he said, "I'm sure it's just a little hole."

"No, I answered, "it is big enough I could put Allegro in it." Allegro was our miniature Schnauzer. He laughed; I did not.

Then I called the painter and told him what had happened. He was silent for a bit, processing the information, then said, "Christine is back again," referring to Stephen King's book *Christine,* "the car that had a mind of its own." It is humorous now, but not even remotely then!

My scooter is my legs. As such, it has been used thoughtlessly.

Since our yard backed to the woods, there was a root system under the sod like you wouldn't believe. So when I started making two beds of rose bushes, I had to first de-root the plot.

Some roots were fairly sizable, but I figured if I could start pulling at the root and drove my scooter fairly fast, I would get roots out quickly. It worked really well until I got into some mud. Then I was stuck.

My neighbor, Don, came and pushed me out of the mud. That in itself should have been a good lesson. But I think I'm a slow learner because a week later I did the same thing in the front yard.

Poor Don! This time, my tires kicked up enough mud to cover him, and he went to his knees. The perils of being me!

My spirit really doesn't fit my body. I am convinced I can do most anything if I can just figure out how my body can cooperate. I never have been fully convinced of the saying "The spirit may be willing, but the body is weak."

Maybe I should now reconsider this!

Freedom

WRITTEN JULY 1, 2016

IN MY MIND, THERE ARE TWO KINDS OF FREEDOM—personal freedom, and the general freedoms granted by the government. My personal freedom is limited in a physical sense, but my mind has no such restrictions. It can take me anywhere.

Driving a car expanded my physical boundaries. In 1980, we—my parents, John, and I attended a major convention in Washington, D.C., displaying every kind of assistive device imaginable for the disabled. It offered freedom in every guise. We stopped at a booth showing scooters, a fairly new product in our world. I tried one. Daddy said he would never forget the look on my face—I glowed! I experienced the freedom to move from one place to another with little or no effort. In my mind, I thought I had died and gone to heaven!

There is something within me that twists into knots when I think of my life in deficit terms. How I yearn to walk the seashore with the river lapping at my feet. Maybe I would discover an arrowhead from a long ago settlement of the Nanticoke Indians.

How I yearned for the freedom to take my baby for a carriage ride or show him the beauty of this earth, squatting in the grass to watch a cricket chirp; a blossom ready to burst open in glorious color. And the freedom to dance when the heart explodes with the beauty of music. So much the normal world takes for granted. I want to shout, "Move! You are so blessed—move to the rhythms of life!

I have become one with my scooter. It gives me the freedom to move slowly, deliberately, or at a racing speed. Life is good then. Yet my life crumbles when my chair is out of commission. I turn into a sharp-tongued shrew. Yet in my book of personal freedoms, the asset pages far out number the deficit ones.

The Statue of Liberty is a beautiful symbol of freedom. On our very first visit, I learned the true meaning of Lady Liberty. It was a cool, damp Fall day with intermittent rain. I sat in my chair next to the other deck chairs. The boat plowed through the choppy water at a steady pace. Next to me sat a fairly short man bundled in a heavy overcoat, Fedora on his head. As Lady Liberty came into view, he said, in a thick Italian accent, "Such a beautiful lady." I replied, "And that she is."

Immediately I wanted to hear more from this man, so I asked had he been here before. He related to me how he had come from Sicily soon after World War II had ended. He was an electrician by trade and had to wait on Ellis Island until his cousin from Syracuse, New York, could come and sign for him. It took two weeks before he arrived in Syracuse, where he established a very successful electrical repair store. He had employment, someone to vouch for him, and he came to thank Lady Liberty. Freedom became more than a concept: it was visceral; it was real.

In the late 1970's, we took Mark to Salzburg, Austria, where he was to study at the *Mozarteum*. It was a picture perfect week for all of us. John and I returned home after the first week, and my parents arrived for the second week. We returned home by way of Munich. While waiting to board the plane, we became very aware of the military guards marching with loaded rifles. It didn't instill a feeling of safety; rather, a feeling of fear. How do people live like that? Never knowing if you would make an unintentional mistake and be shot.

When we landed at J.F.K. in New York City, I wanted to kiss the ground. It is the land of the free. I have always thought that F.D.R.'s Four Freedom's Speech defined freedoms most successfully:

1. The freedom of speech and expression;
2. The freedom to worship in our own way;
3. The freedom from want;
4. The freedom from fear.

Who could forget the Norman Rockwell painting of the Four Freedoms? If only these freedoms could be realized!

Birthdays

WRITTEN JULY 13, 2018

A FRIEND ASKED ME A FEW DAYS AGO—what was my favorite birthday? The answer was almost reflexive—the year I got my first car fully equipped with hand controls. I was seventeen years old, and that red and white Mercury Montego was a real dream boat.

Funny enough, it was a year that my birthday happened to be on a Friday 13th. Now, my father would never admit to being superstitious, heaven forbid! But he artfully managed to get it delivered on Thursday the 12th. His excuse was that it suited Mr. Emerson to bring the car on Thursday rather than on Friday!

At that point, I really didn't care. I was over the moon—my very own car! It presented me with a freedom that I never expected to have. Birthdays were usually family affairs aunts, uncles, cousins, and grandparents.

But another birthday, probably 18th or 19th, my Sugar Daddy gave me a giant-sized bottle of Chanel perfume. He told me, "Every young woman should try wearing Chanel." After his visit, I rushed to my bedroom and looked in the mirror. I don't know what I was hoping to see, but all I saw was plain old me. Yet, there was something different.

Daddy engaged a State trooper to teach me how to drive and the rules of the road. It was like a bee to honey—driving was easy—that Mercury and I became one.

On one of my early outings, Mother, beside me, shouted (or so it seemed to me) "Stop!" I did, the brake almost pushed to the floor and my grandmother and her sister in the back seat thrown forward.

Mother looked at me and I said, "You said, 'Stop,' didn't you"? Fortunately, I learned to stop without squealing the tires.

Strangely enough, John and I had birthdays only six days apart. We fully agreed that our birth year was a vintage one. But since his came first, I would call him "My Old Man" for six days. Then I became remarkably silent.

My earliest memory of a birthday is when I was five years old. All the little boys and girls in the neighborhood were invited. Loraine (my sister of the heart) was spending the week with me. Mother had dressed me in a pretty little dress, and I'm sure Loraine had one also.

We were told to go sit on the porch 'til the other children came. Loraine and I loved paper dolls, and I had a new book of them. So we sat on the porch floor cutting away—until I posed the question, "Dare me to cut my hair?"

Loraine may or may not have answered. Never mind, I wanted to do it anyway, so I cut a chunk of hair right in the front. Let's say it was early spike style! My mother was. . .well, angry. But the party went as planned.

There is a picture of me pulling my dress up to cover my face. Presumably to hide the new haircut. So it's all there in black and white. Modesty would only come later.

Who would have thought that I would live to be seventy-nine? Eighty-nine in polio years. Certainly, no one would have thought John would be the first to leave this earth.

It seems to me that God really does have a sense of humor. All the odds are against me, but here I am, still able to enjoy a glass of wine, share laughter and, best of all, the love of many, many dear friends.

Father

WRITTEN JUNE 17, 2016

It's been six years since I sent my last Father's Day card. I miss him terribly. We had our moments; still, in all, I loved every bone in his body. Daddy was an intelligent man. My love of history started with him.

He was graduated from Washington College in Chestertown, Maryland, and was immediately offered a great position at Dupont Industries in Dover, Delaware. I don't think he spent a lot of time considering the offer because his life-long passion was the seafood business with his father.

He loved the river and knew its every curve. He built the business from a little oyster house serving mainly local Maryland markets to providing oysters to Canada, the Midwest, to Seattle, to Fisherman's Wharf in California. He often left the dinner table to return to the plant to help the men finish loading the trucks. He probably employed about a hundred people at that time.

But what could he offer these people in the off season? Daddy started canning tomatoes. The season started in July with local grown tomatoes, continuing with tomatoes from Virginia to New Jersey, and finished the season in September with tomatoes grown in New York state.

I think he was the most proud of being able to offer year-round employment to members of the community. In the early 1950's, he became interested in canning tuna fish. I'm not sure why. He flew to Oslo, Norway, to check out their freezing techniques. Next, he went to New York City to talk with people about importing raw tuna.

While in New York City, he went to Chase Manhattan Bank and met with David Rockefellow who, basically, gave him carte blanche for this new endeavor. However, there was one stumbling block. There was no one on the East Coast at the time, mainly because California controlled the tuna industry by means of tariffs. So, Daddy, with his lawyer at his side, went before Congress to testify that the East Coast should be allowed to import tuna.

In later years, he spoke kindly of Everett Dirkson and Margaret Chase Smith, saying that they were so well prepared and the committee asked cogent questions. Daddy was to testify twice more, trying to save the treasures of the sea. A bill was passed, and Daddy imported tuna from Peru for the next four or five years. It was a beautiful sight to see those big ships coming up the Nanticoke River. They had to stop at the mouth of the Chesapeake Bay, by the Federal Custom agent, to clear them to unload at Nanticoke.

These ships were rusty and quite weathered. The *Rhumba* anchored outside of the harbor and was met by Daddy and his State Department friend who lived in the Village. Mr. Shoenrick was a linguist and was able to translate the Spanish to English and English to Spanish.

Daddy had some knowledge of Spanish from college, so always had a sense of what was being said. The captain brought gifts, of course, and invited us to dinner. It was a glimpse of life that was completely "off my grid," but, oh, so fascinating.

The faces of the crew reflected their life at sea; their smiles were kind. Daddy made sure that while they were in port, they were all taken shopping in Salisbury, the county seat. The crew was ecstatic. They bought televisions, radios, clothes for their families, and other household items. Somehow, I don't think the weight was substantially reduced on their return trip.

The Norway trip and the connection to Peru started my doll collection, of which there are over a hundred countries that are represented.

Daddy was pleased that I took to driving like a duck to water. He never complained about gas bills. But somehow he always knew where I went and with whom.

When Mark was born, he was overjoyed. John called my parents at 1:30 a.m. to announce Mark's arrival. Daddy's first words were, "Dorothy, Mary Ann has a little boy." Mother promptly replied, "I don't know how to buy for a little boy." She was a quick learner!

We lived in Salisbury for seven years before moving to Radford, Virginia, so that John could teach political science at Radford University. My father saw this as an act of treason. He didn't speak to me for months. After all, I was taking his grandson away from him. It was as simple as that. I knew it was the right thing for us to do, but it broke my heart.

When we moved back to Maryland on the western shore, he acknowledged that I had done the right thing. "Mary Ann, you had to go with your husband." I never doubted that I had made the right decision.

In October of 2009, Daddy called and said, "My Lord, Mary Ann, you have done one hell of a job." It was 64 years to the day that I had been stricken with polio. He never knew how much that meant, coming from him.

Several years earlier, I had gone to a polio specialist in Baltimore for evaluation. After hours of tests, the doctor looked over his notes and said, "What a job you have done! I'm sure you hear that all the time."

I looked at him, tears welling in my eyes, and told him this was the first time. He could not believe that no one had said, "Good job." So, years later when Daddy acknowledged my survival, something crumbled inside me like a piece of pottery. Yes, indeed, I am a survivor, and I still love every bone in his body.

Happy Father's Day, Daddy!

A Tribute to Mother

WRITTEN MAY 6, 2021

I always told my mother that God certainly knew what He was doing when He gave me to her. She was always my champion, always by my side to help me master difficult times, and my number one cheerleader.

Mother, Dorothy by name, was the middle sister of the three sisters. She approached life rather seriously. I never heard her laugh uproariously. She was, however, fastidious about her clothes. She washed and ironed her own clothes at a young age. Every piece was just so.

The youngest sister "borrowed" one of my mother's outfits to play the piano at a Parent/Teachers meeting. So many people commented how nice Amy looked in that beautiful aqua suit. Mother heard this, of course, went to her closet, and found the suit with a grease stain on it. Words were exchanged. Let's just say Amy didn't try that again!

Mother dated my father in high school. She always hastened to tell me that dating in that time was a group thing. After graduation, Daddy went off to college and Mother went to nursing school in Baltimore. Daddy had a car, so I think he made a few trips to Baltimore. She was never clear about that. She left nursing school about halfway through the course work. Why? I really don't know.

I think she had such a hard time physically, particularly night duty. She said many times that it was all so stressful. They actually had to scrub the metal beds, floors, and such. It sounded like forced labor to me.

But, did I ever benefit from her year and a half training. She knew instinctively how to bank pillows around me to support muscles. Medicines were always properly given throughout the day and night. She learned how to do physical therapy for me. I see God's hand in all of this.

After fifteen months in the hospital, I was allowed to go home. A twin bed was put in the dining room so I could rest during the day. Within three months, an elevator was installed, plus a second bathroom on the first floor and a large play room on the second floor. Needs were met before I knew I needed anything.

Mother knew the value of being with other children, so she encouraged other children to visit—and they did. She always had fresh lemonade and pretzels. Homemade cake, cupcakes, you name it, she prepared it all! In addition, she had a large flower garden. I can understand now, that the garden was her escape, her stabilizer.

When I was allowed to return to public school, she came at lunchtime, bringing me lunch and helping me use the bathroom. She did this for eleven years. Not only that, she would lift me under my arms and a schoolmate would carry my legs so that I could be outside with the other children.

You can imagine the worry she had to cope with when I went away to college. For the first time, I saw her cry—she was almost hysterical thinking my needs would not be met. Daddy took her to Canada, but knowing Mother, I was always on her mind. Mother was all about making life better for me. She saw an advertisement for a bath lift. It was ordered and installed. All visitors had to see this marvelous piece of equipment!

She read everything she could find about wheelchairs. Early on, I had a collapsible wheelchair that could be stowed in the trunk of a car. The seat was covered in corduroy! That didn't last too long, sliding in and out of that chair, the corduroy became shiny and smooth! And, oh yes, there was no such thing as brakes!

When my pregnancy was announced, because I threw up on Abraham Lincoln's front yard, mother became stoic. I know they called my orthopedic doctor and were told I couldn't carry a baby beyond five months. She hovered. I can only imagine how conflicted she was. I never, ever doubted that this baby would be born well and healthy, and it was called Abe or Abby thanks to Abe Lincoln!

This mother who gave me life and enriched my life so immeasurably knew me so well. She gave her very life for me. In fact, she herself said, "If I could have breathed for her, I would." A mother's love is like no other!

As she more and more slipped into Alzheimer's dementia, so much of Mother disappeared. Yet, I think she knew me, right up to the end. I stayed at the hospital with her on that last night. At 7:00 a.m., I kissed her and told her how much I loved her. Then I whispered in her ear, "It's time, Mother, to go with God."

An hour later, she was gone but never, ever forgotten...

News flash! I received a phone call yesterday from a high school friend. Of course, we reminisced, then Susan said, "I'll never forget your mother. You remember, she always came to bring you lunch and got to the cafeteria before we did. She would go to the counter and get a serving of applesauce for Susan and some fries for Adrian." Susan said, "I'll never forget that." That was Mother!

One summer evening when I was eight or nine, a severe thunder storm began. Daddy was traveling on business. The lightning came through the telephone beside my parents' bed. Mother jumped up, ran into my bedroom, picked me up and carried me down the flight of stairs.

Now, mother was always slender, some would say skinny, weighing not more than 110 pounds. At that time, I probably weighed 75 pounds. How she did it, I don't know, but she made sure I was out of harm's way.

A Tribute to Mother
Part 2

WRITTEN MAY 13, 2021

I LOVE THE STORY OF MY MOTHER THAT MY FATHER TOLD ME. It was nearing Christmas and Daddy asked her what she wanted for Christmas. Sitting in her favorite rocker, she threw her legs in the air and replied, "You know me, I like furs, diamonds and silver." That was Mother!

Lest you think that was all that defined her, think again. She was just leaving Daddy's office at this particular time when a big sixteen wheeler truck arrived. Someone challenged her that she couldn't back that truck to the designated shipping area.

She took the challenge, climbed up to the cab (no mean feat in itself) and backed the truck, never missing a gear shift to the appropriate spot. Mother received a big round of applause from many employees who had rushed out to see the event!

When I was first stricken with polio, Mother barely slept. Often, she would put on her coat in the early hours of the morning, walk to our little church, and kneel at the altar and pray. Years later, she would tell me that she would beg God to paralyze her, not me. Her love for me never faltered. Mother made sure that I was part of any teenage trend at that time. In Senior High, the trend was charcoal blazers for girls. Mother had one for me early in the "game."

When my dear friend from Bombay, India, came with her parents to visit, they wanted mother to return with them to England on the Queen Mary sailing ship. Daddy begged her to go, but her mind was made up she wouldn't and couldn't leave me.

Mother would go to the library for me, first reading for pleasure books, then for research purposes from the library itself. Steps for both venues prohibited my access.

Mother instinctively seemed to know my needs—physical or mental. She never complained that my disability was a twenty four hour/seven day a week daunting responsibility. She just loved me through it all. I have been so blessed to be surrounded by such love. And it is true that love is eternal.

Pianos

WRITTEN OCTOBER 28, 2016

MARK STARTED PLAYING THE PIANO WHEN HE WAS FOUR OR FIVE. We had my old Spinet piano at the time. It's a wonder that it didn't ruin his gift of perfect pitch! It was of World War II vintage with a metal sound board. I shudder when I think of this.

When my grandmother died in 1980, she left a provision in her will that Mark should get a better piano. After much deliberation with highly respected musicians, we found a Baldwin grand piano. At the time, we lived in Radford, Virginia, so the seller agreed to bring said piano to us.

Expecting to see a medium size truck pull into our driveway, we were blown away to see a station wagon pulling a small trailer and the grand piano wrapped in a blanket on a piano board. There was only the driver in the truck.

Bewildered, I asked if I should try to locate more help. "No," he said, "I've got this." And he did!! He rolled the piano down a truck ramp and headed to our living room. My ramp into the house was an extra blessing that day.

Now, of course, the three legs of the piano had been removed, so first thing he did was put two legs on the piano. Then what? He asked if I had a high chair so he could stand the piano on two legs while he secured the third leg. My brain actually worked then. I remembered my step stool chair (a wedding gift). It was the perfect height and, viola, the piano stood on its three legs!

I believe Mark would have played all night! It made such beautiful sounds. But can you imagine pulling this beautiful instrument up and down the mountains in Virginia? I wonder what he would have done had it rained?

The next piano in Mark's life was his beloved Steinway D that came when we lived in Bowie, Maryland. It really has a magnificent sound even today! I don't think he would ever part from this piano. We had in-house concerts, and at every party there would be requests for him to play or do sing-alongs. It was the focus of all our lives.

So, when Mark moved out and took his piano, I thought life was over. I actually grieved for that piano forever! We were fortunate enough to have the Kennedy Center piano tuner take care of the piano. Percy had great stories of celebrity pianists—one that will stick in my mind forever is the artist bench story.

Maurizio Pollini, a tall, large-frame man, plays the piano like an angel. The Steinway artist bench can be adjusted to any height for the pianist. Pollini likes to almost sit on the floor when he performs. He couldn't get the Kennedy Center artist bench low enough. He was terribly upset. So Percy, our piano tuner, takes the bench to his truck and saws the legs to the desired height!

Now, an artist bench is somewhat costly, but I guess the Kennedy Center wrote it off as the price of doing business. I like to think "anything for the artist"!

Then there are the wacky stories. Friends of John's parents in Andover, Massachusetts, invited Mark to play a little recital on their grand piano for twenty or so friends. Imagine our horror when, with the first note of a Bach prelude and fugue, an ivory from a key popped off and went airborne! It could have been disastrous for Mark, yet he handled it like a pro. Now we laugh, "music in the air" or "the lost note"!

In Radford, Virginia, the president of the Music Teacher's Association invited Mark to do a recital some distance from Radford. John and I were seated right on the front row. Everything was going well until he started Schumann's *Scenes from Childhood.* These were seven little music passages that depicted childhood events. Mark forgot the fourth one. Trying to be helpful, I mouthed, "You forgot number four." Hands on the keys, he turned to me and did the perfect Carol Burnett, "Huh"? It really was a video moment.

Then there was the time Mark played with the Merrimac Orchestra in Massachusetts. Of course, all the local papers wanted interviews. And when asked if he were worried about playing with an orchestra, Mark replied, "I know my part and I know they know theirs."

Every summer for eight years Mark went to Cody, Wyoming, with my parents. They stayed at Bill Cody's Ranch Inn. Bill was the grandson of the famous Buffalo Bill. There were numerous cabins where guests stayed and all meals were served in the ranch house. Mark loved to ride horses, and Bill took him up the mountain for an overnight. Otherwise, everyone gathered at the ranch house after supper for conversation. Except when Mark was there. He was invited and expected to play on an old upright piano, rescued from a house of ill repute! I understand completely why many musicians don't want to be recognized.

There were many times we three were bone weary when we traveled with Mark. We shared, in a somewhat limited way, the stress that Mark must have felt. For him, the applause was rewarding. For John and me, the applause of an audience helped to reassure us that we were doing the right thing.

London

WRITTEN AUGUST 12, 2016

My favorite trip of all times is our trip to London, England. It was the very best way to celebrate our 50th wedding anniversary. OK, I admit I'm a died in the wool Anglophile. I have this deep connection with all things English, Cornwall in particular. Maybe it's because I know that Kennerlys (my maiden name) lived there. There is even a church named Kennerly. I do know I was first in line for any English history course in college and hugely regretted when every class was over.

When we arrived at Heathrow airport, and when I heard all the people with their beautiful English, a big smile was on my face that never left. Our hotel was not terribly far from Buckingham Palace. Unfortunately, the palace was closed for a month. That was a big disappointment, yet we surely made up for that deficit.

Trafalgar Square was exactly as I thought it to be—a straight forward monument to the military. Parliament was absolutely beautiful. If I closed my eyes, surely I would hear some past meticulously argued debates. Gentlemen's rules did not allow for anything too raucous.

Westminster Abbey was regal. To read the names of so many encrypted there was like reading a history book. What a place for royal weddings—all of the pomp and circumstance just fit here.

We went to the British Museum of Art where I wanted to see the Elgin Marbles. They are so lovely—I wanted to stroke those beautiful forms. And I could see why the British and Italians would feud over them.

One day we hired a driver to take us to Windsor Castle. It looked old, inside and out, and massive. But, then, you had to remember that at one time it was lavish living.

I was allowed to ride in the Queen's elevator and I could smell the luncheon being prepared for the day. The guard told us that the Queen Mum first used this elevator—or lift, I should say. The Queen Mum liked living at Windsor Castle for rather long periods of time. It must have been a daily occurrence, back in the day, that someone would get lost. What a rabbits' wren of rooms—some tiny, some huge.

Going into the castle, there was a pelting rain. A most kind security guard rushed over to me and said, "Luv, you will be soaked. Wait here." She literally wrapped me in plastic—so that I was not only dry, I was warm! Good thing, too. The castle was cold and damp.

The famed Doll House of Queen Victoria was a sweet work of art. What little girl wouldn't love it! It's difficult even now to imagine people living there. And now the upkeep of such a large place.

As we left the castle itself, John wanted to visit King George's chapel, while Mark and I opted to go to the gift shop. As we were entering the shop, this dear little lady—who happened to be the sales lady—rushed over to us to say, "Go over there to that fence. The Queen and her ladies in waiting are leaving for the horse races." One of the Queen's horses was running.

Somehow at least 50 or so other people got the same message and were making a mad dash to the same area. Mark was not deterred—he pushed me through the crowd with constant—excuse me, pardon me, right to the front, and there she was, Queen Elizabeth II with all of her ladies in waiting. At 80 years of age, she got into the limousine with the greatest of ease. And what did I do? I cried! Mark asked me what was wrong, and I said that I just couldn't believe I had actually seen the Queen! Mark added that, in the process, we probably set international relations back by ten years!

When we got back to the street, our driver was waiting for us. With a tear-streaked face, I told him we had seen the Queen. He replied, "Blimey, I've been driving out here for over thirty-five years and I have yet to see the Queen."

Churchill's underground quarters were amazing. Everything was so well documented. You could spend days down there and still not be able to comprehend the enormity of that war effort. I am ashamed to admit that, after three hours, my claustrophobia kicked in—big time. Those dear people were often there for weeks!

Saint Paul's, where Princess Diana was married, looked more Colonial America—clean lines, yet elegant.

As a good Methodist, we couldn't leave London without going to John Wesley's chapel. The wooden pews, so austere to my eye, ensured that the worshipers had no choice but to sit straight. Since John Wesley's sermons often lasted two hours or more, worship must have become a kind of endurance test.

What to our wandering eyes should appear but a sea of red, sitting in the balcony choir loft. Lo and behold, there were sixty or more juniors and seniors from throughout Nebraska who had been selected to sing on a tour throughout Europe. This opportunity happens every other year. What fun for them and for us in the audience.

We were ready to leave, standing in the vestibule, when we heard a voice calling "Mark Clinton"! A young woman knew Mark from the Lincoln musical world.

Our ride on the Eye was fun and a great way to orient ourself with the layout of London. The Thames is a sluggish body of water in London. But outside of London, it becomes quite a beautiful body of water.

Greenwich reminded me of Annapolis and the Naval Academy. When we bought our tickets to the Observatory, we inquired about elevators. Everyone said there were elevators, but didn't know where they were! John opted out of walking the very steep walk to the entrance.

Mark said, "We are going." I begged him to go through the Observatory and tell me about it, but my pleas fell on deaf ears. He pushed me up the 45 degree walkway! Later, he confessed that it got a little dicey as we neared the top. It is truly a magnificent observatory. The time pieces alone are staggering and the sailing instruments were so primitive that I marveled how they ever found North America!

As we exited the building, we saw elevator signs!!!

Why weren't we directed to the elevators? Maybe we should have asked for the lift!

Another day we went to Blenheim Palace where Winston Churchill was born. His parents were attending a party at Blenheim when little Winston came early. This was a time in history where it was most important to marry a British noble. Consuela Vanderbilt lived at Blenheim. There is a gorgeous portrait of her there.

On the way back from Windsor, we stopped at the Tower of London. The jewels were spectacular. I still can't understand how any monarch can wear a tiara or a crown for any length of time without getting the world's worst headache. I think there is an aura of sadness surrounding the Tower. The thousands who lost their lives, the citizens who spent their life there, the little prince who spent his life there, the beheadings—all these lost souls there seem to ooze from the very ground.

One of our last sites to visit was Chartwell, the home of Winston and

Clementine Churchill. It is a lovely home given by Lord Beaverbrook to the Churchills. Isn't it sad to think that a man who contributed so much to England and the world never had the wealth to live without financial problems?

We also spent a day in Bath. It was thrilling to see the large pool filled with mosaics dating back to Roman times. Bath is still today a delightful town.

Yes, in two weeks we covered a lot of territory. It was fun, exciting, and so stimulating. I couldn't get enough. It will always be my happiest vacation.

Vignettes and Cows

WRITTEN SEPTEMBER 2, 2016

THE OLDER I GET, THE MORE SOME PRESENT EVENT TRIGGERS A memory of a similar past event, giving credence to "everything old is new again."

Now, I know very little about cows, but I have had some cow-related incidents. My favorite incident occurred in the late sixties when John and I were visiting Old Sturbridge Village in Massachusetts. At some point during the visit, I became aware of a little girl in a red sweater watching every move we made. She really wanted to speak to me, but her parents kept pulling her away and cautioned her not to speak to me.

However, invariably we would meet again at the next exhibit. The tour of the reconstructed New England village ended in the barn yard. There were sheep pens, horse corrals, and cow pens. This little mite climbed up on the rail of the cow pens, flung her little arms wide, looked at me, and said, "I just love 'cowses', don't you?" I assured her that I indeed did love 'cowses', as once again her parents pulled her away from the area.

Her parents were well meaning, but the child had the true read on the situation. Children are naturally curious, and their questions are rarely unkind. My little red sweater girl just wanted to reach out to me. It is still a beautiful memory.

There was in my childhood a board game named "Elsie the Cow." The cow family featured Elsie, Elmer, and Daisy. By throwing the dice, you tried to move your cow back to the barn before anyone else. This game was played so much that the board started to disintegrate!

The current political campaign seems to thrive on mud slinging. I suppose they are not familiar with the saying, "If you can't say anything nice, then don't say anything."

It reminds me of an early polio support group. At one meeting, you were asked to say something that made you glad to have had polio. My first thought was: How ridiculous! I carefully listened as others in the group said: "I got to meet a celebrity"; or high government official. That went on ad nauseum.

At the same time, my emotions reached the boiling point. Finally, I erupted with: "If there had been a choice to have or not have polio, I would surely have passed on this one." I never understood the rationale and I never returned to the group!

When John and I visited Warm Springs, Georgia, we were the first visitors of the day. We stopped at the ticket gate. John handed the lady the necessary amount of money. This tiny gray-haired lady handed money back to John. John was puzzled. Then this dear lady said in her most honeyed Southern accent, "Oh, no, the lady in the chair is our guest." It was an act of kindness I shall never forget.

There is also the other side of the coin. My college roommate and I decided to see a movie in town a short distance from the university. We arrived to discover the parking lot was full. Then I saw a gated lot in back of the paved lot. Surely this was for overflow parking, so I drove in.

I'm sure we enjoyed the movie, we always did; however, when we returned to the parking lot, the gate was closed. And not only that, the gate was locked. It was about 10:00 o'clock, and we had a 10:30 curfew! No one seemed to be around. We yelled and rattled the gate, all to no avail. After ten minutes, here comes a night watchman. I did a Pitiful Pearl act and finally persuaded him to open the gates. Note to self: don't do that again!

We were so grateful when handicapped parking was available. It truly makes life easier. John, as Maryland governor's commission on employment of persons with disabilities, had stacks of printouts that read "stupidity is not a disability." One evening, against my loud protests, he posted said printout on a car illegally parked in a handicapped space. The owner of the car saw John from a store window and rushed out and wanted to fight. Needless to say, we retired those printouts immediately!

In a church, that shall remain nameless, we attended a musical program. There were no accommodations for wheelchairs. John parked me at the end of an aisle. I turned around and inquired if those behind me could see. One lady quickly and crossly said, "All I can see is you." That made me very uncomfortable. So, as the lights dimmed, I moved as far over to the wall, as far as I could, and still leave room for people to walk through.

Sometimes it is better to make do than cause a disturbance.

In another Lincoln church during the children's time at the altar, each child was given a flower and told, as an act of kindness, to give it to someone. Imagine my surprise when some sweet little girl came to me and said, "This is for you." It was a precious moment.

I wish parents would feel brave enough to let their child ask questions or express their caring in many ways.

Years ago, I spoke to a Sunday school class about polio. They were going to trick or treat for the March of Dimes.

One little guy just wanted to know "if I slept in those," pointing to my braces. Or the little girl who asks, "Why are you in a baby carriage"? All good questions.

So many fleeting moments in time, many of which are like tiny jewels locked in my heart forever.

Christmas Memories

WRITTEN DECEMBER 9, 2016

EVERY DECEMBER WHEN I FIRST HEAR CHRISTMAS CAROLS, I automatically go into a nostalgic state. Christmas is a beautiful time. And it's really not the presents; it is the spirit of Christmas—the joy at the birth of the Christ child, the good feelings between all mankind. People smile more, their increased, generous giving reflects that spirit.

As a child of seven, my first Christmas home from the hospital, a gentleman from the village came to our home with a big Whitman sampler box of candy tied in a big red bow and with two beautiful gold bells. It really was pretty. But I sensed there was more than that. Mr. Herman lived by himself with a pittance of an income. He dug deep in his pocket for that gift, and to this day I am grateful. And, even better, those two golden bells are hung on our Christmas tree each year, a beautiful reminder of the true spirit of Christmas.

When John was teaching in high school, he became very close to his students—mostly juniors and seniors.

He is a born teacher and loves teaching. His students loved him, too. Most weekends you would find twenty or so in our living room. I started buying Coke by the case and tins of Charles Chips pretzels and potato chips. That probably sweetened the deal, but it was fun!

One year as Christmas approached, John suggested that they think of adopting a needy family with children. Social Services gave them a family's name. There were two little boys, one of which was quite disabled.

John and one of his students dressed as Santa, visited the family to assess what was wanted or needed. Eddie, the disabled child, wanted a train, but in the same breath asked for something for his little brother.

John described the house as starkly furnished with only one heated room.

What an awakening for these students, most of whom came from good homes and had no idea how some others lived. But they were quick learners. They canvassed businesses for donations, they collected food items, and, once again, with the students and Santa, they returned to Eddie's house a few days before Christmas, their cars filled with gifts. The mother knew that the students were coming, so Eddie opened the door. He called to his brother, "See, I told you Santa would come," and repeated it several times! These students learned a valuable lesson—the joy of giving. I count it as a most special Christmas memory!

I had always been home for Christmas, so in 1972, the first year in Radford, we decided to travel back to Maryland the day after Christmas. That was a very unsettled Christmas day for me, so the next year we thought to do the same. I knew that it was a difficult time for my parents, so late on the 22nd I said, "We are going to Maryland."

We packed, and Santa's gifts were stowed in every inch of the car. Off we drove for ten hours. I did not call my parents to let them know we were on the way. When we arrived, I saw the Christmas tree lights from the road. We knocked on the door, and when Daddy opened it his mouth dropped open. "Mary Ann," he said in a choked voice. And by that time Mark was in his arms. He had just returned from duck hunting and still was dressed in his camouflage outfit.

Mother had gotten her bath and dressed for what they thought would be a sad meal. Daddy called her to "come down immediately, there's someone here that wants to see you." As she came down the steps, I first saw her blue furry bedroom slippers, then a green sheath dress, and then her face first reflecting surprise, disbelief, then this incredible joy as she said my name, "Mary Ann." As far as I'm concerned, that was the best Christmas of all!

Funny, isn't it? It really is all about love, starting with the first Christmas and the Christ child.

Christmas Treasures

WRITTEN NOVEMBER 30, 2018

Christmas is a beautiful season, starting with the very first Christmas, the birth of the Christ child. The first Christmas story is exquisitely beautiful. I never tire of hearing it. All I need to hear, "And it came to pass," and a warm pensiveness settles on my soul.

It is then that love truly came into the world. Throughout the years, I have been blessed by seeing many examples of selfless love.

One of my favorite stories of selfless love I first heard many years ago. At a certain church, the Sunday School decided to have the children present a Christmas pageant. You can imagine their excitement.

They would do this in the big church. Immediately one would say, "I want to be Joseph"; another, "I want to be the angel"; and always there were many who wished to be Mary—because she would get to watch over the baby in the manger.

The teacher continued assigning the roles of shepherds and wise men. Joey had made it abundantly clear he wanted to be a shepherd. But the teacher didn't call his name.

He hung that little head, trying hard not to cry, when he heard the teacher say, "Joey, you get to be the innkeeper." The teacher assigned that role to Joey because he had only one line to remember: "There is no room in the inn."

The bathrobes came out as the principle costumes; the angel, of course, had the tinsel halo; shepherds' staffs suddenly appeared.

The excitement was almost too much to bear. Joey's Mother practiced his line with him over and over. Joey was so proud.

The special night finally arrived. It was going so well. Joey spoke at the appropriate time, with much gusto.

As Joseph, dejectedly turned to leave after hearing there was no room available, Joey literally shouted, "Wait, Joseph, you can have a room at my house!" A little child once again showing that beautiful selfless love.

I can't imagine anyone lucky enough to be in that audience leaving and not knowing that there was something extra special about that pageant.

I am told I shouldn't do a lot of Christmas decorating as I did back in Maryland. I have zero stamina, offset by a ton of determination! Guess which wins? Silly question!

I started on December 14th with five loads on the big flatbed cart. A week later, I'm almost done.

Mark questions my sanity this time of year. Why do I have so much stuff? There is a reason. John taught an adult Sunday School at two of our last churches. I was designated as the party planner.

So, at Christmas we would have fifty-five to sixty people in our home—each of whom brought a Christmas remembrance. These parties occurred over thirty years! I love every remembrance given us.

As I unpack box after box, I am once again overwhelmed by each gift. Some are rather the worse for wear, but in my eyes they remain beautiful. I recall so many good times and feel so very fortunate.

That fellowship spans the years and continues as I unwrap each angel, ornament, or candle. Thus, I surround myself with all the lovely reminders of our Christian fellowship.

It is truly the gift that keeps giving. And weary I might be, but it is more than worth it to see these Christmas treasures once again.

And that's what Christmas is all about, Charlie Brown!

Christmas Cheer

WRITTEN DECEMBER 7, 2018

It is three weeks before Christmas
and all through the house
Signs of the holiday such as my little Christmas wine mouse
All point out that I have been one busy little elf,
So much so that my writing stayed on the shelf
Now the Open House is over, and the house is very quiet
I must return to my routine and perhaps start to diet.
Looking around my home, I am reminded of so many friends
The joy this gives me never ends.
So now the hour is late, and I'm so weary
One last greeting, "May your holiday be cheery"!

Christmas

WRITTEN DECEMBER 21, 2018

FOUR DAYS BEFORE CHRISTMAS, and the frenzy
is not abating. There are still gifts yet to arrive,
and I'm frantically writing.
My Christmas cards all have been sent and many
received. The decorating is done—it's really hard
to believe!
The only thing left is to set the table. I must not
forget that I have dined here for some seventy-
five years. That is certainly something to cheer.
The blessings of that table linger from year to
year. The renewal of family often brings a tear.
But the take away remains the same.
A wish for peace and good cheer. And, yes,
Happy New Year.

Doors

WRITTEN DECEMBER 14, 2018

At Christmas time, doors become even more interesting. Many doors are dressed in many varied ways to reflect the season.

Some plain doors are wrapped in colorful foil—accented with a beautiful ribbon and bow and lighted by a spotlight.

Are they hinting that there are more packages inside?

More traditionally at Christmas time a wreath is hung on the front door. It can be as simple as a circle of greenery with pine cones and a red bow, or it can be elaborately lighted and any motion brings a Christmas carol. All of these door treatments announce that Christmas is celebrated here.

Then there are closet doors. They denote a bit of secretiveness. Are they a glorified jungle, as mine are? Or if you absentmindedly open a closet door, will you find items stored with precision? Not in my apartment. My one talent in life is being able to find storage space in every square inch. I have no shame!

As a child, I wondered where Mother hid my Christmas presents. I still don't know! All other presents were dutifully wrapped and placed on the guest room bed. So, if you happen to open my closet doors, all I have to say is "BE PREPARED"!

The back door of a home is often relegated to being only marginally welcoming. Friends and family just enter—no fanfare. They know they are welcome.

As a child, I sat on our back steps and colored oyster shells with my crayons.

The door into your dormitory room often indicated the personality of the occupants. At exam time, you saw many signs of "DO NOT DISTURB UNDER ANY CIRCUMSTANCES." That was the first commandment of any study regimen.

Walking across the stage at my college graduation, I truly knew I was going through my door to the future. It was really a threshold moment.

We closed the door on life in Maryland in 2012. It was the most gut-wrenching moment of my life. I knew I was leaving a lifetime of memories and all that I had ever known. But my faith reminded me that God never closes a door without opening another.

Then I think of the door to my heart. John certainly found the key. He sent me a long-stemmed red rose every week for two years when we were in college. I can't think of how many he sent after we were married.

The door to old age has definitely opened for me. I wish I had a choice in this matter, but sadly that is not the case.

The next door to open for me will be at the Pearly Gates. I anticipate waltzing through that final door!

Music

WRITTEN DECEMBER 16, 2016

MUSIC IS ONE OF GOD'S GREATEST GIFTS—a form of communication that can, and does, express all emotions. There can be no doubt of the sadness in Chopin's music. *Prokofiev Sixth Sonata* brings forth the stridency of war in 1918 Russia, and also the horror of death. Country music addresses the joys and sadness of everyday life. Popular music does the same, only in more of a poetic way. Elvis Presley's "Love me Tender" certainly got my hormones going. Rap music fascinates me. But I must confess my old ears have trouble following all the words.

Khachaturian Masquerade Suite brings me to tears. I know I'll waltz into heaven with that *Waltz* and *Mazurka* playing. Even today it stirs something inside of me like birds circling in the sky, compelling me into a state of sheer joy, abandoning all that ties us to earth, and dancing and twirling in complete freedom.

As a child, the first music I remember was "Jesus Loves me." Then polio came along and interrupted everything. My parents were so wise to engage me mentally with other children. They brought me a radio when I was able to be in the ward. Quite soon my favorite show was the "Hit Parade" on Saturday evening.

Not just mine, but all who could hear around me.

One of the nurses on evening shift decided to have a contest once a week where any who wanted could sing a song. A winner would be chosen. I think there was a prize—maybe a dollar, I'm just not sure. However, my singing of "The Gypsy" was a winner one week. I don't really think I sang very well—I was too afraid—but being singled out was encouraging. And in the rigid routine of a hospital, it was a good thing.

As a teenager, Rock and Roll ruled. It was important to know each new song and the artist. How clever of the writers to stage a scene where teens in box cubicles had telephones on which they sang to each other. Right out of my teen life, but right out of the Broadway musical *Bye Bye Birdie*.

As was our custom, John and I hosted the Sunday school class Christmas party. I think Christmas carols are the ribbons tying all of our Christmas memories together. My Mother's favorite was "Silent Night."

One year when my mother's Alzheimer's was noticeably advancing, the fifty or so members of our Sunday school class were singing "Silent Night" in our living room, dining room, and hall. It was so beautiful wafting through the house. I called Mother and told her to listen. She was so touched, saying, "I hear it, I hear it"!

I love the pipe organ. One year we were fortunate enough to hear the organ at the Fox theatre in St. Louis.

There's a reason it is known as the Royal Instrument. The pipe organ at Radio City is worth the price of admission.

Now, I cannot write about music without mentioning Mark. His love of music from the very beginning is a gift. He knew from the get-go that music would be his life's work. In the process of his musical education, I also learned a lot. Mark never visited my parents without playing Daddy's favorite piece, Debussy's *Claire de Lune.* So it was no surprise that in his after death instructions, he requested Mark to play *Claire de Lune* at his funeral.

In that small country church, that music soared, and the last note hung in the air for minutes. It was exquisite. Truly, it touched each soul there. And that's what music is all about.

Unexpected Blessings

WRITTEN OCTOBER 20, 2017

LAST WEEK, I RECEIVED A MEDIUM-SIZE PACKET in the mail, and much to my surprise it was from the chairman of my high school reunion committee. Inside were forty or fifty notes from my classmates. John had asked Bob (the chairman) to ask that those, who wished, write me a note.

It was wonderful! I laughed and cried—so many beautiful reminders of times shared. It was eye opening to read the ways they remembered me—even some classmates that I did not know really well. One of my classmates, who shared much of my teen years, wrote, "I miss you every day"! What blessings each and every note was.

On Monday morning, the doorbell rang. I knew John was in the den and would answer it. Then I was summoned by a bellowed "Mary Ann," the master called! In the foyer was a lady of unknown identity. She quickly introduced herself (and, of course, just as quickly I forgot her name)!

She said, "You wrote the article about Hazel, didn't you"? I answered affirmatively. And she said how much she liked the article and identified with my "Type A" personality. She asked if I might write more, and I explained what I was doing. "Well," she said, "I want to read that." I told her how very kind she was to seek me out and say such nice things. She will never know what her words meant to me. I floated on air the rest of the day! I needed those pickups.

I have been on my fall and winter season clothes exchange—sorting clothes that go to the dry cleaners and those that "stay at the ranch" for Mary Ann to wash, five-hour marathon ironings, then storing them away for another year.

I derive a great sense of accomplishment from this. Never mind how tired I get or how many muscle spasms I have. In my mind, by accomplishing normal tasks, I am normal. I was surprised that this feeling was documented in one of the latest Post Polio Survivors Newsletters.

This thinking is so predominant in me. John and I were talking about obituaries. He made the comment that "so many in the paper were cut and dried." I remarked "mine would be short. I haven't done anything notable." John said, "I'll write yours. But what would YOU say"? In a matter of seconds, I said: "She lived, she died; grateful for the ride"!

I am more convinced than ever that these blessings are little reminders from God. Despite what you hear on the news, there are many, many good and kind people who make life better for all of us.

Travels With John

WRITTEN MAY 25, 2018

I have always liked to reflect on life, the people and their actions or inactions, their faith, and, really, all of creation.

But since I am living alone, I have come to the conclusion that men's brains are wired differently!

John was a prime example. He completely disregarded any signs of ill health. I think his philosophy was "if it isn't completely broken, don't bother to fix it."

The first evidence of such mentality occurred when he went on the golf course with my father and played eighteen holes, when he hadn't had that kind of exercise in years. By the time he returned to the house, he was barely walking.

Thank goodness, I was still driving and could handle the two-hour drive to our home. This little venture caused him to have a week of pain pills and muscle relaxers.

When I asked John when he first felt pain, he answered with, "Oh, since the beginning."

"Why would you continue, then?"

"Well, it wasn't too bad."

I think that was his last appearance on the golf course, though!

John always had a queasy stomach. His mother said he was born with it, so any highly spiced foods should not have been on his menu.

But John would not accept that! If he wanted it, he ate it. But then, he always paid later. Case in point. We had traveled to New England for the wedding of one of his nephews. At the banquet the night before, fresh Maine lobster was served. Oh, my, it was good! Ever the dutiful wife, I cautioned him not to eat too much lobster because it was so very rich. Did he listen? Of course not.

Throughout the rest of the, night he was sick. I was close to calling a doctor; as the sun came up, I knew I needed help.

Without braces, getting back in my travel wheelchair was almost impossible, but I did it, and managed to get dressed, and called Paul and Doris who were staying in the same hotel.

We got medicine for John, which put him to sleep a good part of the day. Thankfully, we got to attend the wedding.

On the plane ride home, I gave him an ultimatum. "If you can't restrain yourself, I refuse to travel with you."

That was somewhat harsh, but in an unfamiliar territory, I was helpless to care for him. I always hated that feeling of complete dependence, and I try not to be in that situation, and I could never understand why John would do that to himself.

When John was diagnosed with Type II diabetes, he was devastated. You would have thought the world was going to end. I kept reminding him that life would go on; we would just have to restructure his eating as well as his eating times.

I soon discovered that John's rules were "if she didn't see me eat these cookies, it doesn't count"!

One instance I will never forget. We had gone to my parents' home for probably a birthday or Mother's or Father's Day. We had concluded our visit by going out to dinner.

Then John and I started the two-hour drive back to our home. We were only about half an hour into the drive when John started weaving side to side on the road. He was starting to go to sleep.

Now, my hand controls were no longer on the car, so I said, "Listen to me," and I verbally drove him to a little gas station where he could get water and ice.

I begged him to let me call friends who would come to us. But, no, he would have none of that and, so, I verbally drove him for the next hour and a half, over the Bay Bridge, to our home in Millersville. I was never so grateful to drive in our driveway.

But why would he put himself in such jeopardy? I still don't understand. Maybe that's the difference between the able-bodied life and the disabled body life—or the male brain is wired differently than the female!

However, I must clarify that. All of our trips were not this way. Part of the fun for John was planning for the journey. He would collect maps, inquire what was accessible and what was not. Was there transportation available for people in wheelchairs? Could my travel bath lift be able to go into their bathtub? He was a meticulous planner!

Our last trip in London was a visit to John Wesley's church. John came from a family of Methodists, and was a dyed in the wool Methodist. He even did a one man presentation of John Wesley throughout Maryland churches—so we both were drawn into this site.

Mark was pushing me, and John would slowly go from one exhibit to another gazing intently at everything. Naturally, I was limited in where I could go, so Mark and I finished the tour first.

John said, "Go back to the hotel, and I'll meet you there." He wanted to wander in the cemetery a bit.

So Mark and I went back to the hotel, expecting John within an hour, to an hour and a half at most. After three and a half hours, John came in the restaurant where we were having dinner.

I was a wreck by this time. Those three and a half hours felt like three and a half weeks. John simply said, "I decided to walk back to the hotel." He definitely provided adventure!

Looking back, I think God, in His Infinite Wisdom, called him Home. John was facing eye problems, leg and feet problems, plus kidney problems. He handled my disability so very well, but to handle his own would have been another whole ballgame.

A Faith Legacy

WRITTEN MARCH 29, 2019

I SUPPOSE WE ALL WILL HAVE SOME SORT OF LEGACY, though I can't imagine what mine would be. I guess I'll have to stick with: "She lived, she died; she was glad for the ride."

However, John left a remarkable legacy, starting with many of the kids he taught in high school. He taught a course required by Maryland —government and politics—fun! The United States Constitution was the basis of the course.

His students loved it, and John, too! Often, these kids would congregate at our house on Friday night to continue some class discussion. John took them to Annapolis for a day to watch how state government worked.

Proof of the pudding was that many of these students continued to keep in touch until his death.

John would often fill the pulpit on Sunday mornings when a pastor was ill or on vacation. One pastor allowed him to use some of his public school students to perform a church drama called "Checker Board"; it was about race relations during the time of race riots. Young and old went home with a different perspective. One of the older parishioners loudly pronounced at the end of the drama, "This is good, this is good!"

John did a one-man show of John Wesley, the founder of the Methodist Church. He researched and read and put together about an hour of John Wesley's life and how he came to establish the Methodist Church from the Church of England. He presented this in churches throughout Maryland. It was quite authentic—John in a black robe, with quill in hand, glasses down somewhat on his nose.

One little fellow in our home church was heard to say, as John walked in, "Well, looks like Paddington Bear to me!"

When our adopted granddaughter first came into our lives, it was at church. She was with her mother, and only later did we meet her dad, Cleotilde. He was obviously of Spanish descent, which explained Desiree's beautiful olive skin and hair.

Cleo was from El Salvador. It was a while after we met that Cleo mentioned he would have to leave the country for a time, then he could return. John asked if he had ever thought of becoming a citizen. Cleo said he had, but did not know how to start. John coached him on the hows and whys and explained how a democracy works.

Cleo was a quick learner, and the day he got his citizenship papers, John handed him a flag that had flown over the capitol building in Washington, D.C.

Some ten years later, Cleo's mother came for a visit from El Salvador and died here. John helped Cleo put together a funeral service for his mother. Not surprising is that most of his immediate family came.

Then the problem became how to get her body flown back to El Salvador. John to the rescue! He found the airline that would do this, and helped Cleo through the reams of paperwork.

This was all so John. Wherever he saw a problem, he wasn't satisfied until he found a solution. He really lived his faith. I like to think, as he went through the Pearly Gates, the first words he heard were, "Welcome home, good and faithful servant"!

Old Friends Forever Friends Good Friends

WRITTEN DECEMBER 27, 2018

ONE OF MY BEST CHRISTMAS GIFTS THIS YEAR was a phone call from an old friend. We keep in touch, but not regularly. In some ways it was a distressing conversation. They both have had serious medical problems.

I blame myself for not calling them more often. It seems so easy to tell one's self, "I'll call them later." And later never comes.

Bob and Joan have been in our lives for a long time. We first met them through our mutual church and quickly found we shared a love of music, theatre and the arts.

So, we soon started going to the theatre, concerts, sharing dining, books, you name it. And we had fun. Bob and I share a crazy sense of humor, while Joan and John looked on in disbelief.

One of our early jaunts to the Kennedy Center is a case in point. We had agreed to arrive early enough to go to the second floor of the Kennedy Center for drinks and hors d'oeuvres. That would be our dinner. So, to the second floor we went.

We expected to see food and a bar in a rather large room. All we saw were people. John looks around and sees a rather small room set up for drinks and food. In we went. The food was elegantly displayed and the bar was quite busy. So we joined others and thoroughly enjoyed the goodies.

When John and Bob went to pay the bill, they discovered it was a private party! We had crashed a party at the Kennedy Center. No less, probably an ambassador or some notable had given us dinner.

Of course, Bob and I were laughing uproariously. John and Joan were trying to find a way for us all to leave as inconspicuously as possible. We still laugh at this today.

Bob and I enjoyed thinking of tacky ways to decorate. There was a party at Joan and Bob's home. I put a pink plastic flamingo on their lawn. That flamingo went back and forth from our lawns for months. You never knew when to expect it. The fancier the party, the flamingo was there.

Bob and Joan were good travel companions. We traveled to San Antonio, Texas, when Mark performed there. Needless to say, we explored San Antonio fully.

The day after the concert, we were to fly back to Maryland. Daddy called us at 11:00 p.m. the night before the concert and suggested we leave San Antonio as soon as possible because a blizzard was forecast for the area (at home).

I said we came to hear Mark and we would leave shortly thereafter; thereafter the airport was closed. We couldn't get into the state.

Daddy suggested we fly to Nashville so we would be part way home. I nixed that idea immediately. Nashville is known to be on the freezing line. Call me chicken, but I did not want to end on icy runways.

It became a moot question, anyway, when we learned Nashville Airport was closed also. So we extended our trip four more days. And in our rental car, we drove L.B.J.'s hill country and even saw Lady Bird by the pool on her ranch!

When we finally got back home, we found eight feet of snow. We had to have a neighbor with an S.U.V. transport us to our house and leave our car at the top of the hill! We will never forget that trip.

Bob and Joan traveled with us to France for Solenne's baptism. We managed to see Paris and stop every day at 4:00 for a glass of wine. The outdoor cafes are so charming. Bob and I wanted to redecorate a palace or two. Joan and John stood in the corner and pretended not to know us. What happy times they were!

I feel ever so fortunate to have had such special times with special friends. It is for sure that the delight of that time remains with me even today.

Rites of Spring

WRITTEN MAY 17, 2019

WHO SAYS CLEANING CAN'T BE FUN? I have been looking at my international dolls cabinet for months, always thinking it looked a little dusty in there!

Finally, my conscience made it clear that Wednesday should be the day—no excuses accepted. The job took five or six hours. As we removed dolls from the six shelves, each one reminded me of a time in my personal history.

It started in 1953, I believe. I was in hospital for a muscle transplant, and my parents went to dinner with a business associate. I'm sure daddy did this to keep mother somewhat occupied.

Of course, the topic of children surfaced. And when they explained why they were in Baltimore, Mr. Cassell asked if he could send me a doll.

I think the two dolls from the Dutch West Indies were the beginning of my collection of nearly two hundred dolls from all over the world. Each one has a story.

The rather large doll from Hawaii is a replica of the doll with which the first princess played—a rather rudimentary doll, but one surely loved.

The doll from China is truly authentic his fingers and thumb held in a circle means good luck.

The doll from Japan is beautiful, her porcelain face cracked from her long years with me. I think of the cracks as wrinkles. After all, we are old!

The man and woman from the Philippines are quite regal. His shirt and her gown are made from pineapple cloth.

The lady from Spain is strikingly beautiful. She is seated, dressed in a red and white gown, playing the guitar.

The man from Portugal has a basket of fish hanging from each shoulder. He is a proud man and, should he start to walk, it would be a swagger.

I acquired a bride and groom from Norway in the early to mid '50's when my father traveled there. They are dressed in traditional clothing of a Norwegian bride and groom, which I have seen in recent photographs, rather like the Czech tradition.

The doll from Kenya is carved from solid mahogany, the head egg-shaped due to being bound as a baby.

The fire crier from Turkey, running, with a lantern in one hand and a whip in the other, is striking.

The doll from Trieste (northern Italy) has a straw bonnet and carries a parasol.

The dolls from Ecuador are rather crudely made, but significant to that country—much like the dolls from Peru. The Peruvian dolls were a gift from a ship captain who sailed to Nanticoke Harbor with tuna for my father's seafood business.

The Austrian boy and girl are posed to look at each other, lips pursed in a whistle or maybe yodel.

The Australian Swagman replicates the Nobo settlers, corks on hat helped keep the flies away. The Aborigine represents the earliest settlers, and their costumes are still used on holiday celebrations.

Each time I received a doll, mother made sure we read about the country the doll represented in the World Book Encyclopedia. These dolls brought such joy and opened my mind to so much more. At some point in time, I hope these dolls will pleasure new generations and remind them of the beautiful world out there.

Things That Used to Matter

WRITTEN JANUARY 3, 2017

CIVILITY, OR LACK THEREOF, IS A FAST FADING VIRTUE in our society. That lack was glaringly evident in the past election. I was brought up with "If you can't say anything nice, don't say anything."

Now, I know each life has some negativity, but it shouldn't determine who we are. During the election, it was as if there were two third grade children playing the name calling game.

We see this lack of civility in the words of the school bullies. Somehow they have learned, or absorbed, that anyone the least bit different is bad, and is to be ridiculed and shamed.

Children are not born that way. They are taught. In the musical "South Pacific," the lyrics of a song put it so well: "You've got to be taught, you've got to be carefully taught, before you are six or seven or eight. You've got to be taught to either love or to hate."

So we as a society had best get to work on the school situation the stakes are very high! We see this lack of civility in racial relations. DIFFERENT IS NOT BAD! Given the same opportunities would provide a fair playing field. Everyone deserves to be loved and appreciated.

I was born with a sense of "Underdog," the cartoon character who always sought out the last in line. In elementary school, in order to go outside to the playground, I had to be carried down the four or five steps. My dear Mother would have her arms around my torso and someone else would carry my legs.

This is where Charlene appears—a little girl of seven or eight, not beautiful or outgoing at all, but she wanted to carry my legs. She was a tiny mite, but she waited for me each noontime. Sometimes I think she didn't even eat lunch so that she could be there first. I knew instinctively how important this was for her it made her special. AND SHE WAS.

Why is different such a threat? I have waited at counters in a department store, the clerk looking over me, no other customers in sight. Here comes "Underdog" again! I stubbornly waited probably ten minutes or more. Then the clerk comes by the counter, looks down, and says, "Oh, I didn't see you there"! People of color have been there many, many more times.

People answering the telephone can make or break the day. First, they may talk so fast, running words together so much, that you are left wondering, "What language is that"? Then you request a repeat of the message slowly. In an effort to make my request a little more acceptable, I usually say, "I'm sorry, my ears are old"!

One of my all time pet peeves is dealing with Social Security. That puts me in a bad mood to begin with. Social Security is, by law, supposed to pay for one pair of brace shoes a year. It took me a good many years to get four pairs of shoes—one for each season. At $1,000 a pop, you don't have a whole lot of choice!

At one point, I received a notice that they would not pay for a new pair of shoes. I called the appropriate number and asked, "Why the change of policy"?

"Oh," she said, "we decided that you might walk around in these shoes."

I said, "Yes, I would mainly stand, but these shoes fit on Caliper braces. And, if I could walk, you can be sure I wouldn't be doing it in those clunkers! You do understand what Calipers are?" I asked.

She said very tersely, "Send me a picture."

I did, but still had to go to another level. The first lady obviously did not do her job. I am told they have a book with information on most all kinds of braces or any other equipment for the disabled.

What happens to all the other people who might not push so hard? Why was she so adversarial? The civil way would have been, "Let me check this out and get all the facts together." So much for civil servants!

I am so gratified that, in Lincoln, most people rush to hold a door open for me—young and old. It was not always so in the East. John would never hesitate to ask, after waiting a bit, that kindness adds another dimension to any day.

One of our favorite places to go on Friday night was *California Pizza.* They were always crowded. And one night we had been waiting for quite a bit, when the hostess came to us and said, "If you don't mind sitting at the bar, we have a place for you." We said that would be fine. In the bar area was a lower counter where one in a wheelchair could sit and John with me. What a marvelous accommodation!

Back in the Seventies, when John would take me shopping, I quickly learned to place any item I intended to buy on my lap, very visible. This was done after several times of security following us around. Apparently, people would use a wheelchair so as to hide what they had stolen.

Civility on the road is barely existent! If you are attempting to drive from a side street to a main artery, and there is no light, well, let's hope time is not a factor for you. Or the young person (mostly) using obscene gestures. Is all that really necessary? Is this the negative side of the "me" generation?

It seems to me civility is just a matter of respect. Respect for not only people who agree with you, but for people who don't agree. Perhaps Dr. Luke says it best in his book, "We should all care for or respect the least, the last, and the lost"!

The New Year

WRITTEN JANUARY 13, 2017

I DON'T USUALLY MAKE RESOLUTIONS FOR THE NEW YEAR. I could never keep the new resolutions, anyway! But this year is different. For my own well being, I need to not let myself be stressed out by things completely out of my control. The purpose driven lifestyle is not working for me.

Why do I have to clean the kitchen after every meal? Is there a hidden camera that records that I haven't put dishes in the dishwasher or scrubbed a pan? Is there someone who counts the un-ironed pieces on the chair? Who says I have to iron, anyway? Am I punishing myself because I'm disabled and can't do it all like I really want?

If my scooter is sick, I go into a tailspin to end all tailspins. I have a backup scooter, for goodness sakes. But—here it comes—the dimensions of the backup chair are different from the one I use daily. So? You ask. Well, that means every turn, every position is different enough to cause me to fall or call on new muscle strength that's not there.

I'm paranoid about falling. I had been at The Landing only six weeks when I fell and broke my femur. Mercifully, it healed despite severe osteoporosis and the doctor's view that it would never heal.

If my household help is unexpectedly not able to be with me, I go crazy. I can make the bed, I but can't change it and I have fallen doing so. Smart polios (of which I'm not one) recommend not making the bed! Just pull the covers up part way. That is blasphemy to me. I know, I know. Heavens, it's about mind set. Mine must be set in concrete!

Then there is transportation. Vicki drives me to my appointments. However, if she is not here, then what? The Landing will take me, but I couldn't use my scooter for hair appointments, and it is for sure I couldn't push myself from the van to the salon. Now, I'm sure there are resolutions of some kind for these problems.

In my mind, I think I have adjusted to "Lincoln life"; but it seems I've drawn a line in the sand—no more adjusting! That's silly, isn't it? Life is all about adjustments. We are born, learn to talk and walk, go to elementary school, then high school, then college, adjusting all the way. We marry, have children, and shepherd them through life's needed adjustments. It's rather like a train finally getting to the station and then slowly returning to ground zero.

What to do in the meantime? I think I know, if I but use the resource. Turn the daily challenges over to God. After all, He promises to walk with us always. And He might close a door, but you can be sure He'll open another.

Stop fretting, Mary Ann. Each stumbling block is temporary and the best is yet to come!

Friday

WRITTEN JANUARY 20, 2017

I'VE WANTED TO WRITE ABOUT THIS FOR MONTHS, but didn't for some reason have the courage. I guess I'm ashamed. I've had to adjust one way or another all my life. Does this become more difficult with old age?

It literally pains me to think of our home in Millersville—my dream home. It truly was my creation. We selected the house plans in 1998, and I started fine tuning immediately.

The architect did not take kindly to my request to add a wall between the kitchen and form a dining room until the agent reminded him that, after all, it was our money!

Then I insisted that the garage had to be turned to the side rather than the front, because I didn't want the world to see our stuff stored there!

We moved there in 1994, four bedrooms, three full baths, office, living room, dining room, family room, and kitchen.

Oh, a beautiful foyer with Palladium windows facing east.

Our back yard was bordered by a small woods that became my constant inspiration.

I fed the birds and provided a heated bird bath.

They, in turn, sang to me off and on all day. And I loved when they sang their good night lullaby. I always tried to be on the patio at this time.

Occasionally, a deer would stand at the fence and gaze at me. A beaver would waddle up a hill. A hawk would swoop down and grab a snake. (I would have put him on the payroll)!!!

The humming birds were amazing from the first offering of nectar, they became friends. I would talk to them in a low modulated voice as they would fly back and forth in front of me. Like many creatures, they responded to love. I really thought that I would have one perch on my finger, I was so close.

I talked to the squirrels also. They would approach me and listen, but when they heard the click of my scooter, they left the scene.

I miss the complete freedom of spending days outside, coming in to prepare dinner, and being so tired.

BUT, a good tired!

I miss each and every room of the house. Our bedroom had one wall, all windows, in which my African violets bloomed profusely.

The walk in closet with three hundred books stacked on the floor, alphabetized by author! This closet was a refuge for Maggie in a thunder storm. She and I would sit, Maggie trembling and me reading.

The office was supposed to be jointly shared, but ended up being John's man cave. That is, until Alvin, the chipmunk, ran in the back door through the house to the office. We cornered him, but couldn't catch him.

I called neighbors looking for a crab net, but was out of luck. Then I realized Alvin was so scared, as we were, so I yelled, "Open the window and push out the screen." And out Alvin went!

The Sunday School parties were always great. We tried to have one for each season. One year I announced that we would drink our beverage from a Mason jar and our meal would be in a bowl.

From the back of the room came the question, "What is a hobo"? Naturally, it came from the youngest members of the class!

Christmas parties were the best! We would have fifty five or sixty people, food galore, and unending laughter. I had five Christmas trees inside and three outside. And we usually had some form of entertainment. Of course, we always had to sing Christmas carols.

Several years, when the singing started, I would call Mother and hold the phone so she would share the Christmas cheer.

There are so many precious memories in that house. I loved it so. I loved our church. It was a good life, and I mourn that each and every day. I tell myself "that was then," and I'm so grateful for that; however, I'm living here now. I love, not just like, so many here, and we have shared numerous good times. And, yet, I want to go back almost daily.

The thought suddenly struck me: Has history repeated itself? When my Father sold his seafood business, he soon discovered living in the little village so close to his business wasn't a good idea.

He decided to purchase a home in Salisbury, twenty five miles away. As you might guess, Mother wanted no part of it, so he bargained with her. They would leave the Nanticoke home as it was, completely furnished, for a number of years, until she could comfortably settle in Salisbury. He kept it for seven years.

During that time, she would go back to Nanticoke and call me telling me where she was and how comforting it was to be there. I completely understand her pain. I guess it would be safe to say I was "cut from the same cloth"!

Mother and I both loved deeply, and this love never wavered. It is a blessing...and a curse. It hurts. But, then, someone comes to me and says "thank you for the cards" or "I played the Steinway today," and it is wonderful. And, I am reminded "God's people are everywhere."

Will the pain ever subside? Probably not.

To Love and to Care

WRITTEN JANUARY 27, 2017

TO WRITE OR NOT TO WRITE—that is the big question! My very soul seems to be dry. Have the winter doldrums set in? Has my large supply of empathy gotten me in trouble again?

It seems that so many of my friends are facing serious health problems and their mental capabilities are exposing them to numerous bad decisions. I have no authority to make their decisions, nor do I really want that authority. But it's hard to see someone you love live like a hermit. And because of blindness, let us say things are far from clean.

Reminding me of Mrs. Habersham at her dining table, enveloped by spider webs. Or another friend who has let her offspring drain her financially.

Then there is the friend batting cancer, a battle that she surely will not win. I fervently pray for her each chemo day.

Or the friend with a mentally challenged adult son who is allowed to come once each weekend. As a child, she had complete control of him, but now it's a different story. He gets up at night and cuts all the draperies in half or finds money that he immediately flushes down the toilet hundreds of dollars.

What can a friend do to help? I listen, which is about all I can do. From time to time, I'll send a little gift hoping that it will bring a moment of pleasure and as a reminder that I care.

I do care, not only that I love. I remember as a little girl Daddy put me in the car to ride me through the village and surrounding area after a big snow storm. Snow, five or six feet high. The trees laden with snow. The evergreens trimmed with snow like a Christmas tree.

I said, "Oh, Daddy, it's so beautiful, it makes me cry.

He said, "Then it's not pretty." He understood, I know he did, but I am convinced that love or beauty can hurt. But the joy of love or beauty outweighs any negativity.

It calls to mind Ecclesiastes 3: "*Everything on earth has its own time and own season.*"

My Love of History

WRITTEN FEBRUARY 10, 2022

I HAVE ALWAYS LOVED HISTORY—ANY HISTORY, REALLY. History can show us the present and future. Who as a child hasn't heard, "Well, that is the way it has always been done."

Really? In many cases, yes. And often times with good reason. One of my grandmothers called "recipes" "receipts." A "receipt" was proof that you properly made a certain food item. That was what she learned as a girl and, suffice it to say, she never veered from her understanding of the term.

One of my earliest vacations was a trip that included a visit to Hyde Park, F.D.R.'s home. He was born in a very humble house somewhere in the vicinity of Hyde Park. His Mother adored him and ruled his life.

She was, by all accounts, a social climber. So when her husband was able to amass a sizable income, Hyde Park was built. After all, it was only fitting for this new aristocrat.

"Mama," as she was called, dictated Franklin's every move. The only reason she approved of his marriage to Eleanor was that Eleanor was related to Theodore Roosevelt, and Mama sought to be a part of Theodore's legacy.

Mama never liked Eleanor, and always made it abundantly clear. She put them in separate bedrooms when Eleanor and Franklin came to visit.

Then, polio came and Mama did everything to deny or hide this fact. She refused to install an elevator for her son. At one point, he bumped up the steps (which I have done), and Plan B was to ride up to the second floor on the dumbwaiter. The president of the United States!

She did everything in her power to deny his disability.

Could that be why so little was written or photographed of the President's disability? They went to great lengths to have the public believe that our President was hale and hearty.

Thank heavens, this kind of thinking has changed. It is hard to believe that many in the United States had no idea the President was disabled at all. Even when his medical staff insisted he be taken to Warm Springs for rest, the public knew nothing of this time out. How different it would be today!

Seeing Hyde Park and all the efforts made to make F.D.R. look so called normal, adds a dimension to my understanding of the man. In this area of his life, I am amazed that, in addition to the problems of the nation and the world, he had to always appear able bodied.

I have visited probably thirty Presidential homes, and all of them give clues to the man who was President. One of the most recent Presidential homes we have visited is that of President Lyndon Baines Johnson. We first drove by his birthplace—a rundown (at best) home with a wringer washing machine on the front porch. I'm sure a washboard was close by! It was stark!

My first thought was "no wonder he worked tirelessly on a rural electrification program when he was in the Senate. He had lived that life of poverty and saw, first hand, how hard life could be. Not far away was the L.B.J. ranch reflecting his financial success. And, yes, there sat Lady Bird by the pool, and who waved to us!

His Presidential library is awesome. We seem to forget how savvy he was. He is a great example of civility and uncivility in government. When he wanted to get a bill passed in Congress and things were not going as he wanted, L.B.J. would call Tip O'Neill, then Speaker of the House, invite him over to the White House. After a few drinks, Speaker O'Neill would "begin to see the light" and they would bargain. That's how Washington works! It's called civility.

The President's choice of words sometimes were not printable. That was a part of his life when he was climbing the rope to success. However, he never forgot his roots. I saw President Johnson dining in the dining room of the Shoreham Hotel in D.C. He was an imposing man.

I'm sure I could go back to revisit these Presidential residences and discover more indications of the men who lived there. It was fascinating then and just as fascinating now.

The Year was 1935

WRITTEN FEBRUARY 24, 2017

LET'S TURN THE PAGES OF THE CALENDAR BACK. To be specific, back to 1935. It was that year a certain young man was graduated from college. His soon-to-be wife drove a brand new car, a gift from his parents, to the college. She had had a year and a half of nurses' training, but chose to leave nurses' training and work in the retail business.

They married on August 1, 1935. After the honeymoon, they rented half of a house, right on the Nanticoke River. It was an old house, even then. And when it snowed, the snow covered the floors of their home.

The house still stands, and has been renovated with a lot of insulation, I hope! Strangely, this house has always spoken to me. I played with my best girlfriend there. I still dream of living there and sitting on the partial wrap around porch, gazing at the river.

In the next four years, they bought a property and built a home, to which I came in July of 1939. This young couple had the world in their hands. How optimistic they must have been! A new home of their dreams and a little daughter to complete their family circle. The oyster business was growing beyond all expectations. They were good people. They loved their home, their church and each other.

It all came crashing down October 7th, 1945. Their daughter, who would have everything, was diagnosed with infantile paralysis that left her completely paralyzed. All the dreams for her came to a screeching halt. No pony for her seventh birthday. What chance would she have to attend Vassar, Radcliffe, Smith or Wellesley?

And, horror of horrors, there would be no more children. From my old lady vantage point, they must have felt that this was some kind of cruel joke. My dear Mother always assured me, "we only wanted you to get well." But all their dreams were annihilated. Not only annihilated, there was no play book for life ahead.

Yes, they were intelligent, but the increasing needs of their daughter would challenge them for years. It called for unbelievable sacrifice, but they never blinked.

That first year, Mother had told me they would visit me in the Contagious Disease Hospital, outside the window of my room. I don't remember much communication, but I knew they were there.

After standing there for a few hours (in rain, sleet or snow), they would drive three hours back to Nanticoke, and many times would turn in their driveway, look at each other and, without saying a word, back out the driveway and return to Baltimore. As a parent today, I doubt that I could have had their strength or courage.

And the journey was just beginning. Fifteen months later, I was allowed to return home—to a two story, one bathroom house. Steps at all three exterior entrances. Daddy carried me up the stairs at night and, after a bath and some therapy, down the stairs in the morning.

Within six months, a two story addition was added with an elevator and a first floor bathroom. How did they ever cope with all of this? Whatever happened to normal? Their adjustment to this new situation was far greater than mine. After all, I was a child, and children accept change more easily.

There was soon a need for a collapsible travel wheelchair. Then I could go to church and on a few occasions visit family members. I still remember the brown corduroy seat, worn to a shiny surface. I had to be re-introduced to the world. This "hospital alien" had forgotten so much.

During a summer thunderstorm, lightning struck the telephone by my parents' bed. Daddy had gone to the harbor to check on the warehouses. Mother grabbed me from my bed and carried me down a fairly long flight of stairs. I was a hefty size and dead weight, but Mother ran as if she had wings.

Daddy wanted so badly to share his love of the river and would often take me in one of his boats and explore. The marshes were alive with life. If you were lucky, you sometimes would see a school of fish come to the surface to feed.

This one Sunday afternoon we were enjoying the river, when the motor stopped. Daddy could not restart it. Using the oars, he pushed us to a marsh with which he was familiar, and said, "Let's go"!

My question was, "Where?"

He told me that he would carry me through the marsh to the little village of Waterview. I can't even imagine how he did this—the marsh sucks at your feet with each step taken, never mind the snakes and turtles!

But, he did it. He knew who in the village had a telephone and who did not. It all worked out. Most people would not have taken me alone on such a trip, but he really wanted me to experience the tidewater.

And I did. And I still do!

The Year Was1935

Part 2

WRITTEN MARCH 3, 2017

AFTER CARRYING ME THROUGH THE MARSH, Daddy made the S.O.S. call to Mother, who arrived within ten minutes to pick me up. Daddy had his car so he could go pick up one of his employees who would go with Daddy back to the stranded boat and tow it back to the harbor. After it was over, I quite liked the whole adventure!

In those early years home from the hospital, Mother always managed to have other children come to spend the afternoon with me. We played games and, at some point, Mother would appear with fresh lime or lemonade, pretzels or cookies—always most welcome. She knew I needed that socialization.

Mother made it all seem so effortless. Now I can only marvel at her stamina.

One of my best girlfriends would visit, and Mother would come to the door of my play room to see why it was so quiet. Nancy and I were reading! We found it to be so companionable and did it often.

When Nancy moved with her family back to New Jersey, I was inconsolable. Nancy came back to visit me the next summer. Unfortunately, she brought the mumps also. By the time she was to leave, she had recovered, but a day later I had the mumps.

Poor Mother! But she never complained. For once, I wasn't horribly sick. However, when my Mother got the mumps a week later, it was a different story. She was SICK!

When I was discharged from the hospital, we were instructed to return monthly for a muscle evaluation and general check up. I dreaded those visits. In fact, I became very quiet and couldn't eat breakfast on that morning.

We drove to Baltimore the day before, stayed in the hotel overnight, and returned home after the hospital visit the next day. I didn't trust those visits—they might want me to stay. Fear took over my body. I think I responded well enough, but all the time I was begging God that I'd go home with Mother and Daddy.

Then the visits went from one month to three, then to six, then whenever needed. I never verbalized that fear, but I'm sure it was quite evident. It was eight years before I heard that I was a candidate for muscle transplant surgery and would return to the hospital. I am convinced that at stress-filled times, I go into a suspended animation state. I'm there, but not really.

The surgery did what they wanted, stabilized an ankle in preparation to reduce some bracing. A second surgery the following summer was to complete that goal. Alas, it did not work—muscles often lose their strength when moved. Even then, I realized the effort was worth it.

At fourteen, I had become aware of the very active teen life—a torment that is still there. I can only imagine the drain on my parents' income. My Father would never divulge the cost.

He did say, when they had the first interview with the one who would be my orthopedic doctor, that they were a little apprehensive. After all, Dr. Johnson was one of the best orthopedic doctors at Johns Hopkins.

I was told he was so very gracious in that interview, but his goal was the same as my parents—to rehabilitate as much as possible this little girl's body. Daddy asked to pay after the interview. But the secretary said they would mail the bill—a bill of five dollars!

Daddy always teared up when telling this through the years. We have found the greater the man, the greater his compassion.

My dear parents traveled back and forth twice a week for years. They drove an Oldsmobile when I initially was taken to the hospital. It probably was well traveled at that time and, after too numerous to count trips to Baltimore, the Oldsmobile died—right on the Hanover Street Bridge in Baltimore with my Mother driving! She called Daddy, who came as fast as he could—but three hours is still three hours!

That day, or the next, Daddy went to a large Chevrolet dealer in Baltimore. Now, this was still war time, so the dealer said, "I have no cars to sell you." It's almost as if I were there!

Daddy said, "Let me explain my situation. I have a little girl who has had polio and is at Children's' Hospital. We visit her twice a week. She's been very sick. She's only six years old, and we need transportation."

The dealer thought a minute and said, "Follow me." There was a five floor underground garage. Daddy has said he thought they would never stop, but they got to the bottom and the salesman walked over to a little four-door car, and he and Daddy shook hands.

This young couple was tested at every turn and they never once failed.

Off to College She Goes

WRITTEN MARCH 10, 2017

THE FIVE CLOCKS ARE TICKING THEIR MEASURED BEATS, giving structure to each hour. I like that sound. It is steady and reliable. In the middle of the night, they comfort me—life goes on.

Time for that young couple who were my parents to have felt shattered. Mother, driving to Baltimore each Thursday and returning with Daddy on Saturday or Sunday. She took my clothes home, washed and ironed them, to return on her next visit.

You can imagine how enraged she was to find my dresses on other children when she came to visit one week. Suffice it to say, it didn't happen again!

In the spring of 1946, the hospital allowed my parents to take me for a ride in the car. It felt surreal. It felt like an overgrown iron lung!

Daddy drove through the Baltimore Zoo. I could see some of the larger animals, but I was confused. I had never been to a zoo and, frankly, didn't know what to think. Probably, my parents realized at that point that in just one year I had lost so much mentally.

Lying in bed, month after month, staring at the ceiling, was so very limiting. I did not know joy—just fear. What an awesome task faced this couple.

But the future began to look brighter. There were plans made for me to be discharged early summer. I heard the words, but didn't fully understand. Home was a vague concept to me.

Then the whole plan went on hold when I was thrown out of my chair coming from a therapy session—one broken femur and one ankle chipped in three places. So that meant another six weeks flat in bed, then another four to eight weeks to regain what strength I had.

Homecoming did arrive, but not until December of 1946. Christmas that year was a blur. I seem to remember a doll, but little else. It took some time for home to become home again.

And after the addition to the house—with an elevator—I could go everywhere. It was really home again!

Being able to return to the public school was in many ways the best "medicine" ever. Children are so accepting, and they certainly were in my case. Slowly but surely they learned that I was a child only packaged a little differently.

Mother never missed a day coming at lunch time with my lunch, then a trip to the bathroom, and down the front steps for play time.

Of course, public school brought the measles and flu and colds. I had them all, and always severely. I recovered from them all due largely to Mother's T.L.C. How many times she went up and down those stairs with food, medicine, or a special treat!

Junior and senior high school time presented altogether different problems. Nanticoke (our village) was twenty-three miles away from these schools. So Daddy had a two bedroom rancher built just down the street from Mother's sister in Salisbury.

We were home (Nanticoke) Friday after school, and returned to Salisbury on Monday morning. The rancher was quite nice, but it wasn't home.

Daddy would occasionally come for dinner and spend the night. Otherwise, he was by himself in Nanticoke. What a sacrifice that must have been for them both. I never heard them complain, but as an adult I'm blown away by their undying devotion.

Their love has always made me stronger. There was never any question that I would go to college. They both agreed that this would happen, and they would make it happen.

They contacted the Lovejoy Agency in New York City, who did college placement. We went for an interview, and Mother and Daddy presented their requirements—first floor dorm room, no steps into the building, a room not far from the bathroom, and a moderate climate and classroom accessibility.

It had to have been quite a challenge in 1957. If you found a college with few steps or elevators, it was a geographical area that had frigid winters—strike that. If you found a college that fit the bill for accessibility in the South, academically, Lovejoy would not recommend it.

Somehow, Drew University in Madison, New Jersey, came to the top of the list. There was a possibility of some bad winter weather, and there were steps to the classrooms. But all this was overcome by Daddy having the school choose some male who needed financial help. This young man would take me to classes, to the dining hall and/or to the library. This young man was John, who I categorized as "like a brother"! But I married him, anyway, in 1961!

Then my parents had Drew select a young girl to room with me who could make the bed and assist me in any way. They also added to her scholarship. The first year's choice didn't work so well, but the final three years my roommate was perfect.

Can you imagine the cost that my parents, without any sign to me, encountered? God blessed me beyond all riches with these parents.

In his last years, I would phone Daddy and identify myself as his "million dollar baby"! I don't think he really liked this because, in his mind, he felt he just did what was needed.

Au contraire, Mother and Daddy, you went far beyond what was needed. You gave, to the fullest measure, every step of the way!

Drew University

WRITTEN MARCH 17, 2017

THE DECISION TO ATTEND DREW UNIVERSITY and my acceptance there was certainly a watershed moment for me as well as my family. The beginning day for freshmen was about a week before the upper classmen returned.

The Kennerly caravan arrived fully loaded. I had my kidney-shaped cherry desk, a small extra bureau, lamps, and my Franklin wheelchair (thanks to F.D.R.), and clothes!

Lest you think this was a bit much, one other freshman brought her entire bedroom set! My roommate, thankfully, brought just the basics.

We arrived one Sunday and quickly settled in. Then it was time for goodbyes. My dear Mother just went to pieces. As her tears flowed, she kept saying, "Who will know when she is weary and needs more help? Who will help her with braces? Or getting dressed?"

One of the councilors put her arms around Mother and said, "Please, don't worry, Mrs. Kennerly. We will keep an eye on her."

Mother was hysterical, and Daddy hustled her back to the car. He took her to Canada, hoping to distract her. It really didn't work very well, and a week later on their return trip to Maryland, they stopped to see how well I was doing. Of course, I was fine—still a little tentative about the days ahead, but confident I could manage.

College presented many life lessons as well as academic. A day or so after arrival, all freshmen were put on buses and taken to a camp in the New Jersey mountain area. This was intended to help develop relationships and become a united front. It did just that. Several of the guys adopted me to ensure I could get around.

Now, you can imagine that the terrain was anything but flat! I remember Dick, who insisted on carrying me up a steep hill to a flat rock where we sat surveying the mountains of North Jersey. That was the good part!

The rough part was having a guy take me into the bathroom, sit me on the toilet, returning minutes later to put me in my chair and down the steps. I was embarrassed beyond belief! But it did get better a few days later.

Then there was the bunk house. Of course, I got the bottom bunk. The first night there, as I gazed up at the top bunk, I saw only one peg holding the top mattress. I yelled for the councilor who pulled the girl from the top bunk. She weighed twice as much as I and could have easily made me one dimensional!

At eighteen, all I could think was, "Well, I'm glad that problem is solved," and promptly went to sleep. But these were valuable life lessons.

I had to have help to the bathroom—it was a necessity—so you do what you have to do. At all times you have to make judgment calls on the safety of the situation. It is the key to survival.

A polio friend of mine from India visited us in the United States three or four times. We would compare our attempts to solve problems in adapting to situations in the normal world.

Pam never really used her braces, so she had to be carried more than me. I remember asking her what she did on long airplane flights. "Oh," she said, "I just look for someone with a cleric collar and then I feel safe and less embarrassed!

Asking for help is never easy, but what other choice is there? I guess one could become a recluse, but, oh, what you would miss! Sometimes you just have to tell someone what to do.

Case in point. I had to have a breast biopsy. The doctor and I really enjoyed our conversations. In fact, I think he forgot I was disabled! So when I was rolled into the surgical room, he looked down and said, "Okay, let's get up here." And the words flew out of my mouth, "If you want me up there, you'll have to put me there!"

We laughed.

When I finally woke up, he was sitting by my bed. Months later, he phoned me to say he had accepted a position at a big hospital in Oklahoma, "But feel free to continue my visit for his care!"

I will never find it easy to ask for help. Not asking can sometimes end up making one look very silly, such as carrying a "boat load" of papers in your lap, not asking for help, and somehow the papers slip to the floor, spreading everywhere! A little voice inside of me will say, "Gotcha! Next time, let someone else help!"

Mother was my guardian angel. She literally lived and breathed for me. I would mail my laundry home from college and she literally would receive it one day, wash and iron the clothes, and mail it back—all in three or four days—for five years!

Mother and Daddy would visit me every month. Sometimes we would have a weekend in New York. Often there would be theatre tickets—oh, how I loved that! But, always, things were done to enhance my life and broaden my horizons.

Mother would buy a new evening gown for me, bring a seamstress with a portable sewing machine, and I would have this beautiful gown to wear at a Fall or Spring event.

Talk about selfless love! I can't think of a better example!

Life With Child From a Seated Position

WRITTEN MARCH 24, 2017

CHILDREN COME INTO THIS WORLD much like a blank piece of paper. If all of their physical needs are met, they are content. So, I carried Mark next to my chest with one arm while pushing my chair with the other. He thought all mothers came with wheelchairs! We shortened the legs of the changing table to make it easier for me, and, of course, the side of the crib lowered, which was perfect.

Still, my greatest fear was that I would do or not do something that would harm him. You can imagine my panic when Mark—on his tricycle and the little neighbor child, Cathy, on her tricycle—went missing. They were supposed to stay on the sidewalk of our block.

Chris, my daily helper, and I went up and down the block calling their names. An elderly neighbor heard us and said, "Oh, I saw them heading for the cemetery." There was a cemetery across the alleyway behind our house. And, yes, we could see them pedaling away. They had no idea that there was any problem at all.

Thank heavens I could always reason with Mark. We sat on the sidewalk and I tried to explain that big cars often came to the cemetery and could run over them—they wouldn't mean to harm them, but it could just happen.

It never happened again. If I were a cat, I could say I lost seven of my nine lives that day!

When other children came to play, they stopped short when they saw me. Some would immediately ask Mark, "What's wrong with your Mother?"

Now, most adults try to stifle such questions. But it was an honest question, and Mark would most often reply, "Her legs don't work so she uses that chair to move." The visiting little friend might say, "Oh," and then run with Mark to play. The short, straightforward answer was all that was needed. Children are so accepting.

While we lived in Salisbury, Mark was under the care of a group of pediatricians. The senior pediatrician had quite a reputation as being really short tempered with parents. One time Mark developed an ear ache, so I tried all the old remedies—like a heating pad, a tiny drop of oil, but nothing seemed to help.

The last resort was to call the pediatric service at night. Of course, the senior pediatrician was on call. When he called me back (I can hear him now), in his West Virginia twang he said, "Mrs. Clinton, what seems to be the problem?"

I dutifully reported what I had done, and waited for his input. It seemed like ten minutes before he spoke. "Mrs. Clinton, you've done all you can. Call the office tomorrow."

Well! I had expected that he would have called the all night pharmacy and we would have some kind of relief before office hours. So, I ended it all, "Well, I'll hang out my shingle in the morning!" Mama Bear has no shame.

The next time I saw the senior pediatrician (in an elevator, no less), he eyed me up and down, I did the same, then he smiled and nodded his head as he got off the elevator. Little did he know that if Mark had had any serious illness, he was the only doctor I would have wanted to treat him!

I think my concerns for a child from a wheelchair position would be fairly common for that segment of the disabled community. However, I always wondered if he would love me despite my chair, my braces, and my awkward movements.

After all, I did not measure up to the other children's mothers. If he experienced any of these thoughts, I never heard them. And any time he was part of a class performance, that little blond head would scan the audience until he located me and then wave. Who wouldn't love that?

When it was time for Mark's first haircut, I was told by my father and my husband that, "A woman did not enter a men's barber shop." I thought that was ridiculous, and said so in no uncertain terms. If the barber shop hadn't had steps, I would have taken him myself.

Nevertheless, he was given his first haircut, and I stayed home. The haircut was awful. It looked as if they had put a bowl on his head! So when it came time for his second haircut, I drew in pencil on his head the style I wanted. Perfect! It was the Beetle hair style I wanted!

Years later (I had one of those days!) that I dropped everything I touched, something slid down the disposal that was not supposed to, and I spilled tea. I muttered, "If I could move my feet, I would jump up and down and stomp my feet."

Here comes Mark, jumping up and down, stopping to say, "Well, do you feel better?" How did this junior high student know to do that? I laughed a long time, and it still brings a smile to my face when I think of it.

This just confirms my belief that the power of love is beyond anything we can imagine. It won't change the unchangeable, but it will soften the sharp edges and make life fuller in ways we could never imagine.

Oops! I Went in the Wrong Direction

WRITTEN MARCH 30, 2017

I HAVE MET THE FLOOR OR THE GROUND IN NUMEROUS WAYS and numerous times. Fortunately for the most part, there were no serious injuries, just embarrassment and humiliation.

They say "pride goes before the fall." Not in my case!

My first thought is, "Okay, I'm not hurt." And the second thought is, "How do I get out of this with at least a shred of dignity? Is anything showing that should not be? And how do I rearrange myself?"

Remember, this was the age of dresses. As my father would say, "That is most unladylike!"

One of the most challenging falls happened in the spring of 1980. John was in Florida at an A.D.A. convention, and Mark was to be graduated from Rice University, receiving his Doctor of Music degree in a few days.

The plan was when John returned on Sunday, we would leave for Houston a few days later. Somehow, I slipped and fell in the kitchen while washing dishes. I was able to reach, very painfully, into my basket for the phone and called my neighbor. June managed to help me back in my chair after numerous attempts. I was hurting, but assured my neighbor that I would be okay.

Wrong! With each passing hour, I hurt even more. I made it through the night, and John returned the following day. For once in my life, I said that I needed to see a doctor. I don't know how I got in the car. The x-ray revealed the source of pain—a cracked pelvis!

The doctor said I should go to the hospital. That probably was Plan A, but my Plan B was to stay home in bed for a few days, then we were flying to Houston to see Mark receive his diploma.

I stated my case—a few pain pills so I could sleep at night and I could manage the rest. After all, we had waited for this special time for years, and I wasn't going to miss it.

The dear doctor realized I fully intended to do this, so he just had one requirement—that my legs should never be allowed to dangle. My feet must be on a stool so no pressure would make the crack worse.

We went to Houston, and it was dicey at times, yet I was so glad to be there. What's a little pain next to seeing your son receive his doctorate?

When Mark was in kindergarten, he had his "bestest" friend over for a play date. Of course, at that age you don't walk anywhere when you can run. Unfortunately, my chair was midway down the ramp at the front door when Mark and Keith barreled out the door, pushing my chair almost over—with my right foot mashed back to my shin. I don't think Mark realized what had happened.

But, by the time Mother unexpectedly came an hour later, my foot was black. I didn't wear braces for a day due to the swelling, but after that—with an active little boy—I needed to stand for certain chores.

Thankfully, time took care of things. But I always wondered if I broke anything! I have fallen so many times and hit my head that I should be brain dead. Come to think of it, maybe I am—at least once in a while!

My latest fiasco was falling in a most public place, of course. I was leaving the P.E.O. Christmas luncheon at the Lincoln Country Club when, in my voluminous winter wraps, a friend inadvertently picked up my legs thinking I was mostly on the car seat. Except I wasn't. So I just slid down to the edge of the car where the door closes.

With all my winter garb, I could scarcely move, let alone get up. It seemed like thousands of people were swarming out of the door. Several of the young men who parked the cars rushed over to help. Wonderful! Except I must direct the help. If you try to stand me up, in my present feeble condition, I'll probably jack knife—with my rear up in the air!

When that almost happened, they realized that they should listen to my directions, and I finally made it to the front seat.

Some of the same young men have given me such nice smiles on my most recent visits. I am hoping that we have no duplication of that excitement at the Country Club.

I hate falling, but it just happens to be a part of my life. Usually I can laugh at the ridiculous positions I end up in, but inside I always feel somewhat diminished—reduced to stumbling, drunken-like form.

It takes time for me to adjust to the fact that, by chance, these things happen and will happen. The lesson for me is not to live in fear. I would rather think FULL STEAM AHEAD!

Unforgettable Friends

WRITTEN APRIL 7, 2017

IN 1953, I HAD MY FIRST MUSCLE TRANSPLANT SURGERY. That was a rough one. I went into shock. And when they looked at the cast, they found it soaked in blood. Mother later said it looked like the entire staff ran into my room. I don't remember a thing. They were able to stop the bleeding and the healing process could begin. My parents immediately made arrangements for a private nurse to be with me day and night.

Enter Milly, a slender woman with dark hair—very attractive, really. She was an excellent nurse who cared for me physically and mentally. I loved it when she shared stories of her family—two little girls and a husband.

She idolized her husband—except it was never reciprocated. And from my now adult mind, I suspect she was abused. When I was allowed out of the bed, she would push my chair throughout the public areas of the hospital. She was fun.

When I was finally discharged, it was very difficult for me to say goodbye. She had made all my days so very nice.

It was about a year later one of my parents read in the Baltimore Sun paper that Milly had been charged with murder. She had killed her husband. Apparently Milly discovered he had been unfaithful.

It wasn't more than a week later that Milly called Daddy asking for financial help. It was most unusual for Daddy to bring up such matters at home. He took care of all things at the office.

Of course, my response was "help her." But my Mother, always the cautious one, said, "You don't know what he did."

But I do know Milly was found guilty and put in prison. Years later I learned she had died from tuberculosis. What happened to her children? I don't know. What I do know was that she was special. She treated me as a young adult. I was only thirteen.

And through our many conversations, I came to understand the importance of equal partners in a relationship. I'm sure Milly tolerated a lot, but the time came when all the passion, all the love, was not enough. A good lawyer could have probably gotten her off with a plea of temporary insanity. I feel somewhat guilty about that. Rest in peace, Milly.

In high school, I became good friends with a classmate who carried my books from classroom to classroom. I was walking on crutches, and Ann solved a real problem for me. Ann was in a great many of my classes, so it was an easy solution. She was a bright young girl who loved a party and became quite popular.

On many of our family vacations, Ann was invited to go with us. We both loved to read and would pass books back and forth all the time. On one of our trips, we were staying in a lovely hotel. Ann and I decided to check out the drugstore, where we headed for the book area. This was the time period when Dale Evans wrote a book called "Anger Unaware."

Ann and I each grabbed a copy, and when we saw the price decided we really didn't have the funds for this at the beginning of our vacation, so we each took our copy.

Ann sat on the floor and, of course, I was in my wheelchair. We proceeded to read the entire book, with tears running down our faces. The little girl born to Dale Evans and Roy Rogers lived a very short life, but had a powerful impact on many.

I've often wondered what we looked like, reading a book and crying, At the time, we were oblivious to the world around us.

That was the same trip Ann, as only Ann could, made a negative remark about a teenager's yellow slacks. I think she said something like "A little too much mustard, don't you think?"

Two young boys were gassing up their car at the same time Daddy was filling our car's gas tank. Well, one of the boys heard Ann's comment and replied, "What? You don't like my pants?" Being normal teenagers, we blushed and looked everywhere but at them.

To finish off the trip, we were dining at a lovely restaurant when I noticed Ann sort of clutching her throat. She was wearing a mint green scoop neck dress. "Is something wrong?" I questioned.

With her free hand, she pointed to the ceiling. It was all mirrors! We giggled and continued enjoying the evening.

Ann was a girl for all seasons. She loved—and played—sports. She played the piano. She was always a good dancer and singer. She was such a delightful friend.

Our paths seemed to separate at the time of high school graduation. Ann left home to go to a school of nursing in Philadelphia, Pennsylvania. I left to go to a liberal arts school in New Jersey.

We got together the next Christmas, but it was too different. Her world had become quite different from mine. We both were trying to find our place in the adult world.

We got back together when John and I lived in Salisbury. Ann had not married. I'm not sure why. She had had several serious boyfriends, but all ended abruptly.

Ann was the one who met us at the hospital when Mark was born. I remember asking her, when I awakened, if my baby was all right. She said, "He has ten fingers and ten toes. Do you want to count them?" I groggily said, "I'll take your word for it."

After that time, I heard that Ann left Salisbury and at some point married a divorced man in Tennessee. She never had children and later divorced and came back to Salisbury where, when her mother died, Ann stayed in the house.

Somewhere in this time, I realized she was back in Salisbury—I heard a classmate call her a drunk. I called Ann and we talked. Nothing was said about drinking. She called me a few weeks later and said, "You know, I've always had a dog. Would you get me a dog?" I said that I would try. But, what kind of dog did she want?

The old Ann that I knew came through loud and clear, "I want a parti cocker spaniel." So I found a parti cocker and took him to her (a two hour trip each way). This was a very loving dog. He laid in my lap the whole way and would respond to every loving stroke. My hope was that this loving dog would help her alcohol problem.

It was then she told me she was dying from cancer. I tried to keep in touch, but not always successfully. Then I got a call from Ann. She begged me to get her some whiskey. She was not far from dying, and I said, "Ann Faith, I'll see what I can do."

Then she instructed me to have someone leave it at her back door. Of course, I knew why. God forgive me if I was wrong, but she only had a short time to live, so why not? My father, bless his heart, took the bottle to her back door. If it brought her a few hours of relief, then I'm glad.

She died a week later and was buried with only a small foot marker. I have plans to change that. She will have a true stone. That's what friends are for.

Two women I truly love. Both had so much to offer, but somehow they got off the right path. They came to a fork in the road of life and chose one that could only end badly.

Still, they will always be precious to me.

Mary Ann Kennerly Clinton

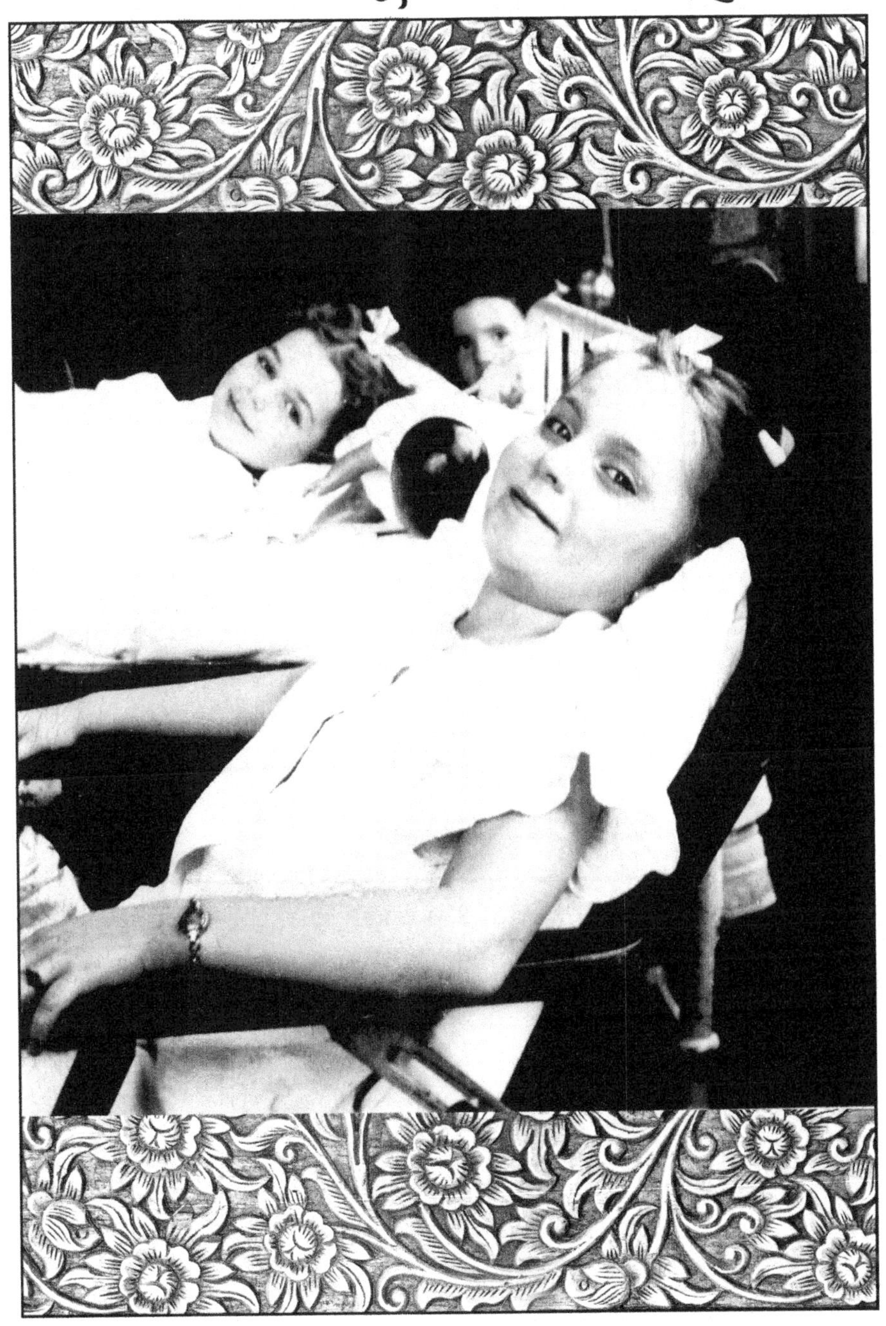

MARY ANN AGE 8 AFTER HOSPITALIZATION

I still want to be me.

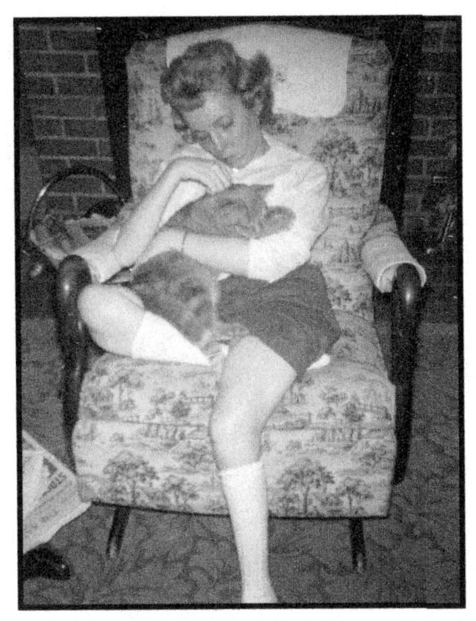

AGE 16

My love, "Sandy Danker" (Alexander)

AGE 17 - HIGH SCHOOL SENIOR

Life is good!

17TH BIRTHDAY

It really is mine!

Below, my friend Betty poses with me on the hood of my 1956 Mercury Montclair with hand controls

Betty and I were the cat's meow!

College Fall Weekend Formal 1957

John and I were Freshmen at Drew

Spring Weekend Formal

My mother and grandmother brought their sewing gear to my dorm room and altered my gown for a perfect fit

JOHN TOOK THIS PHOTO AT DREW

Dreaming of a future

Mary Ann at 17

Stepping into my future

JUNE 10, 1961 - FIVE DAYS AFTER WE GRADUATED FROM DREW UNIVERSITY

A happy bride

The happy couple married in my village church

Mother and Daddy at our wedding

AT THE CODY RANCH IN CODY, WYOMING

Bill Cody and my son Mark
with me and Old Roy

OUR SON MARK - AGE 8

My joy!

MARK CLINTON
AGE 8

My little prodigy

BRITISH EMBASSY - WASHINGTON D.C.

The day Princess Diana died. Every inch of the embassy lawn was covered with flower tributes.

PEPPER AND ME

Note the phone in the basket of my scooter!

Ready with my passport photo and headed to Salzburg, Austria

OUR SON MARK CLINTON

AS A CLASSICALLY TRAINED PIANIST, MARK HAS PERFORMED AROUND THE GLOBE.

HE IS CURRENTLY HIXSON-LIED PROFESSOR OF PIANO AT THE UNIVERSITY OF NEBRASKA.

OUR BEAUTIFUL GRANDDAUGHTER SOLENNE

My favorite companion for brunch

Mary Ann, John, and Mark Clinton

With our gift of this grand piano to The Landing, it was our wish to let the music play on...

Unforgettable Friends
Part 2

WRITTEN APRIL 14, 2017

I CALLED TO WISH HER A SEVENTY EIGHTH BIRTHDAY—my dear friend since 1953. I'm glad we can't foresee the future. Even if I could have, I don't think I would have done things differently.

We met in the eighth grade. Alicia was tall, slender, coal black hair, and brown eyes so dark they were piercing. She was a good student, but very reserved.

Somehow we managed to connect and began to visit each other. Reading was important to both of us. Being outside was not. When she spent the weekend with me, I decided it was time to tan, so we got our towels out and headed to a sunny spot with my transistor radio in hand.

I, of course, enjoyed it and Alicia did, too—for a while. I had grown up with mosquitoes and really was almost immune to them, but Alicia became a delicious target. Soon she was scratching. Then, upon examination, it was discovered she was covered in bites. Return to house pronto!

Mother worried that she had somehow been negligent. Alicia and her mother lived with Alicia's grandmother in a beautiful old brick home with wrap around porches. Her father had died when she was only six (she remembers him, but vaguely, as someone who let her have a sip of his beer!) So the matriarchy held Alicia VERY closely. She was their world.

Our Mothers would take us to Baltimore for "back to school" shopping. Alicia and I loved that, and lunch at Hutzlers Tea Room was the best.

In those times, department stores had revolving doors, so if someone on the maintenance crew could not be found to flatten a side, I couldn't enter. That's why we always stopped at Hutzlers—they had an underground garage, elevators up to the store. And any of your purchases in the store could be sent to your car.

The other big department store across the street also had revolving doors, and you had to go through the whole process again. Mother managed it all—always in high heels. On the way home, we would go through each and every one of our bags, admiring our purchases. We did that for four seasons.

Alicia applied to Baldwin College. And since another of our classmates had done the same, the roommate question was nicely solved. Or so we thought. Alicia couldn't adapt to dorm life and perhaps the different style of teaching. In two or three weeks, she was home. There was a local college, but I guess she was "gun shy."

She found a job and liked it. She was with people she knew and she could go home at night. I always thought that there was an insecure little girl inside.

We always kept in touch. And when I was home on vacation times, we usually got together. On one such vacation, I had called and said I would pick her up and we would get a coke and chat. As Alicia got in the car, her mother appeared and told me in no uncertain terms that "it was too late" (it was 7:30 p.m.!) "to be going anywhere."

I quickly said that "that decision was between her and her daughter." Alicia was almost mute. Then the mother said, "Well, no later than 9:30." As if that was the sinful bewitching hour!

Alicia never referred to the incident, nor did I, but I think I was given a big clue. You raise your child and part of the glory is watching them grow, but the hard part is knowing when it's time to fly.

Alicia continued to work and met a man who would become her husband. They were very happy. And when their daughter was born, they were both over the moon. Two years later, Alicia had twins, one of whom died shortly after birth.

The living twin was critical and was flown from Salisbury to Roanoke, Virginia, where a special preemie machine would possibly save his life. As it so happened, John and Mark and I lived a half hour away from

Roanoke. We said, "Come stay with us, I'll care for your daughter and you can go be with your little son."

He survived. The trauma of it all was almost beyond belief. Then, four years later, another son was born and was developmentally challenged. They did everything possible to help him, but by the time he was eight, it became clear he would always be a child.

Alicia managed it all so well. I marveled at how well she could control him. He now lives in a group home. He goes to his mother's home for an overnight, but is finally really too much for her.

Alicia was struck by a car as she walked to her car from a restaurant. She walks very poorly and uses a walker. Her life is challenged even more by blindness. Her husband died about four years ago. Her grown children pretty much ignore her.

We still chat frequently. I want to help, but how? I offered her a player for books on tape. No, she didn't want to sit and listen. I located a person who would take her wherever she wanted to go. No go. For the last two years, I have had a birthday dinner delivered to her. Two crab cakes, new potatoes, vegetables, and a birthday cake.

I love her. She is my friend. But, as the old saying goes, "You can lead a horse to water, but you can't make him drink!"

In 2012, I got the news that Ted and Alicia's home had completely burned. Nothing was left. John and I took them to dinner a few weeks later. They were still in a state of shock. My father had died and I was getting ready to clean out their house. I asked, "Do you have any bedroom furniture?"

"No."

My response was, "You do now. Do you have any dishes or pots and pans?"

"No."

Again, my response was, "You do now."

When Alicia came to get the dishes, she started to cry and said, "I always wanted this pattern."

My mother was smiling down from heaven!

Village Characters

WRITTEN APRIL 21, 2017

EACH TOWN, CITY OR VILLAGE, HAS ITS SHARE OF CHARACTERS. Nanticoke was no exception. To me, characters are the spice of life.

Take our town handyman, the self proclaimed mayor, as a prime example. He was extremely smart, read vociferously, played the piano, and sketched whatever interested him at the moment.

He was married and had two sons. His wife, early on, fled the oh-so-casual lifestyle. Fortunately, she was an R.N. and could be self-supporting.

The two boys, one a madcap type of fellow, the other a more traditional boy. These two were the ones who hid in the giant maple trees until some poor unsuspecting person walked by and they would drop a rubber snake or some scary looking bug. I'm sure their father encouraged this behavior!

Always on call, Mr. Joe would come to take care of any crisis. I pulled a bathroom sink out of the wall as I started to fall. Thankfully, it didn't fall on me. Mr. Joe was called and came very quickly. When he finished re-attaching the sink, he commented, "She'll never get this one out of the wall." As far as I know, it is still standing.

Mr. Joe would often attend a gathering of men at a gas station each evening. When he read the new book that categorizes people by class, he proceeded to categorize each household in the village. The other men would laughingly disagree that some families did or did not fit in said category. They probably spent a week figuring each family's place on the social scale.

He is unforgettable, a charming man who always marched to his own drummer. The picture of him sitting in a rocking chair, feet propped on the railing, reading a newspaper, with his prominent sign "The Mayor" on his front yard, said it all. It is an indelible memory.

Mrs. Sadie was another Nanticoke character. She had a husband, but I don't remember him at all. Mrs. Sadie drove a 1930's vintage Chevy in a strange way—one eye looking out the front window, the other looking out the side. I tried riding my tricycle her way, but Mother quickly corrected that.

Mrs. Sadie had been involved in a local bank scandal. I don't think she served any time, but she became somewhat of a recluse and a hoarder. She loved dolls and had the five Dionne quintuplets. When I came home from the hospital, she gave me Cecile. Her house was filled with old toys, beautiful furniture pieces and old farm pieces.

Her life had to have been sad. As a young girl, I believe she was quite pretty. But when I knew her, she had lost a lot of her teeth, had white, stringy hair, and a general wizened appearance. Yet, her smile for me was, oh, so kind. That's how I like to remember her.

The Stone family was at one time a prominent family in the community. They lived in a beautiful old house with the original part having been built during the Civil War era. There were three girls and one boy—all very musical. The girls never married—they were too busy feuding.

As the family grew, so did the house. The additions were built to accommodate the feuding females—they each had their own pathway to the dining and sitting rooms and kitchen. They could actually move through the house without seeing each other.

They had a full dinner at twelve noon on a table with a linen tablecloth and white linen napkins with silver napkin rings engraved with their names.

The land around the house was farmed. They were always thought to have the best asparagus.

After the family died, the house was sold to a middle aged couple who dreamed of restoring it to its original grandeur. Imagine their surprise when they found a map of the original plot of land and discovered a covered well. The well was dry, so someone went down there and discovered china and silver hidden there since the Civil war.

Inside the house was a tremendous grand piano. You couldn't get your arms around the legs. It was solid mahogany. I bet the sounds from that magnificent instrument must have filled many an hour.

The house still stands—in a derelict state. It is still a beautiful testimony to days gone by. I just hope there is someone who would love it enough to restore it and actually live there.

I saw it as Nanticoke's own "Tara" from "Gone with the Wind."

These characters made a contribution to the life of the community—each and every one, with every twist and turn playing a part in creating the fabric of life in the sleepy little community.

Village Characters

Part 2

WRITTEN APRIL 28, 2017

The house still has its secrets. One of the daughters was locked in a room most of her life. The other sisters would bring her meals—unlock the door only to lock it again when they left. There is no one now who knows of her disability.

Thank heavens attitudes changed by the time I was born. But, still, think of that poor soul locked in four walls all her life.

The only son married a very sweet lady and brought his bride back to the house. She surely was a saint. It was made very clear to her from the beginning that it was not her house, and one sister was in charge of all things at all times. A relative of mine remembers her as the "Drill Sergeant." If only the beautiful wooden floor could talk!

Mr. Finn was another of the village characters. He and his wife bought waterfront property with a lovely house and pier. He was a Shriner and a magician (a very good one, I'm told).

For some reason, I thought magic was evil. I was always uncomfortable when he would pull things from your ears or change a yellow scarf into red. He entertained many times at hospitals for children, who applauded and laughed. Why I was so different, I don't really know.

One summer day I and my friend, Ann, were at the beach. We were enjoying the splashing and going under water to see if we could see anything exciting, like crabs maybe. All of a sudden we heard this loud male voice shouting, "Get out of my river!" We laughed and waved. So then he issued a warning, "If you don't get out of the water, I'll pull it out from under you."

I don't think we stayed at the beach very long that day. I eventually realized that his words and actions were his way of teasing. He actually was a marshmallow at heart who cried easily.

Mr. Finn and his wife were neighbors. Now, Mr. Finn was never what the locals would call "ambitious," so it was late in life before he bought his first automobile.

Like many of the citizens in the village, a twenty-five mile trip to the county seat was a much anticipated event each Saturday, so Mr. Finn would be ready to leave long before his wife was ready.

She dressed beautifully and always looked so put together. But each Saturday, rain or shine, Mr. Finn would bring the car in front of the house and, in measured time, blew the horn. Sometimes it went on for thirty minutes.

My father would be so irritated at this, he would grumble. I, on the other hand, thought it was hilarious. It certainly reminded us of what day it was!

Now, I can't stop my character narrative without mentioning a most beloved character in my life—my father. He had this very strong sense of right and wrong, which never wavered. There was also this little boy devilish character. As a four- or five-year-old, he found a pistol in a trunk from a long gone Kennerly. He took the pistol in hand and announced he was the Kaiser and would shoot!

My grandmother nearly died. She had a house rule, "absolutely no weapons, particularly loaded weapons, in the house." How this loaded weapon found its way into a trunk, no one ever knew.

In his adult life, the little devilish boy still reigned. He was returning to Nanticoke when a farm truck, for whatever reason, started to tailgate, getting way too close to Daddy's Cadillac. He tolerated that for a few miles, then gently tapped the brakes.

The truck, trying to avoid crashing into the Cadillac, veered into a farm field, muddy from recent rains, and promptly got stuck. Daddy never stopped, thinking now that "justice was served"!

I must admit, I love these characters. They were a blueprint for my life.

Mr. Finn, our neighbor, felt it important to make a resounding statement that he and his wife were traveling to the city.

Mr. Holston wanted to amuse me by teasing.

Daddy, he was in a class by himself. He seldom denied a request for a pay advance on a Saturday afternoon or a substantial donation for a new church organ. Yet, he polished his shoes every week, almost until he died.

I sometimes think that all those characters are like a ball of variegated yarn—each contributed to the whole me and what I am.

Old Things

WRITTEN MAY 4, 2017

I GUESS I'LL START WITH THE OBVIOUS—ME! I'm old. I am seventy-seven in calendar years, but in polio years I'm eighty-seven. Some days I would swear that I'm ninety-seven. Either way, I'm an antique!

When I mention to the younger generation that the advent of television was a spectacular event, they look at me, and I see in their faces, "How weird is that?" Then I hasten to add there was no color, just black and white. Surely, to them, we lived somewhere in a cave and clubbed animals for our food.

Central air conditioning was nowhere to be found. Window units were the high tech of the day. I hated them because they drastically reduced the amount of light in any room. I guess that's why I didn't live in a cave!!

Rotary phones were treasures, and not everyone had a phone. There were party lines with several homes on the same line. The switchboard operator knew who said what and why.

Some people who would listen to other people's phone calls would forget and break into the conversation. That had to be embarrassing, yet not enough to change their way. I have heard my father say many times at the end of a conversation, "You can hang up now, Annie!"

Maybe all of this is why I really do like old things. One of my most loved "old things" is a dropleaf table in my living room. It has a slightly warped leg from being on a ship that sank. My grandfather and his brother sailed the Chesapeake Bay, and their boat sank due to a bad storm.

Some months later, my grandmother insisted that they return to the site and retrieve anything they could. They returned with the drop leaf table. It shows its age, and I love it. As they say on HGTV, "It has character."

Another piece from my Kennerly grandparents was a wash stand, marble top, but missing the back. I often wonder how many of my grandmother's sisters preened in front of this piece. Now it is home to my beautiful parlor lamp, whose date goes back to the 1800's. To me, they are as beautiful as the day they were made, and loved because they were part of my family's life.

Two other old things are the rosewood chairs in the front hall. They are truly beautiful, and will one day reside in the Maryland Museum of History. These chairs were part of a group of six that were sent from England to White Haven, Maryland, to a doctor who was my great, great grandfather.

Mother discovered these beauties at the estate sale of a home lived in by the sister of my great, great grandmother. There was one chair with a broken leg tossed on a pile of junk. She chastised herself until the day she died that she did not collect those pieces of the remaining chair. I think there still exists the shipping bill from England.

I have earlier written of my love for clocks. One of those clocks (a

Regulator) hangs in our den. Its date easily goes back to early 1800, and once hung in the custom office by the wharf on the Nanticoke River.

On its back are the signatures of five generations of Kennerlys. It has a gentle, soothing tick and, oh, how I wish it could talk!

Another of my clocks is a mantle clock. In 1912, my grandfather sent a hired man to a general store on Christmas Eve to buy this clock for my grandmother. Did I forget to tell that this was during a snow storm and it was a two-mile walk each way?

Old things and old people have stories to tell that enrich our lives beyond belief. I sense that I'm just a bleep on the history radar. But maybe, just maybe, another generation will find "my bleep" and enjoy my links in a family history.

The Down Side of Life

WRITTEN MAY 12, 2017

I'M GOING TO BLAME IT ON THE WEATHER, but that is just convenient. I don't want to re-evaluate my situation, yet that won't change anything either. I'm on a downward spiral, and each new frustration seems to bring out the worst in me.

I can't even find a pen that is easy for me to use. So, as I try to write, I find myself comparing it to chicken scratching. My Triple A personality finds little that I do acceptable.

I am losing strength so fast it seems. To turn over in bed is pretty much out of the question. Transferring from chair to toilet, to bed, to tub, is quite an effort. I am so fearful of falling that each time I'm successful in the transfer, I breathe a "Thank you, Lord"!

Standing up with braces is a challenge now. In the past, I could manage to stand easily with braces. Now I wobble like a drunken sailor. It calls for mental courage just to try to move.

Sitting has become problematic. As you could guess, sitting so much causes pressure sores. So then it seems I have ants in my pants! I have such a curvature of the spine that it has caused my rib cage to be pulled askew. One side is only half the size because the other half is in the back.

What this is doing to my internal organs, I can only guess. BUT THERE IS NOTHING THAT CAN BE DONE TO STOP THIS! Many have offered the advice of using a corset. All things being equal, that would help.

The down side is that by immobilizing my trunk, I could no longer move my body. I need side to side freedom of motion to move.

With a corset, I could not even bend forward to lock my braces to achieve standing position. Still, I can't hold myself in a proper sitting position for any length of time, then I slump, so I don't breathe properly. It is all a vicious circle!

What makes this bearable? Faith and the love and support of friends. My faith reminds me constantly that I'm not alone. I have a bad habit (one of many, I might add!) of denigrating myself when I don't perform a task as perfectly as I want—"Okay, dumb dumb! You idiot! Can't you do anything right?"

Not too long ago, I was reading one of my two daily devotions and it hit me right between the eyes. God was saying, "Don't be so hard on yourself. After all, I made you. You are a child of God."

I went back and re-read that passage two more times. On really bad days, I revert to the anger, but I am trying!

Fellowship

WRITTEN MAY 19, 2017

I HAVE BEEN BLESSED WITH SPECIAL FELLOWSHIP MOMENTS. Or, as I like to think of them, a gathering of kindred spirits.

John and I are born and bred United Methodists. We went to college where a Methodist seminary was located. I guess you could say we are steeped in that faith.

The services were fairly traditional. So when we moved to Radford,

Virginia, we quickly found a Methodist church. The pastor and lay leader visited us within ten days of our arrival. The pastor was invited into our home and immediately headed for a rocking chair. He had a newspaper in his hand.

We were enjoying our conversation when Miss Sniff, our cat, wandered in. Well, immediately Jerry, the minister, started rocking and folding the newspaper. I could see he was in battle mode when he said, "I'm afraid of cats." Somehow Sniffy recognized his fear and tried to twine herself around his legs, purring at high volume.

I realized this conversation was going nowhere if our cat stayed in the room, so I scooped her up and put her in the garage. We joined Jerry's church and enjoyed being a part of that church for two years.

At one point in time, we began to hear of what was considered then a momentous event, a "Lay Witness Weekend." A team of people visit the church, starting on Friday night, with a dinner and an outline of the program beginning and ending with prayer. They offered study groups, activities groups, music groups all with faith objectives. And, yes, there were groups for teens and small children.

This style of worship was foreign to me and I felt a little afraid, but we attended. The final piece of a "Lay Witness Weekend" was the service on Sunday morning. I didn't know what to expect and went with a great deal of trepidation. The sermon was quite good, after which there was an altar call.

Now, I had never been in church where that was done, so this was way out of my comfort zone. But like a rising ocean wave, the congregation rose as one and started to the altar. It was a beautiful sight—eerily quiet, the organ playing in the background and all the people waiting for a final blessing.

There was a serenity there that I didn't want to leave. It was so real that it was almost palpable. The fellowship of that church was beyond belief.

When we left Radford, I wrote a note to the church expressing my gratitude for helping me grow in my faith. The pastor read it to the congregation on Sunday. I hope that same spirit is still alive today.

We quickly found a church home in Bowie, Maryland, where we located after Radford. The sanctuary had just been completed and, when we arrived on that first Sunday after services, a member came to us and asked if there was anything the church could do to make it easier for me to attend. John immediately said "a curb cut." Monday morning the "curb cut" was made!

We worshipped here for the next twenty years. Mark became a part of the music program. He gave recitals at fund raisers. And anywhere he performed, many church people attended. He accompanied singers from the choir.

And when he won a competition giving him the chance to play with the National Symphony Orchestra at the Kennedy center, they hired a bus in addition to dozens of private cars to attend. When he walked on stage (at 16), the applause was thunderous. When he sat down on the bench, adjusted it—I felt it. It was like a warm cloud of love—and more—"we're here to share in your music."

Rachmaninoff 3rd Concerto, last movement swept me away. And I guess the audience felt the same. It was a standing ovation. Later, I asked Mark had he felt that warm loving support? He looked at me with surprise. I know my fan club was there. Kindred spirits. When the last person boarded the bus back to Bowie, hands in the air, Norman said, "WE WON!"

There were lots of special moments at St. Matthews. The day the hostages were released from Iran, John and I heard the news and headed to church. Apparently, fifty or so other people felt the same. We had a special "tolling of the bells," making a joyous sound throughout Bowie. People were so thrilled. It is good for people to fellowship in joy as one.

Storms in West Virginia destroyed homes and hundreds of cars. One of our church members spearheaded a drive to collect cars. He did over three hundred of them. The church parking lot was full. Parishioners drove them to West Virginia, and Gordon even managed to get the use of some car carrier trucks. It is amazing what these kindred spirits can do.

Our last church in Maryland (Severna Park United Methodist Church) was another blessing. It has a long history of Christian outreach. What they didn't have was an active Sunday School class for adults. And I missed Sunday School. So, John, after speaking with the pastors, started an adult Sunday School class at 9:30 a.m. every Sunday. It was a diverse group, which made for great discussions.

I was the support system, providing four or five parties a year at our home. Everyone seemed to enjoy them, particularly the Christmas trees. I started decorating the day after Thanksgiving. There absolutely are not enough words to describe the joy that this gave us.

When 9/11 occurred, it was automatic to head to church. And like before, the parking lot filled with cars. One family actually had a son working in the building. He had not gone to work that day. You can imagine their horror until they learned their son was safe. Grief and joy bring people together and somehow bring out the best in them.

I did a farewell dialogue with the minister on my last Sunday there. We had three services—8:30, 9:30 and 11:00 a.m. Each service was filled. Never have I gotten so many hugs and tears.

But these faith communities sustain me. They all exemplify that faith is not a passive way of life, but an active one to be passed to the next generation.

Special People—Family & Friends

WRITTEN MAY 25, 2017

WHEREVER I GO, I FIND PEOPLE TO LOVE. Of course, my parents and grandparents were first on the list. My sister of the heart's mother was another. She called me "droopy drawers"! You can guess why. I was four or five and in too much of a hurry to get on with life to carefully pull up my pants!

My grandmother's neighbor who, until the day she died, called me "young un"! I wonder if she really knew my name. My maternal grandfather called each of his grandchildren "Skip." I have no idea why, but Skip it was. Skip was the first word I heard as I came out of anesthesia from my first muscle transplant. These names are special, but reflected love for me.

Of course, I named myself "Susie Brown" because a grandmother-like lady asked me what my name was and, knowing she knew my real name, I felt compelled to try to confuse her. These people were all given to me from my birth. I think they were lovely role models for finding others in the future.

I loved my elementary school teacher. It was fun just to be in her class. She really made learning interesting. I cried when my years with her were over.

High school years—adult relationships were few. For me, it was a time to come to terms with what I liked and what I wanted. "Circumspect" best characterizes it.

College was a different story. I was totally free to pick and choose all aspects of college life. One lady stands out as a real love. She was a hairdresser. I found her somewhat accidentally. I rode by her shop, went in, and made an appointment. We became good friends. And when I needed something in an off time, she was always available. Elveretta was caught up in our wedding plans and came to our Maryland wedding from New Jersey. You can't forget people like that.

John's mother was another love. She was smart. She cooked, oh, so well. She could take little or nothing and make table decorations that blew my mind. She could play the piano. She had the sweetest ways.

One summer she was visiting, while John was in D.C. working on his doctorate, and we decided to play Scrabble. We both had our eye on the space that would triple our tile.

Mother Clinton said, "I can make jowl."

And I quickly said, "You can't do that. There is only space for three letters."

We went round and round until she finally played her three letters, "j a r". The New England accent does not pronounce R's! We laughed about this for many years.

Aunt Maxine (John's mother's sister) was a most favorite person of ours. We loved visiting her and Uncle Jack and having them visit us. Mark adored her.

Aunt Maxine was visiting us when Princess Diana was killed. We had been to church and had dinner at home, all the time listening to the tragic news. All at once we decided to go to D.C. and the British Embassy. Thousands of others had the same idea.

But it was an experience like no other. The flowers were piled as high as the fence, beautiful flowers. And it was quiet except for a few sobs here and there. The only other sound of the enormous crowd was a shuffling sound as they moved down the sidewalk.

For those who wished, they were allowed to go into the embassy and sign the book of condolences. John signed and Aunt Maxine signed and I stayed outside. It was one of the many times we were glad to be so near our capital, and glad we had our Aunt Maxine to share in this event.

After Uncle Jack died, Aunt Maxine lived alone. So when she had to have hip surgery, I suggested that after she regained a little strength and stitches were removed, she come to our home to recuperate. After all, we had the perfect setup—no steps. So in due time her son brought her to Millersville.

We had a great time. At the end of the two weeks, she wanted a tub bath. I helped her until she was sitting comfortably. Never will I forget the love reflected in her face when she said, "You're a good woman, Mary Ann." Love makes all matters easier.

She later moved to a senior residence that was quite nice. And then she had kidney problems. She had to go on dialysis until she said, "This isn't living." We went to see her for the last time. Recounting our history together made the time go quickly, but soon we could see she was weary.

This lady was a role model for me in many ways. She was always ready to learn or try something new, and had an infectious laugh. It was a privilege to know and love her.

When I worked for the Maryland State Employment Service, I met Mrs. B. We were friends from the very beginning. She was easy to talk to and we shared many lunches and dinners. She knew I was pregnant almost before I did. When I asked how did she know that, she said, "You looked green around the gills." That I did. Food was the enemy for a while.

We moved to Salisbury in June and my obstetrician said I could travel to Hyattsville no later than early November. We made arrangements to visit Mrs. B and were excited about the visit. On the Thursday before we were to leave, I didn't feel well. On Friday the Kennedy assassination occurred, by which time we had canceled our trip.

I have always thought that if we had made that trip with all the hysteria, I might have gone into labor and lost my baby. As it was, he came a month early.

Mrs. B was wise and nurturing, and I loved her. I can still hear her say, "Now, Mary Ann Clinton," and off she would go.

These are a few of so many wonderful people who will always reside in my heart. They made my life better, and maybe I added something to theirs.

My Love of Flowers

WRITTEN JUNE 1, 2017

I WENT ON MY ANNUAL PLANT HUNT THIS WEEK. As always, it brightens my world, and my spirit rises. My car once again becomes the plantmobile. I'm not quite finished, but the balcony—instead of a stark, dull looking platform rising to the sky—is becoming a welcoming bower of color.

The giant fuchsia geraniums, surrounded by white bacopa, caught my eye immediately. "That one," I said, pointing at the hanging basket.

And so it began—the red geraniums and red verbena, the mandavilla (I got two) and a hanging basket.

Dear friends had sent us a giant pot of miniature petunias and lacy greenery that started my landscape. You are probably thinking, "What a riot of color." Exactly! The Lord God gave us all this color in plants, and I enjoy each and every one.

There are still a few more plants to add—five pots of geraniums for my towering plant stand, some bacopa for the two planters hanging on the chimney, and maybe something mostly green. That should complete things nicely.

I went back on the balcony about 11:00 p.m.—what a satisfying moment, surrounded by sheer beauty and, yes, one of my family treasures is here—a white bench that sat on the wharf over the Nanticoke River where my great grandfather was the custom agent. Perfect!

I have always loved flowers and throughout my life had been showered with them. When I was hospitalized for muscle transplant surgery, my hospital room looked like a floral shop.

At age thirteen, I loved receiving them, but when my doctor would take a rosebud for his lapel, he got a serious frown from me!

On my sixteenth birthday, many of Daddy's business customers sent me gorgeous baskets of flowers. I felt very adult. From my senior vantage point now, I was just a babe in arms.

In college, when John and I began to date each other exclusively, he would bring me a rose each Friday.

For all my familiarity with receiving flowers, I did not always get the names right. Nor am I much of a prankster. What made me do this, I don't know. John and I had gone to my parents for the weekend, and when I returned to Drew on Sunday, I told my roommate that we had eloped!

She, naturally, asked questions. "What did you wear?" And, "Didn't you have any flowers?"

I made things up as I went along. "Oh, I just had a church dress on and I carried "bidians," thinking I was carrying an orchid, which would have been cymbidium.

The joke was on me. Carol believed me and even went so far as to buy me a gift. Did I ever feel ashamed! I still have the gift.

And I'm still ashamed!

When we lived in Bowie, a high percentage of residents worked for the Federal government. Every Friday between 4:00 and 6:00 p.m., a floral vendor was at the bus stop where residents come home. It was sweet to see many workers stop and buy flowers to take home. It would have made a great Norman Rockwell painting.

John and Mark quite frequently bring me flowers. They are well aware of my love for them. It gives me great pleasure to take a flower of welcome to each new resident on our floor.

How better to say "welcome" and "I care"!

Mother Nature's Creations

WRITTEN JUNE 9, 2017

I HAVE A DEEP, DEEP LOVE FOR MOTHER NATURE. Or, as I am more apt to say, "My Dear Lord."

Spring is such an obvious great awakening. I constantly check to see the first swelling buds on the trees, the daffodils adding their accent of yellow, the clamor of the ducks and geese.

How do they know when to return? Does God email them and say, "It is okay to?" It all seems such an orderly process, not random at all.

We are just as awesome as one of God's creation. Because of my disability, I tend to watch how people move or struggle to do so. Some people walk, one leg always leading; others walk with a measured gait, properly swinging from the hip.

Most dancers seem to be made of rubber. They twist and turn at angles that defy gravity.

Children running, heads back, are perfect examples of freedom of movement—and it is all done naturally. We don't program anything.

Watch an infant who discovers his or her hands. It takes time and a good deal of effort. I have a picture on my fridge of my sister-of-the-heart's one year old great grandson gazing at a geranium. His intensity is amazing. He is completely lost, looking at that flower.

How wonderfully the human body is made. And how wonderfully this human body tries to heal itself.

In my case, my body was paralyzed completely. In an effort to return to normal over a few years, it completely re-wired itself with the remaining healthy nerve cells and muscles. Imagine that!

How did the humming bird remember to come to my kitchen window for a period of three years? She would arrive about Mother's Day and fly back and forth in front of the window. I would quickly make the nectar and serve it to my feathered friend.

When she left in October, she always came to say goodbye, flying back and forth in front of that window.

Look around. It's a beautiful world.

And look—with a grateful heart!

The Fears With Which We Live

WRITTEN JUNE 16, 2017

I, long ago, made a vow to myself to not let fear control my life. Fear is a natural emotion: FLIGHT or FIGHT. Obviously, FLIGHT was not a choice for me, so I've done a lot of FIGHTING.

I became acquainted with fear at an early age. The "Sister Kenny" treatment for hot packs may have been the worst fear of my young life.

From the moment I saw the silver colander on wheels, I knew what was coming. When the lid was raised, steam poured forth and the cloths were retrieved with tongs. Then they were wrapped around my legs.

I don't think any of the cloths were ever used on my arms. And why they didn't cause blisters, I will never know. But maybe they did, I had no way of knowing.

What I did know was that those hot packs burned, as if my legs had been set on fire. That was as close to torture as I ever want to be.

The benefit of the Sister Kenny treatment was soon proven false and was less and less used and finally discontinued altogether.

I had to re-enter normal life, and it took me a while. At meal times, I ate one thing at a time—all the peas, all the mashed potatoes, then all the meat. Dessert was easy—I had been fed like that, and when I was able to feed myself, I followed the protocol.

It was months after I got home before I revised my eating habits. It was scary. I had forgotten all sorts of food. When they thought I could re-enter a normal gathering, church was the first choice. I didn't know enough to be afraid, but after the first Sunday School class, I knew I was different and I really didn't want to leave the safety of my home again.

Wisely, my parents kept taking me out in the community, and soon children were not as interested in my difference as they were in who would push my chair.

When I finished elementary school, I cried like a baby. I was comfortable there. I wanted no part of that three hundred student high school.

AND A BOY WOULD CARRY ME UP AND DOWN THE STEPS! It was so very humiliating! It's a wonder I never had stomach ulcers.

The degree of fear was ever present that year. I refused to use a wheelchair and so walked on crutches, with someone carrying my books. It took almost a year for me to be at ease and accept the new situation.

When I started driving, I told myself, "Self, you have to be a better driver than anyone else on the road. You already have one strike against you."

So you can imagine my overwhelming fear when I was caught in a chain reaction accident. I was in bumper to bumper beach traffic when the car in front of me came to a screeching halt. And, try as I did to stop, I hit the car in front of me.

Now, the scary part—I did not have braces on. There were no cell phones then, so I had to ask the driver of the car I hit to call my father. I don't know which was worse—having to reveal my disability or having to ask the young guy whose car I hit to call my father.

To be truthful, I hated being helpless. Everyone has accidents and gets out of their car and takes care of business. I had to sit there, alone, and wait to be carried to my father's car. That really rankled!

I still, today, have a fear of being helpless. Hence, I always want a Plan B in everything I do—a way to get help. The cell phone is the best medicine for my nerves.

Helplessness—a battle I can never win. Post polio syndrome is taking me back to 1945. Little by little I lose strength in every part of me. If I could declare war on the medical system, I would.

POLIO IS NOT NEW. It is still rampant in the third world countries. Yet, most doctors do not know how to treat polio survivors.

Case in point—true story—a female polio survivor in her sixties was taken to the hospital having trouble breathing. She told them about polio and that initially she had been on a ventilator. They insisted they could find nothing to cause her breathing problems.

It took her twelve days to convince them to put her on a ventilator. (She probably had to threaten to sue)! In the meantime, she lost a lot of strength, and her oxygen level suffered a real blow.

Immediately she began to breathe easier. Eventually, she went home with a ventilator.

Now, this is real fear for all polio survivors.

Flight or Fight

WRITTEN JUNE 23, 2017

"THE ONLY THING WE HAVE TO FEAR IS FEAR ITSELF," so said Franklin Roosevelt. But fear is a natural emotion. Even the animals know fear. FLIGHT or FIGHT! In my case, I can neither fight nor flee, and that is a source of fear.

My world here at The Landing offers me freedom that I never had before. When I was still able to drive, I could visit friends, as long as there were no more than two steps into their homes.

Even in our last home in Maryland, I could not go in any of my neighbors' homes. They came to me or I got as far as their front steps and we would commune there.

I have never shopped in a mall by myself. I don't drive and I don't know directions in Lincoln. Give me certain landmarks and I might, just might, be able to point you in the right direction.

All this is to say that the first time I left our apartment by myself, I felt entitled to a panic attack. All these floors look alike. What if the elevator stops between floors?

Then one day I convinced myself that I should really visit outside areas. I took a deep breath and reminded myself I was, after all, a grown woman—even if an old one!

Head high, I rolled through the garage and out the door. I must admit the world looked, well, big. And from a seated position, I guess it would.

I checked out the garden plots and continued around the pond. I watched the geese and they watched me. After a bit, I headed toward 34th street. Halfway to the street, something told me to look back—and here were the geese following me in a straight line. It was a sweet moment in time.

However, when I got to the door by the garage door, I couldn't get it open. "Think, Mary Ann. Okay, my fob would get me in the front door." But, along came a car that I followed into the garage.

I realize this seems strange, but I had never, since I was six years old, been able to do much of anything in the outside world by myself. I missed the learning experience of navigating the outside world. Hooray for Independence Day!

Were it not for John, some sales clerks would not have waited on me. Maybe that's why I have never used my scooter in a department store.

I am confident I would do well in Barnes and Noble, but I won't let myself go there until I have finished the unread books in the apartment.

Fears, real or imagined, are powerful. My greatest fear is once again being completely helpless. It may happen.

My father knew my fear and he promised me that I would always be cared for.

What love I have been given! What hope my faith provides!

Continued Life Lessons

WRITTEN JULY 6, 2017

I GUESS YOU NEVER GET TOO OLD TO ADAPT OR CHANGE. But the frustration level still soars.

It has always given me great pleasure to entertain house guests. I would polish silver and brass pieces for weeks before the guests arrived. I would create menus for each day and schedule activities that would be suitable for each particular guest.

And I delighted in having fresh flowers in the bedrooms, and especially on the dining room table. It was fun!

Living in the Maryland area that we did, there was always lots to see or do. I can't do that anymore. Besides the fact that we don't have the room, I don't have the energy.

But I miss the elegance of a beautifully set table. I took great satisfaction in all of this. And cook! It was glorious! No end of pies, cheesecakes, bread pudding, homemade ice cream, and so on. Always, we had fresh fruit and assorted fresh vegetables and seafood—crabs, fish, oysters, etc.

I wouldn't last a day doing this now. So when John's brother and wife visited this past weekend, there was no evidence of past levels of entertaining. It really bothered me. I had scheduled meals out or bringing meals in. We had tourist places to visit as we wished.

At the first meal on Sunday night, I realized we were joyously laughing and enjoying each other. It was what I call a "Light Bulb Moment"! We were together, and that's what mattered most of all. Lesson duly noted!

Now, the guests have gone, and I get to play catch up, except my plan and reality didn't agree. I was helping our caregiver fold sheets when, all of a sudden, the back seat of my scooter went diagonal. Apparently, there is a large crack in the back and an out and out break where it is joined to the seat. Lovely!

Well, I thought, I can stand this until we get a new seat. But wait, suppose I need a new chair? By now, my head and stomach are like a Kitchen Aid mixer. The still small voice that lives within me says, stop, you do have a backup chair. Yes, but it doesn't fit as well as my old one. Then, what if the seat from the backup chair would fit the old scooter?

Down to the garage we go. Greg helped remove the broken seat and, EUREKA, the backup fit on the old scooter!

You think, problem solved. But nay, nay, the backup seat is wider, the seat back doesn't fit me very well, the whole seat doesn't go as low, so putting dishes away blindly is problematic—just one of many moves I made in a day.

Getting up and down from this different level is a real challenge. I must be super careful not to misgauge any move I make. Tiresome, at best; lest, I fall!

Now, I know the lesson I should learn. Lord knows, I've been there often enough, but patience was never one of my strong attributes.

Actually, it is probably my greatest flaw, and I don't seem to deal with any restriction that causes me to be helpless.

But, then, this comes to mind: *If God is for you, who will be against you?*

IN GOD'S TIME, NOT MINE!

Another Birthday

WRITTEN JULY 13, 2017

"One year older and probably deeper in debt," as Tennessee Ernie Ford sang. That's me today. The years settle on me like a mantle of achievement. I never expected to live past the age of seventy-five. After all, in polio years I'm ten years older than the calendar says. But God must have more in mind for me, I guess.

I have been showered with blessings this week. My chair on the scooter has been repaired. No one can know the trauma of losing this big part of my independence. The arms of the chair were too large for me to grasp and push myself to a standing position. So it was a fight to get into bed, get on the toilet, or to stand at the sink.

Because the backup seat was a fuller cushion, my braces got caught on the lip of the cushion, requiring more struggle. My shoulders would give way. So, in mid transfer, I was neither off nor on.

I can yell with the best—think "entering a pig calling contest"! The back of the seat protruded at least three more inches, so I barreled my way around hitting furniture, walls, and door frames. I explained to my neighbor that I was going for the open concept in our apartment.

Then my eye doctor thought I was a candidate for eye surgery. He made the surgery sound quite tedious, so we went to the eye surgeon armed with all the do's and don'ts for polio survivors.

I was so pleased and thanked him for looking at the material, and he actually thanked us for the information. The best part was his statement that no surgery was needed. WHEW!

Then the beautiful birthday cards and phone calls that I received are astounding. The messages, many from east coast friends, THANKING ME FOR BEING A PART OF THEIR LIVES! It doesn't get better than that.

Blessings, each and every one. Problems were solved in that physical mishap. Eye treatment determined to be status quo.

And the big reminder that when all is said and done, friends are what counts most of all. Their love provides support and joy and brings equilibrium to my days.

Give In or Give Up

WRITTEN JULY 20, 2017

THAT HAS BEEN MY DILEMMA MOST OF MY LIFE. Do I just accept things as they are? Or, do I adopt an "I don't care" attitude? I wish it were that simple.

I am so not in control of our apartment. And I'm not satisfied if it isn't cared for the way I did for some fifty years.

I loved the way glass and crystal sparkled after being washed in ammonia. I routinely did that every three months.

I love the way wood gleams after polishing. My living space was and is my little corner of the world. Now I find I just don't get around to dispensing breakfast dishes, and sometimes that pattern continues right through dinner.

What is wrong with me? I get no pleasure in seeing dirty dishes on the counter, and it would take so little time to do.

Is it that it takes too much energy to lock my leg braces, maneuver my chair so I can pull myself up? I could raise my chair and work from there, but then my shoulders complain big time at the unnatural position.

Our furniture is arranged pretty much so I can access each piece from my chair. I have been known to wipe the baseboards with a damp cloth as I drive my scooter down the hall, turn, and do the same for the other side.

A yardstick works to reach in between areas of furniture. You have no idea how many yardsticks I have broken. I am contemplating using a shortened boat oar. That is, if I can marshal the energy.

Silver! I love it. We got a boat load of silver when we were married. I have enjoyed using it all, and silver and brass were polished every three months. Now the Revere silver bowl and silver candle sticks used at Christmas have taken up residence in a dining room chair. Shame, I keep telling myself that I will polish them and put them away. Any day now!

Bureau drawers were always neatly filled. Now, they look like an egg beater has tried to whip up all the colors.

I'm always in a hurry. Why? I don't know. What I do know is that lack of order is unsettling. Acceptance is supposed to be the key to good mental health, yet I'm still at war.

So, I guess the best I can say is, "Don't give in without a fight."

But there is a time when normal changes into a new normal.

A Guide to the Disabled Psyche

WRITTEN JULY 28, 2017

MOST PROBABLY HUGH GALLIGER, HIMSELF A POLIO SURVIVOR, said it best in the title of his book "Splendid Deception" about Franklin Roosevelt's refusal to be seen in his wheelchair—or standing with crutches when he entered into national politics.

He did not want anyone to think he was too disabled to serve as Governor or Cabinet Secretary or President. He was right in the sense that—at that time—the public looked at any permanent disability as retirement to an armchair.

Family whispered news of his condition in morbid tones. This would be his lot in life. Two of his sons would "walk" him to the podium, stand behind him as he spoke, and return him to his seat afterwards.

The Secret Service built a ramp to the speaker's platform so his handicapped controlled cart could drive to the speaker's platform. Flanked by his sons, moving to the podium, the public was never aware of the "splendid deception."

I think F.D.R. was never truly at ease anywhere but Warm Springs, Georgia. Reports are that he loved to frolic with the children in the pool. He had great upper body strength, so in the pool he could "hold his own"!

Deception for the disabled is necessary. The more we fit in with normal society, the better our life becomes. Sometimes it may reduce our activities to a shorter time, but for most of us it is worth it.

My dear friend, Pamela—who had polio and was in the hospital in 1945 the same time as I—participated in the Para Olympics in Australia. She only had the use of one arm, but rolled her chair around the track. All were winners that day. We all share the spirit of, "Yes, I can do whatever!"

In high school, we had a campus-type layout. Use a wheelchair? Not on your life. I walked those miles every day on crutches. It was part of my "splendid deception." Boils under the arms from constant friction—no problem!

One of my teachers constantly challenged me, asking obscure questions or making stern remarks on my paper assignments. I decided he would give me an "A" or else. When the next exam was given, I was ready. I shall never forget his face when he called "Kennerly, you outdid yourself."

My feeling was one of exhilaration—my body may not work that well, but my brain still does.

This deception is a built in vice for the disabled. No one wants to be *less*, so we try harder. And more times than not we succeed.

Who says we can't "keep house"? We try just a little harder, but the end result is acceptable.

Who says you can't have a child, work part time, take care of the household? Yes, I can.

Driving a car like F.D.R. made us both equal to all the other drivers on the road.

A.D.A. has been quite an equalizer for the disabled, but it still has miles to go. And, contrary to what is generally thought, it often can be quite unobtrusive. In the case of many old buildings, a ramp to the side concealed by landscaping is very possible.

Such was the case of the Governor's mansion in Maryland. Only from the air is the ramp visible.

I have seen elevators installed in closets, pantries, and the history of the building was not disturbed at all. To me, that is a Splendid Deception.

I think all polio survivors would agree that we walk a very fine line. And since we have a large percent of seniors, we guard every last inch of our independence most vigilantly.

Caregivers need to understand that our last shred of independence resides with them. And we fight. Don't tell me you can't pick up four gallon jugs of water when I pour them into my watering can every night. No big deal.

Or you have a twenty-five pound limit when moving a client. How would you push a wheelchair? Aren't they taught how to manage positioning a client? And worse, just walk away.

My trust has too often been broken. Yet, still I believe in the basic goodness of people. It would all be so easy if there was honesty on both sides.

State your needs and expectations, and let the organization listen and lay out what they can and cannot do.

There can be no splendid deception here.

Sugar Daddy

WRITTEN AUGUST 1, 2017

I WAS SO FORTUNATE TO HAVE A SUGAR DADDY. He was such a fine man. He had a home on the river in our village and a home in Florida.

His wife was an antique authority and had her business in New Jersey. His two adult daughters lived in Montana. His father invented the fish reel on the fishing rod.

I never really knew what "Uncle Bob" (I called him) did for a living. But what I do know was that he would take me (and my girlfriends when they were visiting) out on the river in his outboard motorboat. It was always fun.

You really couldn't converse when the motor was operating, and I liked that. You could just think, with no interruptions, and carefully look at the river and marshes. You were isolated in your own little world.

Over the years, you knew where to look for the eagle's nests. They seemed to return each year to the same area. Oh, yes, we fished sometimes. I even caught a rock fish (better known as a striped bass) weighing thirteen pounds. It felt as if I had caught a whale! In fact, Uncle Bob had to help me land this fish. But what a prize!

Uncle Bob had a housekeeper who traveled with him to each of his homes. She cooked and took care of his house and laundry. I think she had family in Virginia. Liza was a dear, who had a very high pitched voice.

I shall always remember her chiding Uncle Bob by exclaiming, "Mr. B, a man of your stability!" I don't remember what caused that outburst, but Uncle Bob laughed each time she used the phrase.

We visited him in Florida one year before a surgery. It was to be my vacation. Uncle Bob was generous with his time. He did not lavish me with many gifts, but when he gave me a gift, it was always very nice.

He would send me fresh fruit from Florida in the winter. For some occasion, he gave me a miniature silver tea set. I'm sure it was old then and even more so now. It really is lovely.

For high school graduation, he gave me a piece of jewelry. But the gift he gave me before I left for college was a giant bottle of perfume. I thought I was ready to take on the world.

Uncle Bob brought a lot to my life, enjoying the simple pleasures of the water, the give and take of conversation. He was never ostentatious, and I really liked that.

I never heard of a good definition for "Sugar Daddy," but in my book he filled the bill!

Looking for Hazel

WRITTEN AUGUST 4, 2017

WHY CAN'T I FIND HAZEL? You know, the cartoon that featured Hazel as keeper of all things—the house, the food, the child, the dog, and somehow she even managed her employer, "Mr. B"!

I loved that television program. I suppose I would blame Hazel for my somewhat high expectations for our personal and household help. Hazel became family. And that's the way it should be, I think. Unfortunately, there were no clues how one could find Hazel.

My search for Hazel has dominated too much of my married life. And I am once again dealing with such a problem. I keep saying I'm too old for this.

It is so draining to follow someone around, hour by hour, explaining the routine in A309 and showing the products and equipment I use.

I do have a schedule, but there are always little things that can change the day, such as "I will do this for you, but I'm really not supposed to." I think caregiver agencies are dominated by a fear of litigation and a lack of heart.

Our most adventurous search for household help occurred in the mid '90's. When we built our house in 1994, we added a bedroom, bath and sitting area, specifically for live-in help.

John read in a local newspaper of an attorney who was bringing people from the Ukraine to be a nanny or a housekeeper. We met with the attorney, and she assured us that it would be fairly easy to find someone. She bought a plane ticket from Lithuania for "Maria."

Maria was a young woman who understood English, but could barely speak a sentence. She seemed excited to be here and willing to learn. So far, so good!

Her background was slowly revealed. She didn't know what a toaster was. She did know a vacuum.

She assured me she did know how to use a washer and dryer, and promptly proved it by doing the laundry while we slept that first night. I have no idea as to the amount of detergent or bleach she used!

She did everything quickly. Or, as I call it, "fool the public cleaning." The tops of furniture are dusted, not moving any objects on the top.

She was eager to do all things pertaining to American life. She said she could drive our car. My first question: "Oh, do you have an international driving license"?

"No," but she knew how to drive. I suspect she drove in Ukraine without a license. When I explained that she would have to learn the rules of the road here and we would enroll her in a driving class, she flatly refused.

Then we learned she had a seven-year-old daughter who she planned to bring to Maryland and live with us. This is not what we had planned. We were certainly not ready to have a seven-year-old live with us!

The next bombshell happened when she informed us that she would only be with us for three or four months. "After all," she said, "I am a doctor."

"A medical doctor?" I asked.

"Yes," was the reply. Then she proceeded to tell me she did the physical tests for her local police department.

I gently told her that she could not be hired anywhere in the United States as a doctor without eight years of training.

She looked at me like I had three heads!

Things began to unravel quickly. She wanted a car. Night after night she went into her room and talked endlessly on the telephone (our phone bill)!

I did learn a lot from this life episode. Life in the Ukraine was hard. Lying and stealing was a way of survival.

She spoke of illegally driving into Hungary, buying all sorts of things, and bringing them back to the Ukraine to sell.

In the Ukraine, she told me, they used mayonnaise as a facial cleanser.

She spoke very little of her daughter, leading me to question if she even had a daughter.

Maria actually "cooked her own goose"! She informed us that she thought she would leave us and go to New York City or Los Angeles.

We reminded her that the Immigration and Naturalization Service is very specific that if she left our employ she would have to return to the Ukraine.

She wasn't deterred by this at all, even knowing we legally would have to notify the I.N.S. She stayed on the phone all night, calling contacts throughout the United States.

We put her on a plane from Maryland to New York City, then Moscow the next day. We made sure she was on her flight.

I felt sorry for her, even though she was a conniver. Yet, in order to get a halfway decent life, she had to connive.

She even admitted to me that she told Ukraine authorities that we were part of President Clinton's family!

Hazel, oh, Hazel! Wherefore, art thou???

Citizen Alert

WRITTEN AUGUST 18, 2017

IS EVERYONE AS UPSET AS I AM AT THE STATE OF AFFAIRS in Washington, D.C.? I can't think of another time in our history that any other President acted so badly.

Well, there was Warren G. Harding who was discovered with his mistress in a White House closet.

The Kennedys were certainly in the "fast crowd," but the dignity of the office was there. The intellect was there.

There has always been wheeling and dealing in the White House. We just call it COMPROMISE.

Now the President wants to remove statues that reflect our past. We are all aware that as a nation we have made mistakes. But as the quote by Santa Yana says, and I paraphrase, "If we don't understand our past, we are doomed to repeat it."

Many of the statues are works of art. Will we go to Statuary Hall in the Capitol Building and remove any statue that remotely has scandal attached to it? If we do, Statuary Hall would probably be empty.

Like Demosthenes, are we searching for a completely honest man? And who will define honest?

This week has been a "great awakening" for me. When I heard groups, marching in Charlottesville, mention Jews in a derogatory manner, encouraging their eradication, I immediately saw the gas ovens in Germany. Such horror was visited upon thousands of Jews.

My mind really can't grasp the enormity of it. Yet, in 2017 there are still groups that call for Jewish extermination.

I thought we had annihilated that idea. Slavery! We fought a war over slavery and our eyes should have been opened for all time. Perhaps we should have had CNN show us the turmoil and daily wretchedness of slavery.

Reunion—Sixty Years Later

WRITTEN AUGUST 25, 2017

ON SEPTEMBER 15TH TO 17TH, there will be a celebration to mark our 1957 graduation from Wicomico Senior High School. Unfortunately, we cannot attend, although I would love to see many of my classmates—sixty years later.

In my mind, it seems not that long ago. I have so many memories:

a.) Mr. Nims, the Latin teacher who always wore his glasses halfway down his nose. Who, for some reason I'll never fathom, frequently called me "Bertha"!

b.) No one can forget Adriene Nock in our Junior Class production of Thornton Wilder's "Our Town" saying, "I just love weddings." Tom Gray did a great job as stage manager.

c.) Do you remember the desk being thrown out of the window at the original Wicomico High School?

d.) I vividly remember Barby and Vicky Thomas constructing something for a geometry project. And driving their car affectionately called "Genevieve."
e.) Who can forget Ann Hill? She had such a zest for life and was always fun. I will always mourn her premature passing.
f.) Then there was Bill Morgan who jumped into my car and started to drive away. My Mother had left the car idling when she saw me coming and struggling with my books. I bellowed like a sheep herder. And, oh, yes, Bill stopped!
g.) Allison Pennewell, my dear friend, who sat behind me in Miss Moore's French class and would whisper forgotten translation.
h.) Or, Betty Jenkins, who was riding with me the day I backed into the hedges around the Parsons Cemetery. Said hedge entwined itself around the back bumper. No way could Betty pull it out, so I drove down the street to my uncle's home, sounding like I was driving on the rims. He had to use an axe to free my bumper from the hedge!

I would truly be remiss if I did not mention that my Mother loved you all. She thought of you as her children. She never hesitated to take someone to a dental or doctor appointment or just to meet someone downtown. It was not at all unusual to have a car full of girls!

Those were the days I would remember.

John and I moved to Lincoln, Nebraska five years ago. John was having some health issues and we thought it best to live closer to our one and only son, Mark.

Mark is chairman of the Keyboard Area at the University of Nebraska.

Lincoln is still "small townish," yet has friendly and caring folks always eager to help in any situation.

If Bob has read all of this, your ears are probably ready to fall from your head! But please know I remember the Class of 1957 with great fondness and wish you all God Speed—till we meet again.

Lovingly,
Mary Ann Kennerly Clinton

Stormy Weather

WRITTEN SEPTEMBER 1, 2017

I WONDER HOW MANY BABIES WILL BE NAMED HARVEY after this week? It is a name that will be remembered by many folks, not the least of which were those monitoring the storm on television. It reminded me of the stormy weather times I had experienced.

Hurricanes were a troubling time at least once a summer. The watermen seemed to sense when it was a "bad" one. They would head to the harbor and tie up their boats.

I have watched Daddy do this many times, maneuvering the ropes in an intricate pattern that I saw as art. It was like a bow on a package. Wonder of wonders the ropes would keep the boats safe. However, if one boat came loose, damage to the other boats was bound to happen.

And there were other bad effects also. The river, like a large washing machine, was agitated so that fish and crabs were scattered, and that would affect the supply for the watermen. Even the oyster beds could be affected by the wind shifting those little mollusks around. There was never an organized evacuation, but people helped each other. That is what is so precious about little villages.

My father sent a truck to pick up an elderly couple (he was a severe diabetic) and bring them to our house. Their home was on the waterfront and the water had gotten about four feet from their porch.

Mother had a gas stove, so could prepare meals. She had to boil water before using it. Even then, I knew that this was as close to camping as I ever wanted to be. You filled the bathtub with buckets of water in order to flush the toilets. It felt like I was living in the dark ages.

In the winter, every seven or ten years we would have a blizzard. No electricity, no heat. Only a fireplace. Roads completely blocked. My father, knowing if there were a medical emergency, it could be fatal.

He remembered that there was a piece of equipment owned by the state not far away doing road work. He was able to get there, and by that time another man showed up, and they got that grader running and opened the main road in and out of the three little villages.

The ambulance was called out for an elderly gentleman who lived in another village. By the time the crew arrived, he had died.

Storms of any kind bring out the best or worst in us. Goodness knows, we have seen both sides this week. I was deeply touched to see two African Americans singing Gospel hymns, not with sadness but hope for better days to come. Just as they did in the slave boats coming to America long ago.

And the faces of those listening—even the news commentator—were wet with tears. Maybe it was the music I heard—Lo, I am with you always.

A Different Time

WRITTEN JUNE 1, 2018

IT'S JUST A BENCH, REALLY—white slats and cast iron, scroll legs. The initial "A" is part of the scroll on each end.

Foundry Research has shown that the bench was made by William Adams Foundry in Philadelphia, Pennsylvania, in the late 1800's. Two chairs from the same foundry are at Longwood Gardens, the Dupont home near Wilmington, Delaware.

My bench, like the other two that Mark has, sat on the steamboat wharf on the Nanticoke River in Maryland.

The steamboats were managed by the Old Bay Lines, and sailed from Norfolk, Virginia, up the Chesapeake Bay with stops along the way such as the Nanticoke and continuing on to Baltimore.

My great grandfather was the custom agent at the Nanticoke Wharf. I suppose this explains why I have the benches. I first remember them in my grandparents' yard. It almost seems unreal that here they are in

Nebraska. If only they could talk. But, oh, they do—to me, at least!

A woman, recently widowed, sailed to the Nanticoke Wharf from Virginia to spend the summer with her sister in Nanticoke. It was always a joyous reunion. Each evening they sat on the porch. Friends would walk by, stop and talk, and neighborhood news or maybe gossip would be shared. There always was laughter.

My bench surely held the grief stricken as well Oh, the horror of the eight-year-old boy who was being chased and ran off the end of the wharf and drowned. That tragedy was never forgotten.

On the brighter side, the wharf was a gathering place for people—just to sit and talk—overlooking my beautiful river. And I can't help but think there were lovers who came—the male casually putting his arm on the back of the bench and then so casually around her shoulders. A stolen kiss—and so history goes!

There were farmers who came with their produce—strawberries, cantaloupes, watermelons, green beans, corn and tomatoes. All would find their way to Baltimore markets.

There were young adults who went on the steamboats to Baltimore to seek their fortunes. Some found wives and settled there.

There were those, being young, who wanted to experience all of life in the big city. One was tragically shot and killed in a bar. No one will ever know why. Was it drink? Money? Or a woman? What we do know was that he had written to say he was coming back home to live.

My grandmother sailed with my grandfather for a year after they married. But after that, she said, "No more!" My grandfather agreed, and he started his own oyster business.

Oh, these benches, what a story they could tell—surviving storms of wind and rain, salt water drying in the sun, ready for the continuing community life. As late as the 1970's, on low tide you could still see the pilings of the old wharf. I hope they are there still—it would be such a wonderful reminder of days gone by.

It was a different era. Yet, it had all the ingredients of a good life—peace, friendships, love, as well as loss and family.

Hurricanes

WRITTEN AUGUST 30, 2019

I CAN CLOSE MY EYES AND I'M BACK IN TIME—time when no summer was without hurricanes. The day before a hurricane would be hot. The air so thick you would think you might suffocate.

Lawn furniture was stowed away. In our case, in the garage.

Cars were parked in garages or sheds, in a manner that would protect them the most.

Bands of rain would start—heavy, like a hot shower—then stop completely.

Trees would rustle in a slow breeze. I can remember thinking, "This isn't so bad," not knowing the storm was barely beginning!

Then the tides changed, water crept higher and higher. The high tide became flood tide. There was a sense of excitement, of danger.

There would be a steady stream of cars and trucks going to the harbor.

Watermen securing their boats in the harbor—lines of rope placed in just the right way, knots tied so that boats in the harbor would not bump into another boat in adjoining berths.

I watched this happen from the car while daddy and his crew tied the work boats, the oyster boats—how many earned their livelihood. There were pleasure boats and small yachts, too.

It was rather like water dancing—boats bobbing up and down, but never bumping each other. Even at best, there were always a few mishaps. Flood ties could strain the ropes and some smaller vessels would be beached.

On land, trees swayed as if they were dancing to an unheard melody. Some trees bending almost horizontal, then swiftly resuming their normal stand. Leaves were shredded like confetti. When you heard a loud cracking sound, you knew a tree had fallen.

Of course, most of the community lost all electricity. I remember so well filling pots of water to flush toilets, wash any dishes that absolutely had to be washed.

You were fortunate to have a gas stove, as we did, that meals could be cooked. Mother often would cook extra so neighbors might have a meal. As a child, I thought this all an adventure, secure under my parents' care.

But for the watermen, it was a serious situation. Without a boat, there was no income for their families.

I always thought that God rewarded us because, after the storm, it was always textbook beautiful—sky blue with not a cloud in sight, and the air sparkled with freshness.

However, the landscape didn't fare so well—trees were down, sheds turned over, yards and roads full of debris, roof shingles missing, and television antennae bent over as if clutching the roof.

Daddy had refused to have an antenna on the roof, so we had an antenna on forty-foot creosote pads. We often pulled in Television Cuba!

It was exciting. Mother Nature had vented her anger, but now it was back to normal living!

Another Piece of the Puzzle

WRITTEN OCTOBER 27, 2017

I LOOK BACK AND SEE MY LIFE AS A GIANT JIGSAW PUZZLE. So many people made an impact on my life, piece by piece. Jessie was one of those people. She was born and raised in Alabama, and never quite lost that beautiful accent. She met her husband, Bob, from Maine, when he was stationed on a military base in Alabama. They had two children—a boy and a girl.

Jessie was one of those people who could make all plants grow and flourish. Poor Bob dug enough dirt to fill a large truck container. Her yard was always spectacular. It was a treat to sit on their patio and just gaze at all of her beautiful plants. She even found flowers that would glow at dusk!

Jessie thought that bamboo would be a great backdrop in front of their driveway fence, only to find out that bamboo spreads—and quickly! She and Bob tried to uproot all the bamboo—without success. Of course, John and I suggested that they keep cutting the bamboo and sell it to the National Zoo for the newly acquired pandas from China. She kept all of these areas watered, fertilized, and pruned. The bamboo was still there when we last visited in 2014.

Jessie was a giver. She planted beautiful things on so many of the city's corners for free. And the planting was such that there was something blooming throughout the year. She had fresh flowers in the church sanctuary most every week—beautifully arranged, of course. The city of Bowie honored her over and over again.

Jessie and Bob adored Mark and traveled to wherever he performed. Bob was the typical New Englander—a man of few words. But those words either made you laugh or marvel at his intellect. On seeing our first miniature Schnauzer, he said, "Looks like an Austrian General to me."

One night at dinner, Jessie said, "You know, Bob, we don't talk as much as we used to." Bob thought a minute, then said, "We've said it all." We enjoyed so many good times with them.

Jessie stopped at our house one morning when Mark was home. I was, ever industrious, washing all the decorative glassware in ammonia and water. Mark greeted her with, "You better keep your feet moving or Mother will have you in the sink also."

Jessie's health was often problematic, but she always fought her way back from colon cancer and other cancer. But the fight was inevitably over in 1980. The community mourned her passing just as we did. She definitely was a sizable piece of my life puzzle.

Jessie's life was no bed of roses. Shortly before we moved to Bowie in 1972, there was a sad incident between her son and a neighbor.

Someone set the neighbor's house on fire. Jessie's son was accused of the crime, and the court system judged him guilty.

Jessie did not believe her son did the crime, and over an eight or ten-year time she did everything she could think of to prove his innocence. She contacted fire marshals from all over the country to review the forensic evidence.

In the end, her son had to serve time in jail. It nearly broke her heart and Bob's also. I think Bob's death was related to the stress of those years. Jessie would have friends picket the courthouse for a retrial.

Thankfully, Jessie lived to see her son released from jail. But by that time, Bob had died. Jessie helped him find a home in a rural area on the Eastern Shore of Maryland. As far as I know, he is still there.

Destiny or Fate

WRITTEN OCTOBER 26, 2018

WE ALL ARE BORN WITH PARTS FROM THE FAMILY GENE POOL, but then circumstances individualize us. Many Kennerlys (my maiden name) have blue eyes (and big ears), as I do. Genetics explain how that happens.

But what about outside circumstances that often redirect an individual's life? One trait comes to mind. Competitiveness. I never liked to compete for anything. Somehow, in the nether reaches of my mind, I felt I could never win anything.

Is that how I protected my esteem? Maybe. But even in board games or card games, winning was never my goal. I just liked playing through the game.

I remember some children would always cheat in some way and I knew it, but I never called them on it. I was just glad they were there to play with me. I never truly understood why they felt it necessary to cheat.

What's wrong with me?

I drove John crazy playing Scrabble. He was cut throat all the way.

Me? Oh, this is fun! In any situation, I always supported the underdog. Did I identify with the underdog? Probably.

In school and college I was a good student. But I got little satisfaction from that. "Big deal," I would say to myself, "where is this going to get me?"

After all, what job is out there that doesn't require some kind of perambulation?

But then I learned an important lesson. There is most always more than one way to accomplish a goal. How I accomplished any given task is not as important as the fact that, no matter how strange the process, I got it done.

That determination is definitely a family trait. So what is my destiny? More of the same, I think. What can I do? Laugh or cry? I like to laugh.

Dreams

WRITTEN AUGUST 19, 2016

DO YOU GET TOO OLD TO DREAM? Certainly your dreams would be different from those of fifty years ago. Then the world was your oyster! Anything was possible!!

Dreams are often wishes for the future. Dreams can also be escapes from reality. I like to think dreams are wishes your heart makes. I cover the waterfront with all my dreams.

I dream of meeting old boyfriends. What was our connection then? Geography ended the connection in most all cases. Was that part of a Divine plan? Or was it a learning exercise? My sense is that they were just that. It was an acknowledgment of the normal maturation process —a goal I desperately wanted in those teen years.

When reality becomes overwhelming, I dream of traveling to London and living there. Or, I can dream through a good book, sometimes pinching myself back to reality back in Lincoln.

Do I dream of walking again? You bet I do! I dream of times past and how different they might have been if I were not handicapped. I probably would not have gone to Drew University. Then, I would not have met John. Would I have been a recluse? A party animal? Or just an ordinary housewife? Would I have had a son? Not like Mark, I'm sure!

There is still a desire to dream—to leave a mark on the world. As I am in the home stretch of life's journey, I more and more question: *What have I done to make the world a better place?* Back to reality, I'm still the searching pilgrim!

My Miracle

WRITTEN SEPTEMBER 09, 2016

I HAVE SAID MANY TIMES THAT I'M A WOMAN OF FAITH. In fact, it is the centerpiece of my life. It's what holds things together for me.

From my early years when I taught another little girl, who was in a hospital bed next to mine, how to pray, to the senior years of my life where I have ongoing conversations with God. But, then, I have always done that.

God surely has a sense of humor. I was alone in our last home when my scooter stopped in the middle of the hallway to the bedrooms—the batteries died!!! No doubt about it, I was not moving. Worst of all, I had left my phone on the kitchen table!

For some reason, what came to mind was Paul's message to the people: "Troubles can be like fire refining gold." I looked up and said, "God, I'm working on the refining. Could you please just get me out of this situation?"

So, after I had vented, I realized the only thing I could do was sit there for five or six hours, or take the chance to stand facing the wall and side step my way to the bedroom and another phone.

Off I went, one step at a time, heart pounding. It took me twenty minutes, but I made it safely. It could so easily have had a very different outcome because if my muscles had "spazzed," I had nothing to grasp that would break my fall.

I have always thought the bonds of love are stronger than we can ever imagine. John and I were going through a rough patch. It was nigh onto impossible that I could work in Radford, Virginia, which left a big hole in our budget.

Living in the mountains during the winter and having electric heat resulted in a bill that equaled a second mortgage! I was so conflicted—do I throw caution to the winds and take any job that is located in a place halfway handicapped accessible?

I couldn't seem to find any solution, so I prayed for help. The phone rang. It was my father. He immediately asked if there was anything wrong. I said, "Why do you ask?" He replied that "something inside me told me to call you."

That was all I needed. I burst into tears, revealing our dilemma. He said, "Let me help you." He paid for my household help. How did he know I was struggling? Divine intervention? Or the gift of love that binds people to each other?

It was a year later when Daddy called about noon time and I picked up the phone; did not say "Hi" or "Hello." Just "It's Gram, isn't it?"

Daddy asked if someone had called me, but, no, no one had called. I just knew I was extremely close to this grandmother—another case of the cord of love binding us together.

I never seriously thought about miracles. I read about them through the Bible, and I saw confessions of miracles happening to celebrities on the covers of magazines. But that was as far as it went. Little did I know!

Six weeks had passed since we had moved to a senior residence. When I fell in the bathroom, I knew immediately I had a broken bone because I heard it snap.

We went to an orthopedic doctor who confirmed my diagnosis. But he gave us more bad news, some of which I knew and some of which I didn't. I knew my leg bones were still child size, but I didn't know that I had osteoporosis so badly that my leg bones looked like Swiss cheese.

There could be no surgery because there was nothing they could pin together. The doctor told me to use a splint to keep the leg straight and come back in five weeks.

We called doctors back in Maryland, and one of the senior doctors told me that I probably would never heal. I just prayed; our church back in Severna Park prayed. I was put out as a prayer request by the Upper Room publication in Nashville, Tennessee, reaching at least three hundred people.

I felt strangely calm. After three weeks, I asked John to make an appointment with the orthopedic doctor. John reminded me that I still had two weeks of healing to do. My response was that I was no longer in pain, so something must be happening.

So off we went. We got the x-ray and returned to the examination room. If ever a doctor danced into an examination room, this doctor did! He put the x-ray on the screen and proclaimed, "You are healed!"

Despite what medical science said, I had healed. I can't adequately describe the joy John and I felt. We floated back to our apartment, and the joy seemed to ooze from our every pore. Once I got in my scooter, I made figure eights in the garage.

Suddenly, I stopped and asked, "You don't suppose there are cameras in here, do you?" John said, "Probably so." I stopped post haste and said, "We must go to the front desk and explain."

Feelings

WRITTEN SEPTEMBER 12, 2016

I AM CONFLICTED ABOUT EXPRESSING MY FEELINGS of anger and frustration. But they are as real as the joy with which I'm so often blessed. I was never allowed to express anger, so I have internalized much. The one and only time I displayed anger physically, I was told, at age eight, that I was hurting my mother, and I couldn't do that. Now, some seventy years later, the filter is off!

I have always had topnotch medical care. If there was a way to cure or adapt, we found it. In 2016, medical care for polio is mighty scarce. In great part, it is because the doctors who treated me are dead. So, if I go to a doctor complaining of back pain, he can't help noticing my scoliosis and treating it as a "spinal cord injury." It is not a spinal cord injury!

The few doctors left that write about polio and have treated polio patients say, in no uncertain terms, "Don't let anyone treat you as a spinal cord injury!" Some doctors have said to me, "We can help you gain strength." The answer to that is, "You can't revive a dead muscle!"

Our bodies are born with a beautiful "electric" system which allows us to move effortlessly. But polio wipes out a lot of those systems; yet, these magnificent bodies re-route that damaged electric system using the good nerve endings to provide limited movement. But here's the kicker: Post Polio Syndrome occurs in middle age and older polios. That is, we have so over-used what electric system we had left that, once again, we start sliding to complete helplessness.

Interesting to me is that medical science has found that most polios are Triple A personalities. We tried harder, sometimes at great risk to ourselves, and in so doing we burned out the little of the electric system which we had left. Boy, do I ever fit that category! And, yet, I would not change a thing. Sure, I shouldn't have raked our large backyard, but it was exhilarating to work outside and the payoff was a beautiful spot. Never mind that my arm, shoulder, and back muscles did a tap dance all night! I just continued on.

Did you know that the polio virus affects the brain, digestive system and, quite often, our capacity to breathe? It's not a pretty picture. And here is where my anger builds. At the end of life, why can't we find someone who knows what is happening and can prepare us for what is inevitable? Are there any detours? In this age of advanced knowledge and technology, surely there is someone somewhere who can speak of these issues.

As always, humor helps to ameliorate pain for me. Not too long ago, I fell off the toilet. My silky slacks just slid me to the floor. I yelled for

John and he came. Now, I knew he couldn't pick me up, but he could help rearrange me. In doing so, he fell! So here we are, two old folks sitting on the bathroom floor. Out of my mouth comes: "Well, isn't this a mell of a hess!" Then we both laughed and called for help.

I choreographed John's moves so he could get himself up. I certainly have learned how best to use the strength we have. One evening John and I were talking about our wills. I mentioned that if my body could help someone else, I would like medical science to have it. We called the appropriate number, explained what information we wanted, and got the response: "We already have enough bodies."

My weird sense of humor kicked in and I laughed uproariously and said, "They don't even want me when I'm dead!" I still think it's funny. The ultimate put down!

I feel stifled by John's not being able to drive. In Maryland, we often spent Saturday afternoon at the mall where we could spend hours in the bookstore. The malls back East were like Main Street of yesteryear. We had planned day trips here where we could explore Nebraska. I wish I could say that I have gracefully accepted this but I haven't. There is still that part of me that wants to see and experience more.

They say acceptance is the key to good mental health. I fail this miserably. At any diminution of strength, I rant and rave to myself and label myself like I would never do for anyone else. I only know to fight on. I do know I don't want to be a grumpy old woman. So, should I just endure? But that doesn't seem right either. Maybe reaching out to others would put me back in the race. It has worked before. The only thing I know, the only thing I'm sure of, is that God does provide and He will provide.

Daddy

WRITTEN SEPTEMBER 5, 2019

My father would have been one hundred and five on August 1st. It seems somehow impossible, because I remember him as a vibrant man, always thinking or doing.

His own mother spoke of him as a character. And that he was! I don't ever remember him being convulsed in laughter.

I don't know from whence I get my humor. Probably humor was my way of dealing with my disability.

He didn't smile often, yet his love for me was undeniable. From his early childhood, it became obvious that he was smart. He had an erector set that looked like an engineer's prop, from which he made actual miniature dams and windmills that would fuel whatever gadget he had at the time.

At an early age, he developed a love of reading. He taught himself to use a computer when he was in his seventies. If he had had Google, he probably would have never left his office.

He was a math whiz. I must have been out of the room when that trait was given! In high school, I would phone him with an algebra problem, and it was automatic that he would know the answer.

Foreign languages may have been a weak area, yet he could read written Spanish fairly well. He would not attempt to speak Spanish. Fortunately for him, there was a retired State Department employee in the community who spoke Spanish fluently.

He was a business man par excellence. Mother would say, "Your dad is wheeling and dealing!"

He was the first person on the east coast to import tuna fish from South America. He had to testify on the floor of Congress to be able to do this.

California tried every way to stop him because they didn't want to lose their exclusive right to bring in tuna to the United States, but Congress agreed that East Coast business could share in that process.

So ships from Peru sailed to the Atlantic, up the Chesapeake Bay, to my favorite river, the Nanticoke. It was an exciting time.

First, the ship was large, rusty and old. The crew, and Captain Jansen, were amazed at everything they saw. Daddy arranged for a van to take the crew shopping in Salisbury, the county seat. Now it was our turn to be amazed.

They bought televisions, dishes, radios, clothing, toys. Daddy had to send a truck to accommodate it all! Needless to say, Salisbury got quite an economic boost that day!

But Daddy's character was always strong. For years, he bought only brown suits. He wouldn't have it any other way. Then, somehow, mother persuaded him to buy a navy blazer. He got so many complements, he soon bought a navy suit.

I have often wondered if he were color blind and life was simpler with only one color in the closet.

Then he was very definite on his sheets and towels. Plain towels only. And certainly not pink!

After mother passed away, he called me to get him a set of sheets, white only. So I dutifully went shopping for sheets and purchased the only white set I could find.

When he saw my purchase, he quickly said he couldn't use them. Puzzled, I asked, "Why?" It had lace (not in any way delicate!) on the top sheet and pillow cases. No, he wanted plain sheets.

But that was all that was available. I offered to return them. "No," he said. He was angry. Somebody found white sheets in Salisbury, I guess, because when I was cleaning out the house after he died, I found said sheets packaged just as I gave them to him. Every time those sheets are on my bed, I laugh.

Traits individualize us. They are a part of who we are and help make us who we are. I see some of his traits in me. We both like our quiet time and share a love of the animal kingdom.

We both loved history and, consequently, my best vacations were visiting historical sites. We both love books.

I will always wish I had his math ability.

Daddy did not praise me much at all. That wasn't his way. But he gave me the sweetest benediction a few months before he died. He phoned me on a Sunday evening and said, "My God, Mary Ann, you have done one hell of a job."

Those words meant more than he will ever know. I knew, then, he recognized all my struggles to be a part of the normal world. It will always be a special blessing!

Mother's Love of Animals

WRITTEN APRIL 1, 2019

IN MY WRITING LAST WEEK, I DISCOVERED A TRUTH that has rocked me to the core. As an adult, I often asked mother, "Why on earth didn't you have Kitty Tab spayed?"

She never answered, really, but with a somewhat embarrassed response, "I don't know." But I think she did know. Mother and daddy wanted more than one child. Mother had a problem becoming pregnant. The spring before I had polio in the fall, mother had to have a complete hysterectomy. There would be no more children.

What a horrible situation for this young couple. No wonder she didn't want Kitty Tab spayed! Mother probably didn't realize how this influenced her decision to not spay Kitty Tab. She would watch this cat and, when she went in heat, would confine her in a room in the garage.

Kitty Tab would sit in the screened in window and howl for hours, and the male cats would gather outside the window.

Mother carried that burden, or what she felt was her weakness, throughout her life. And she just couldn't get any pet spayed or neutered.

That was my mother!

My Gram and Gran

WRITTEN FEBRUARY 16, 2019

THE OLDER I GET, THE MORE I REFLECT ON THE PAST. Nothing unusual about that. My paternal grandparents were typical of the time, I think. They held hands until the day he died.

My grandmother called him "Sug" (short for sugar). Anything Gram wanted, granddaddy made it happen. It's a good thing she asked for so little!

In their early marriage, granddaddy sailed the Chesapeake Bay and Gram went with him. That was an act of devotion because she hated the water. After my father was born, Gram never went back to sailing with granddaddy. From the stories Gram told, she had her hands full just keeping up with my father.

Gram never drove a car. I think she may have attempted to drive, but was frightened by the power of it all.

They had a routine of life that never changed. Their big meal of the day was at noon, and at exactly twelve o'clock they sat at the table.

I remember asking how did they know to be at the table at exactly noon time? Her answer was "our belly clock." It sounded reasonable to me.

I loved spending time with these grandparents. Who wouldn't? We often would have our noon meal under a big maple tree in their yard. And at night, after bumping up the stairs and getting into bed, Gram would sit in a rocker (that I have now) and, at my ardent request, tell me stories of when she was a little girl.

I never grew tired of hearing about her and the other seven siblings. She would tell me of the peacocks roaming their property, of the children picking strawberries, of the little one room schoolhouse they all attended.

Gram probably had a fourth grade education. She was ill for quite a while and couldn't attend school. I don't know what the illness exactly was; and, with a big family to feed, I'm sure the children had to help harvest the crops. School wasn't seen to be that important.

Yet, even with a lack of education, she was a very wise woman. Her counsel, maybe instinctive, was just and true. How many times have I heard, "Now, Mary Ann."

There could be no fibbing to Gram. She always knew, or maybe my excuses were just plain poor. Yet, I never saw her angry. The closest to anger she got was when she called me a little independent hussy when I wouldn't let her help me do something.

She was so embarrassed that she apologized and quickly left. I suspect she shed a tear or two. I deserved that label. But, as always, I wanted to do everything myself.

Gram was always a big part of my life. She adored Mark and often kept him while I went to work in my father's office.

When we moved from Maryland to Radford, Virginia, it was a death knell over the whole family. I felt so guilty taking Mark away from Gram and my parents. But it was a good opportunity for John and that had to be my deciding factor.

But on one of our visits back to Maryland, I convinced her to return to Radford with us. She was in her early eighties. And, looking back, I believe the pancreatic cancer had started to spread. It was at least a ten hour drive if you didn't stop for more than ten minutes.

I thought I had really caused her harm. She stayed in bed the following day. Thankfully, she rallied. But in a week's time, we had to take her back to her home. As she got in the car to leave Radford, she said, "Mary Ann, I needed to see where you lived and that you are all right, but I won't be back." She died a few months later.

She was my role model. She saw the positive first and would just shake her head at the worst. She helped her brothers and sisters in their bad times.

My grandfather was a kind man, too. I think alcohol was a problem in his young life and I suspect he was quite the "dandy," but no one ever doubted that Gram was the love of his life.

I remembered him from pictures—dressed to the nines, bowler hat and all.

I also remember his admonition as we were sitting in the rockers on his front porch, "Mary Ann, don't sign a note for anybody" meaning, "don't sign for anybody trying to get a loan!"

He loved to buy new clothes and always wore cologne except when he went to work. Gram measured the sugar for his coffee and laid out any medicine.

Every Saturday they drove to the county seat, Salisbury, where they visited, shopped and had dinner. The lasting memory is that they held hands every time they were in the car.

Recently, I had another reason to remember my grandfather. I wore his bowler for a New Year's Eve party. I am sure it was the oldest hat there!

One day as Mark got out of the car, I reminded him to be sure to practice the piano. I told him that Gram would surely love to hear him.

Later, when I finished at the office, I called Gram and said that I would pick up Mark in about ten minutes. I could hear Mark at the piano.

The rest of the story was Mark had not practiced at all. But when he heard the phone ring, he told Gram to wait a minute before she answered the phone until he could get to the piano!

The little rascal had great help in his intended deception!

A Flight of Fancy or Phate

WRITTEN OCTOBER 8, 2019

I HAD TO SHOW MY BALCONY SNOOPERVISOR LICENSE AGAIN. I was sitting on my balcony with my guest from Tennessee when our conversation was interrupted by hysterical shouts from an office building across the pond.

Shouts of "Stop, let me out," and at one point a gun was mentioned. The banging noise was so loud that one wondered what she (yes, she!) was hitting with and what she was hitting. There seemed to be some metal sound, not just wood sounds. She screeched ten or fifteen minutes. I never knew the voice could last that long.

People came out of the building and just stood on the parking lot.

Finally, a policeman came on his motorcycle. Another fifteen minutes passed and out of the door came three people: the woman with her hands handcuffed behind her back; flanked by a policeman; and, I assume, a security guard. They put her in a car and drove away.

I don't expect to ever learn the true story. But that never stopped me before! Soooo, let's suppose: Did her employer fire her for poor job performance? Or for failure to complete a project?

Or maybe her husband/boyfriend called to announce he was leaving town? Or maybe she secretly took something from the office that wasn't hers?

I don't like that one—it seems so blatantly wrong. But whatever the motive, she was in a melt down state!

Back to normal time—I had been lamenting that I couldn't take my visitors around Lincoln and show them the city.

However, after the screeching, hysterical, woman event, I told my friend that I always try to provide good entertainment for my guests, but this time I outdid myself!

Joyce reminded me that she came to our house to see my first scooter. I had forgotten that. She asked me if I had taken it outside yet. And I replied that I was a little fearful to do that. She said, "I'll go with you."

So out I went down the driveway to the sidewalk. To move by myself was exhilarating and, of course, I took off full speed. Then I turned my head and shouted, "Where are the brakes"?

Running, she said, "How should I know?"

By this time, I was at the Presbyterian Church and just slowed down. We laughed so much. Friends are treasures of the heart.

And my heart is filled with just such treasures!!!

Another God Incidence

WRITTEN NOVEMBER 15, 2017

WELL, IT HAS HAPPENED AGAIN—ANOTHER GOD INCIDENCE. And I surely needed to be reminded that the world will not end if my scooter is not working properly.

I charge my chair battery every night. My theory is that by keeping the battery charged, the batteries last longer. There have been times they lasted five to seven years, which surprises everyone. And I use my chair—I am like the Energizer Bunny!

So, when I noticed that the battery wasn't fully charged yesterday, I panicked. I told myself that a full night's charge would fix everything. But, no, it didn't. Now I go in full anger mode. "This can't happen now, I'm too busy! I already have twelve hour work days," I grumble and fret, fret and grumble.

Yes, I have a backup chair. However, it is just enough different that when I have to transfer from it, I can't get as close to the toilet, bed, or sofa. Think: FALL! I'm terrified of falling. I try to be so careful. But a different chair just reminds me of how finite my life is. Grumble and fret; fret and grumble.

Then John left a folded newspaper at my place on the kitchen table —the man from the Ivory Coast in Africa who had polio. Yes, God, it puts it all in perspective. I have two scooters—why am I so perturbed? My answer is almost automatic—because I am waging war again.

In polio years, I am close to ninety. I am once again losing strength and I don't like it a bit. I have led a life of restrictions and I made peace with that. Now, I am old and forgetful and I don't want anymore restrictions.

Dear God, I sound like a petulant child! I look at that newspaper article again. It's okay to be angry unless it consumes me, but it is beneficial to understand others have struggled just as much if not more than I.

And life is hard for them—their resources are limited. Bravo to this young man for his determination to succeed and give back to others in need.

Once again, God has reigned me in. I needed that. If only I look and listen, the bumps in the road are reduced—not removed, but they become manageable.

Most of all, I hope every parent that reads this newspaper article will reach for the telephone and make an appointment for their child to receive the polio vaccine.

I am most passionate about this!

The End of a Chapter

WRITTEN DECEMBER 8, 2017

MY DECISION TO MOVE TO LINCOLN has been validated. It was because of John's health that said decision was made.

I sat in front of our Palladian window in Millersville looking skyward as the sky changed from black to orange. I had watched as John was loaded into the ambulance barely conscious. He lost nearly two-thirds of his blood.

I was a ball of fear thinking, "Would they have enough information at the hospital to treat him properly? Would they know enough to call me? They didn't call, and I couldn't rouse a friend to take me to the hospital at this hour. So I waited until 8:00 o'clock, called Mark in Lincoln and asked him to come. My housekeeper and friend arrived at 8:30.

I called the hospital and they told me they were working on him and I couldn't see him until he was taken to his room. I was at his room by 9:00 a.m. That time was agonizing. The question in my head was, "Would my disability cost John his life?" I vowed to myself that I would change whatever needed to change to ensure his safety. My parents had died earlier—one year apart, so I really had no close family there. To Lincoln, we came!

It was a drastic change. John had a forty-year employment record there. He was super involved in many things—be it church, Maryland Bible Society, State Governors Commission for Americans with Disabilities, teaching Sunday School classes, and supporting the Orioles. He was a season ticket holder, and I would often suggest that he get a second mailing address at Orioles Park! I know that he missed those Orioles games terribly at Orioles Park.

Mark and John made a weekend trip to Kansas City to see the Orioles play. They had a fabulous time. My, was he a happy camper. And when Adam Jones caught a ball that kept Kansas from scoring, he looked in the stands, saw Mark's and John's orange and black, and threw the ball to John—who made a magnificent catch, of course!

The next morning when Mark and John entered a restaurant for breakfast, some man came to John and said, "That was quite a catch you made yesterday!" That was such a special time for them both.

When I heard John make a strange sound shortly after we had gotten into bed on November 18th, I automatically asked if he was all right. When he didn't answer, I turned the light on, transferred to my scooter, and saw that he was only partially in bed. I couldn't move him, and it seemed to me that his right leg was paralyzed.

I called Assisted Living, and eight minutes later I called the ambulance. They called me back an hour later and said they were sending him to Immanuel Hospital in Omaha where a procedure to burst the blood clot in the brain could be done.

Mark and I arrived there the same time as the ambulance. It was 5:00 a.m. before they were done with him. We were told the procedure was a success and he probably would recover. Prayers of gratitude! We saw him with hope in our hearts.

I then decreed I would be coming here every day. Mark looked at me askance. "How are you going to do that?"

"I'll make it happen."

An angel from the Landing, and Mark took time off from teaching. Mark gave the order to move him back to Lincoln. And, despite various roadblocks, John was moved back to Lincoln on Thanksgiving day. He received such wonderful care at Bryan West. But when the time came, and the breathing tube had to be removed, decisions had to be made.

John and I had living wills drawn up some twenty years ago. He never regained consciousness, and the doctor said he never would. Our dear son helped me stand by his bed, and I repeated the words I had said to my mother. "John, it's time that you go to God." And with a kiss, I said, "It's only 'til we meet again."

But God, in his never failing love, did not leave me comfortless. The nurses suggested that Mark and I go get dinner. We did. Coming out of Misty's, I looked skyward and exclaimed, "Mark, look at that shooting star. I've never seen one before."

Mark looked at me and said, "That's Dad."

Nothing else was said until five minutes later when the phone rang and the nurse said, "Mr. Clinton died about five minutes ago."

Through my tears, I knew he would go in a blaze of glory! Mark and I laughed and cried, cried and laughed. What a beautiful benediction to his life.

There is a song, CATCH A FALLING STAR AND PUT IT IN YOUR POCKET, NEVER LET IT GO. That falling star resides permanently in my heart 'til the end of time.

GOD IS TRULY GOOD.

A Work in Progress

WRITTEN JANUARY 26, 2018

AS I ONCE AGAIN RESUME WRITING, a certain peace comes to me. The words from Ecclesiastes float in my brain (and I paraphrase):

> "There is a time to live,
> And there is a time to die.
> There is a time to grieve,
> And a time to again reclaim the
> joy in living.
> It is God's promise, after all."

All of this is not to say everything is okay and back in order. It isn't and never will be. So, my new normal is a work in progress.

Like always, my impatience gets the best of me. Is there no end to paperwork? There should be a Philadelphia lawyer for families of the deceased.

The thank you notes! Yes, I could sign the cards given to me from the Funeral Home, but that seems cold to me. The least I can do is write a personal thank you. I did it for my paternal grandmother, my mother, and my father.

I figure I've written at least three hundred and fifty such notes. Not to mention gift thank you's which are a whole different category. But it takes time—days of time.

At first, I was just overwhelmed. Now I think I see the light at the end of the tunnel. Then there is the physical adjustment—little things, really, but it all has to be figured out.

Mark was vehemently adamant that I not be alone at night. I vehemently disagreed. Let's face it, I could fall at any given time with or without anyone with me. I know how very important it is to be careful.

I have gotten almost paranoid about the issue. But I am careful, and enjoy my space.

There have been times of unique happenings. The first was at 5:00 a.m. I was awakened by the sound of bells. I got out of bed and investigated, but found nothing. The next night, the same thing, about the same time. So, I had a little conversation with myself: "Self," I said, "there has to be a logical explanation."

So, I pondered and I pondered, then it came to me. Along with the Christmas wreath on the door, I had real sleigh bells hanging there. So, when the paper boy came, he threw the paper, hitting the door, thus causing one jingle.

I can imagine that leaving newspapers at The Landing is pretty boring, "so to spruce things up, let's try to hit the door midway from the opposite side of the hall." Case solved!

About a week later, I was awakened by a swishing sound, then a clatter. I didn't even get out of bed; I just looked up and said, "Cut it out, John," then went back to sleep!

The next day I checked the entire apartment. Wonder of wonders, I found the source. I had a big aluminum dipper hanging in the laundry room with small bags in it. For whatever reason, the hook had pulled away from the wall, the dipper came down, hit the metal drying rack and, thus, the clatter.

I guess I can say I really do sleep well—but, obviously, my ears don't! It's a new beginning, not one of my choosing, for sure. But I can still glean moments of joy. I can laugh again. It is a beginning!

John...My Life Without

WRITTEN NOVEMBER 23, 2018

IT DOESN'T SEEM POSSIBLE THAT IT HAS ALMOST BEEN A YEAR since John died. Yet, in other ways, it seems an eternity.

I will always hate returning to an empty apartment. I still automatically look for him at the computer. And now I have to use a dictionary for spellings instead of bellowing from my desk, "John, how do you spell this or that?"

I miss our discussions of politics. Usually we were on the same page, but not always.

He knew I loved watching Dr. Phil. So in an attempt to halt whatever I was doing, he would loudly announce, "I've poured you a glass of wine—it's time for Dr. Phil." That never failed to get a response!

I thoroughly enjoyed teasing him just to see that sheepish grin on his face. But, like most married couples, there were times I could have rung his neck.

He loved rich foods such as lobster or crab, and there was never a dessert that he could pass on.

Case in point. We had traveled to New England for a family wedding. Naturally, the first evening meal was full of lobster dishes. I knew his tummy had been bothering him, so it was my wifely duly to caution him against eating any lobster dish.

My protestations fell on deaf ears—not unexpectedly, I must say. All was well until midnight, when he was violently sick. It went on for four hours.

At times like this, my disability becomes maddeningly apparent. I could not help him in any way. I was almost insane with worry. Should I call 911? John nixed that idea every time I reached for the phone.

At 7:00 a.m. I called Paul and Doris (John's brother and wife) who were staying in the same hotel. Doris is a nurse and was able to get medicine to calm his digestive tract. John was weak as a kitten. How he got us to the airport the following day, I don't know.

Provoked?

That wasn't the half of it. Illness can strike anyone at any time, but to deliberately take a chance on something so serious is just plain crazy. I probably could have flown the plane myself that day!

John repeated this several times in my life. It led to major bleed-outs which came close to taking his life. He never really fully accepted his diabetes. John would have been happy with a full diet of desserts. Only in his last years did he learn how to monitor his sugar intake.

John was always active in our church.

One year he did a one-man presentation of John Wesley—black robe and white wig included. Naturally, it was good, and he traveled to many Maryland Methodist churches to do his John Wesley.

He also did a presentation of the disciple Andrew, dressed in a yellow slicker. One little boy sitting on the front row was heard saying, "He looks like Paddington Bear to me!"

John loved doing this. He would diligently research the topic of the day and turn it into something pretty amazing. So it should come as no surprise that after seeing the play "Love Letters," he wanted me to join him on stage. It took some doing to convince me, but when he had the idea for a fundraiser to purchase a new organ at church, he had me.

It went well, and we repeated it in five or six other venues. I called him "Stage Door Johnny"!

I miss John reaching for my hand whenever Mark performed, so it was touching that when Mark played last week, Lou reached for my hand.

We take so much for granted. You live with someone for nearly sixty years, and for some misguided reason you think it will never end. Foolish me.

But, then, I remind myself how very blessed I have been. Count your blessings, Mary Ann!

The last years, John became very controlling. If I said one thing, John would jump in to tell me that what I said was wrong and how I said it was wrong.

Though he encouraged me for years to write, when I did he wanted to correct my feeble attempts. That was a defining moment. He would no longer read anything I wrote!

He couldn't understand that my writing was quintessentially me. It was how I perceived and understood my life.

Get Over It

WRITTEN JULY 20, 2018

THERE IS SOMETHING ABOUT THE PHRASE "Get Over It" that I find demeaning, a slap in the face. We use "Get Over It" as if to say "Your so-called problem isn't important, of no consequence."

To the speaker, it isn't a problem; or at the very least, isn't worthy of attention. But to the one who sees a problem, it is a problem, and it doesn't help to trivialize their emotion.

To the child who struck out at his baseball game, and his team lost, it seems like his world has ended.

But his coach or father can change that in seconds with "I know you did the best you could do. You will have another time at bat."

Or, "Perhaps we can practice hitting at home."

Or use a major league player by name who most certainly does not get a hit every time at bat.

It almost goes without saying that whenever I came on the scene, I was scrutinized and mostly found wanting physically or mentally. I can almost hear an adult saying "Get Over It!"

That left me with two choices—retreat to my home base or put myself out there and suffer the consequences over and over again. I guess I was too dumb to give up. It just wasn't my nature.

I have heard people say, "It is time to get over the grief of losing a loved one." I don't know if you ever get over such a loss. Nor do I really want to do that.

Grief does not consume me, but I still grieve for John. After all, he was part of my life for sixty-one years.

Some two years ago, the very first sentence I wrote was that I grieve for that little six-year-old girl who had polio, and lost so much; and for her parents who lost a normal healthy child, and completely rearranged their lives around that little girl.

I think it is hurtful to abandon the emotions of a time. I think it is rather blasé to believe our reactions are not significant. It is only when we acknowledge the situation that we can continue to grow and hopefully be a better "me" or "you."

Get over it? No! It is the fabric of my life. Difficult times? You bet! Joyous times? Beyond belief!

Things happen—some good and some bad. It is up to us to look for the silver lining behind the clouds.

Finding Joy Again

WRITTEN FEBRUARY 9, 2018

I'VE ALWAYS BEEN FAIRLY OPTIMISTIC, with only a few bouts of pessimism. I'm definitely not a Pollyanna, either, who tried to be glad over everything. And, yet, since John died, I'm different. My focus is different. Dare I say calmer?

Long ago, I wrote that "acceptance is the key to good mental health." It was easy to let John go—I didn't want him to live the rest of his life in bed, hooked up to breathing and feeding tubes. It was time!

Because I am a somewhat reflective person, I choose to see and feel moments of joy. The pristine snow, smooth as cream, is so beautiful. I smiled as I saw two dogs, released from their leashes, run, leap, and frolic in the snow. It was utter abandonment to the joy of being free.

Or the newspaper article that caught my attention when I saw the name Forrest Stith. I was immediately transported back to my freshman year at Drew University as a part of the university community. So, seminarians, as well as college students, ate in the same dining hall. That's where I met Forrest Stith—the son of the man in the newspaper.

"My" Forrest had the most beautiful singing voice, which often could be heard as he waited in line to enter the dining hall. He became a Methodist minister (like his dad) and is now a United Methodist Bishop, retired, in Maryland.

That was such a sweet, happy moment.

The mountain of cards that I have received from high school classmates, college classmates, parishioners (with whom we worshipped during the fifty-six years we were married), all brought comfort and delight. It was like once again being linked to these people from the past. The hours and hours of phone calls offering their condolences.

Sometimes—actually, more often than not—I became the consoler rather than the consoled. But John was appreciated, and that soothed me.

Probably the most joyous/sad moment came when I found a small package on John's desk. It was a Swarovski moose with his rack of antlers—just like the moose on a silver spoon of my Mother's with my name on the bowl of the spoon. "Mary Ann Moose is on display!"

Solenne

WRITTEN OCTOBER 20, 2016

I AM A GRANDMOTHER. But my granddaughter calls me MamaDear. I regret that our times together are so few.

Solenne and her mother, Ann, live in France not far from Paris.

Early in 2007, John and I flew to Lincoln for one of Mark's performances and to see Ann who was also visiting. She had told Mark that she was pregnant, and so Mark wanted to tell us in person "the big news!" I pitied him. If that had been me telling my parents, I probably would have been shipped to Siberia post haste! We just asked, "So what's the plan?"

We had first met Ann in New York City the previous year. We took them to lunch at *B. Smith's,* a trendy eatery at the time. *B.Smith's* is in the theater district and we expected to see some famous person or persons there. We were not disappointed. Denzel Washington, baseball cap pulled low on his forehead, came in and was promptly escorted to a table on the balcony level. Of course, John saw him and in due time went to Denzel's table and got an autograph for Ann! We still speak and laugh about this time.

I insisted that Mark break the "big news" to his grandparents. I did clean up. By this time, mother had long since been diagnosed with Alzheimer's, so it was difficult to know what really registered with her. I tried to make it as matter of fact as I could.

Daddy, on the other hand, was angry. One day as we were eating lunch together, he used a term about this situation in anger—I cannot repeat it. I thought a minute, put my hand over his, and said, "Daddy, this little baby will have your genes and mine. This will be our link to posterity."

He spoke not another word, but I could see he was pondering my words. I can't say he was ever over-joyed, but from then on he did accept the situation. Mark took his sabbatical the fall semester of 2007 to be with Ann when she gave birth. He gave several recitals and did some networking. When the call came on November 30th that we had a granddaughter, we were ecstatic.

I called our friends and shared the good news. Within thirty minutes, they were coming in the front door, champagne in hand. It was so heartwarming to share our joy with our friends. They made a special time even more special.

The following summer, Ann and Solenne met Mark in Maryland for a week. I located a crib and we were ready. One afternoon, I had an open house so that everyone could meet our "angel child." The thirty or forty people must have been a bit overwhelming for her, yet she managed quite well. We also introduced her to my parents. Daddy was quite charmed by her; and mother, who was almost blind by this time, with a beautiful smile reached to touch her and said, "Oh, that soft little baby skin." We were so grateful to have this grandchild in our home.

The next time we saw Solenne was when she was baptized in June 2008. One of our favorite couples went with us. It was a beautiful Catholic ceremony. The priest was adorable—he held Solenne aloft and declared "Solenne is baptized." Then he sang the Battle Hymn of the Republic for the Americans. Isn't that wonderful? We thought so.

In between the baptism and all the parties, Bob, Joan, John, and I did the sightseeing bit. What fun!

Each afternoon Bob would point at his watch at 4:00 o'clock and say, "It's gin and tonic time." Then we would make our way to the nearest sidewalk cafe. Bob and I share the same kind of zany sense of humor and we were never at a loss for a comedic interpretation of life in France. What a good time we had, and what wonderful memories.

Christmas 2008, Ann and Solenne came to visit us in Maryland. She was crawling faster than a speeding bullet by then, so we child-proofed everything except the Tupperware cabinet. It is a God given right that all children have the right to investigate all cabinets open to them. And Solenne found the Tupperware, pulled it all out and sat in one of the bowls. She was so proud of herself! And we have the pictures to prove it!

Solenne also loved our dog, Maggie. We were somewhat leery of the impending visit, but we should not have worried. Maggie let Solenne pat her (not exactly a gentle pat!) and followed her everywhere. That child remembered Maggie more than us.

Our first Christmas in Lincoln, we had all of our little family together. The first word from Solenne's mouth was "Maggee." Even in her old age, Maggie accepted Solenne putting ribbon through her collar and leading her around the apartment.

Then, this fall of 2016, Mark met Ann and Solenne in New York City for a week. Solenne will be nine late November and is just a good age to travel. She ran from customs to Mark with such a happy face. She loved the boat ride around Manhattan and knew that the Statue of Liberty was from France.

They had a tour guide at the Empire State building who spoke French. She loved seeing the city from such a high place. Alas, her mother doesn't like heights! They had lunch at *Alice's Tea Room* with all the *Alice in Wonderland* characters. Solenne knew the story and was delighted from beginning to end.

The *pièce de résistance* was third row aisle seats at *Lion King*. Mark said Solenne was mesmerized. Her choice of souvenirs was a Baby Simba.

Mark called one morning and said, "Mother, she is definitely related to you." Which made my heart sing!

Mark told me they had been to the Gap, and Solenne picked out many things she liked. Mark is on my credit card, so I had instructed him to get whatever she wanted. And she did! In most everything she does, she has, as the French would say, *joie de vivre*. I do not want to think about having to say goodbye.

We Skyped twice, and when I saw Solenne the first time my eyes filled with tears. She has that cute little girl giggle, and Mark said that everywhere they went, people could not do enough for her or would comment on how pretty she was. I told her on Skype how much we loved her. A child hears this and really has no idea of the depth of those words. What I know is she truly is a child of my heart.

Solenne

Part 2

WRITTEN MARCH 30, 2018

I ORDERED A LITTLE DRESS, HAT, AND PURSE TODAY for my granddaughter. It will go to "Aulnay su bois" with her Dad in May. She is a girly girl, which pleases me no end. She loves to dress in new clothes.

In addition to this, she will receive a rosary made from the flowers that I had in the church from her for her grandfather's funeral.

I treasure everything about this little girl, who scarcely knows me and probably never will. She will be making her first communion in May and, in France, this is a time of great celebration. Family comes from everywhere.

I wonder what she thinks about her situation? I know she really loves having Mark there. And when they are together, they seem to really bond.

She is a bright little girl, but I see a sadness in her eyes. The eyes are often said to be a window to your soul. She knows her situation is somewhat different from most children.

Her teacher in school told Mark, the last time he was there, that Solenne cried when other children talked of times with their papas. What a price this child is paying. I know there are millions of other children in like situations, but that doesn't make it any easier.

How do you make a child know she is so very much loved when she really doesn't even speak English and is three thousand miles away?

My case is made even more difficult because I am disabled. Our first meeting was okay, but she was eager to get away from me. Maggie, our dog, made things a little easier. I'm sure Solenne asked her mother a gazillion questions about me.

In France, such things as disabilities are not talked about. In fact, they are ignored, swept under the rug, which makes you feel "out of place" or "out in space."

Solenne and her Mother were to come to Lincoln last summer, but temperamental issues got in the way. Now, John never got to see his granddaughter, let alone interact with her.

John and I were so excited to think she was coming. I had said, "Let's get some games that we could all play," and we were eagerly planning some fun times together. Then the trip was cancelled.

Mark thinks when she is older, she will want to visit. I'm not sure. Yet, I keep reminding myself that there is a little bit of Kennerly and Clinton in this child and maybe one day she will want to know more about that side of her heritage.

I pray that some way, somehow, she will come to know she is so very much loved.

Solenne
Part 3

WRITTEN MAY 11, 2018

OUR GRANDDAUGHTER, SOLENNE, will make her first communion on May 20th. Mark will fly to France for this big event. This occasion is a big deal in France. Family comes from near and far, and it is one continuing celebration.

I love buying for my granddaughter, so I was delighted to find a little blue and white dress with matching purse and a white straw hat with streamers. For a ten year old, she is well aware of her feminine wiles. And I love it!

Her other gift is a rosary made from the dried rose petals of the two dozen red roses with baby's breath that I had on the altar at John's funeral from Solenne. The dried rose petals are boiled, made into a paste, then formed into beads. It is so very beautiful.

Initially, I doubt she will really appreciate the depth of love that this rosary represents. My hope is that at some point she will understand how precious they are, that she will consider this rosary as a treasure made just for her.

As a devoted reader, it was imperative that I send her some books. So Mark and I selected six age appropriate books that I have instructed Mark to help her read daily. I think it might help her with her English.

Solenne e-mailed Mark a list of things to bring. At the top of the list was French's mustard and Q tips, neither of which can be bought in France!

The last item was the *pièce de résistance.* "And for my confirmation, I would like a Samsung 9—A telephone, with said telephone picture posted!"

Mark has a Samsung 9. His response was "no ten-year-old should have a thousand dollar phone to drop or lose!"

He then checked with Solenne's mother, who was not even aware that she had e-mailed such, and agreed such a telephone was not needed.

I hope her mother did not chastise her too much. I like her spunk—no harm in asking!

I firmly believe that the world offers us such joy if we only allow ourselves to see it. This little granddaughter brings me such pleasure.

The little robin, Rosie by name, who has determined that our balcony is strictly her territory, has completely captivated me. She will dive bomb any other bird who tries to join her.

If I don't get the raisins out early enough, Rosie flies in and looks at me as if to say, "Well, where are they?"

One morning she must have been famished. Rosie landed on the balcony, looked at me, and loudly squawked!

The next two mornings I made sure to have the raisins out before I had breakfast. As I was putting the raisins down, I called, "Come and get them, Rosie." Before I could get through the door, she was there!

For her pleasure, I have a bird bath filled with water. She loves to drink, but I have never seen her attempt to bathe. I have seen her preen herself.

Most times, she doesn't stay very long—she has babies back in the nest. I think Mr. Rosie watches them, too. But that's as far as it goes. Rosie chases him off the balcony.

My little window on the world delights me. All creatures, great and small, display such wonders, bringing joy to those who take the time to sit quietly and watch!

Brown, as My Grandmother was Called by My Grandfather

WRITTEN NOVEMBER 5, 2016

THE CLOCK IS BOLDLY TICKING AS I WRITE. Actually, it was her clock that I have heard all my life. It is a comforting and calming sound—life goes on as it measures each quarter hour.

My paternal grandmother, or Gram, as I called her, was a major influence on my life. She loved me with the purest love. But when I needed it, she could stop me in my tracks with "Now, Mary Ann"! She had only a fourth grade education, but she was so very wise. I loved the time spent with her.

When I stayed overnight, I would bump myself up the stairs without braces and crawl or slide to my room. Often she would insist on my sitting on a rug and she pulled me to the bed. She called this my magic carpet.

Then came the best time of all—each time I would ask, "What was it like when you were growing up, Gram?" She would sit in a rocker (which I have now) and tell me stories of her childhood. Gram was one of ten children. Her mother came from a good family and her father was from a hard working family. They lived on a large farm where peacocks strolled the grounds. She knew how to call them and told me they slept in the trees!

All of the children helped with farm chores. They had a persimmon tree that lived till the late 1960's. We would go to see it each Fall. The house is still there, still livable. Oh, if only those walls could talk! Surely, silence in that house seldom reigned!

I think Gram met Grandaddy at a church social, and from then on they were a couple. If ever there was a king of his castle, it was Granddaddy. The first year they were married, they lived with Granddaddy's parents in their home. That couldn't have been the easy way, but I never heard her complain of that at any time.

Granddaddy was captain of a boat that brought supplies from Baltimore. His father was the customs agent at the wharf where all boats, docked in the area, came. So, Gram, who hated the water, sailed with her husband for a year. She must have been terrified on that ship sailing down the Chesapeake Bay in winter storms!

A few years later, Daddy was born. And by that time, Granddaddy's parents were older, so Gram became a mother, caregiver, and chief cook and bottle washer. The one thing on which she differed with my grandfather was sailing. He finally agreed to give that up and started an oyster plant. I don't think he could ever imagine how successful that little oyster house would become.

Each Saturday Granddaddy and Gram rode to the county seat, Salisbury, where Gram would go to the movies—her idol was Clark Gable—and Granddaddy went where men gathered and smoked (and probably more), then they went to dinner.

When Daddy was young, he loved that time. He roamed the beach, made a fire and cooked his dinner. Or, in bad weather, he would cook at home. Gram would tell me that it always smelled so good when they arrived home. She would ask for samples—Daddy was like a dog with a bone—no deal!

When I was sick with various childhood diseases, Gram would come sit with me. Sometimes we talked, but more often her presence was the best medicine. She could sit and not move for hours. In my feverish state, that was so comforting.

Gram's oldest sister, who was a widow, would often spend summers with her. I loved Aunt Net—she loved to play Chinese checkers, so the three of us would play game after game. Beforehand, Gram would instruct her to let me win. And if it looked like Aunt Net was winning, Gram would pinch her leg under the table! One day Aunt Net could not refrain from saying, "Mary, I'm black and blue already." We didn't play checkers as much after that!

After Mark was born, I went to work for my father. I drove the twenty-three miles with Mark in the car seat by me. Most of the time that first year I would drop Mark at Mother's. I don't know who enjoyed it more, but I suspect it was Mother. In the years to come, Gram often kept him when Mother wasn't available. Mark loved it. After lunch, they would watch Art Linkletter and the soaps. I often wondered what the conversation was. But maybe it's better that I don't know!

When we moved to Virginia, Gram agreed to give my little Spinet a home, so when we were back in Maryland Mark had a keyboard on which to practice. He was visiting her on one of our visits to Nanticoke. Mark was told he must practice as he was preparing for a program. I called to say I would be picking him up. That little rascal knew it was about time for me to call, so when Gram answered the phone my first question was: "Has Mark practiced"? Gram took the receiver from her ear and in the background I could hear Mozart. He was pounding away.

I was told Mark closed the deal by saying: "Now, Gram, that's our secret!" Gram was delighted by the whole event, but years later she did confess and we both laughed.

On another trip home to Nanticoke from Virginia, I begged and begged Gram to go back with us so she could see where we lived. Reluctantly, and after much pleading, she agreed to go with us with the promise we would bring her home the following weekend.

I didn't realize how debilitating a ten-hour-plus drive would be for her. She somehow got herself into our house and promptly went to bed. She didn't do much that entire week. Truthfully, I was scared. I didn't know what was going on. Now I believe that this was the beginning of her pancreatic cancer. I don't think she was ever the same. When Gram left Radford, she said, "I'm glad to see where you are living, but I won't be back!"

A few months later, she was in the hospital and then to hospice. We made a quick trip to see her. She so wanted to hear Mark play the piano, but couldn't get out of bed. So, we found a piano in a lobby and pushed it out to the hall and told Mark to play as loudly as he could.

She smiled her sweet smile and said she heard him. I don't know, but we gave it our best shot. She died three weeks later. I was crushed. She was such a force in my life. But, somehow, she is still very much with me. I can still hear her voice, "Now, Mary Ann!"

My grandfather died in January 1956. He had been at Johns Hopkins for a month. Gram was quite simply inconsolable. She no longer wanted to live. Aunt Net came back to stay with her.

In July, on my birthday, I was given a car, per instruction of my grandfather. One of my chief responsibilities was taking Gram to the cemetery each and every day. Her love and devotion never faltered. Even though there had been times that a lesser love would have perished, love can bring such joy but also such grief.

Granddaddy was laid out at his home, and I'm sure Gram sat by him through each and every night.

Changing

WRITTEN JUNE 22, 2018

IT CONTINUES. Just when you think you have your life fairly well organized, along comes another curve ball, and you are once again back to square one.

John and I had become very comfortable with our new life in Lincoln, Nebraska. Then, wham, John dies, and my entire life is turned upside down.

Once again, I must find my way to survive, living as a disabled single. I can't tell you how many times I've looked heavenward and exclaimed, "God, I'm too old for this!"

First, I need to acknowledge, I am a rebel! I fight any change as if it is a life or death issue. Major or minor, I see it as a battle to be won.

Example. I decided late one day I would watch the sun go down with a glass of wine. Unfortunately, I first had to open the bottle of wine. I knew right away it was going to be a challenge, but that never stopped me before.

I pulled and tugged on that cork—it didn't move. Then I got a bottle opener (church key, as it is often called) and tried to pry it open. At this point, I said to myself, "If you had an ounce of sense, you would put the bottle back in the refrigerator."

Obviously, I didn't have that ounce of sense, since I was even more determined. I got the sharpest knife in my arsenal and attacked that cork with a vengeance.

Surprise, surprise! The victory was mine, even if I battled for most of an hour! That's how my life is without John. He was always there for anything I might need from a high shelf, open bottles of any sort, look up information on the internet.

I, on the other hand, could move any piece of furniture with the greatest of ease. Move the cedar chest? Just push it with my scooter in the desired direction.

So now I make lists, if I remember to do so, which makes me a little angry. If I want something, I usually want it now. I've been thinking about the device that, when commanded, will pick up crumbs from the kitchen floor, or the earring back from the bathroom floor, or paperclips, pills, or any piece of paper that I drop on every floor.

My physical strength is decreasing rapidly. John, in some way, would help me compensate for the loss.

When we would attend a Landing function, he would always find a spot where my scooter could go and be as unobtrusive as possible. Or he would have me be on the front row—not my first choice.

Early on, when we were quite new here, there was a function in the Williamsburg room, where I was directed to the side wall. I followed orders well. However, when it was time to leave, I started forward and I heard shouting. I didn't know the drapes were on the floor, and my chair was ready to roll those drapes like a spool of thread.

It was humiliating, to say the least. At best, I have become a one woman wrecking crew! I try to be as careful as I can using the scooter. I listen as I go down the hall for the clicking sounds, which means someone is leaving their apartment.

Or the patch of light you can see on the carpet, if a door is opened. If it's all clear, I rev up my speed. I explained it to Jack Moors: "I like to feel the wind in my hair." We both had a good laugh.

When my memory is most challenged, I must remember everything I might need when I transfer from my chair. Transferring once is somewhat daunting, but having to transfer numerous times is almost impossible. It's always changing and, God willing, it will continue changing.

I just pray that I will have the ability to accept such changings.

Who We Really Are or in This Case Who I Really Am

WRITTEN JUNE 29, 2018

I THINK EVERYONE HAS A PUBLIC SIDE AND A PRIVATE SIDE. I can put on the public persona at the drop of a hat. I've had to do that—smile and hide your fear or distaste and you are bound to get a positive response.

The forlorn are pushed to the back of the bus. All of this is to say you mask too many of your emotions. I try not to mask negative emotions without first understanding them.

This quite often leads to rather painful realizations. Like, "Why is appearance so important to you?" My immediate answer, "I want to be a part of society."

Years ago, the disabled community was seen as dowdy—clothes ill fitting because of some disfigurement. The public dealt with that by putting these disabled people as far out of sight as possible—"homes," they were called.

Their philosophy was that the disabled did better living with their own kind. Isn't this awful? To define someone by their limitations. Yet, it happened.

I was more than fortunate that my parents saw mainstreaming as quite necessary for the development of their daughter. Understand, it was not easy to be mainstreamed after being out of circulation for about two years.

I was different from everyone else. There were whispers. Laughter behind my back. It hurt. Somehow, I knew I couldn't let anyone see my pain. Instead, I invented things I could do within a group, and in time I drew in many of my classmates—at least they would speak to me.

Acceptance has a lot of faces. In high school, my difference caused me a lot of grief. First, I had to be carried up and down the stairs. Then along came puberty.

Couples appeared. Who would look at me? Pretty much all social life was for couples. I felt like the token handicapped when I did attend any event. I hated it all.

I started seriously dating when I was sixteen going on seventeen. It was serious. My parents were not exactly happy with this. I wondered what college would do to us?

Somehow I survived the ordeal of leaving. But that relationship helped me realize that someone other than my parents would find me interesting enough to actually date me. That relationship was a real boost to my self confidence.

Lauro Halstead wrote in one of his books that polio patients grew up believing they have to try harder in every way. You believe that you are just not good enough.

That's a rather negative viewpoint, but I can attest that those emotions were in most all polio survivors. "I am not good enough, smart enough, pretty enough to really matter. How could we compete in a normal world?"

I remember in junior high school responding to a question and giving a wrong answer, and that one student spoke that polio affected my brain. Well, it did affect my brain, but not like he was suggesting. These were the times when I wanted to be invisible.

College became my years of enlightenment. A whole new world was opened to me. I was pretty much accepted in the girls' dormitory.

But, oh, the dating situation! At first, counselors made sure I was involved in all activities, which made me feel like a charity case. Slowly, I made my own way through campus life.

I quickly learned that sometimes I was asked out mainly because I had a car. I was the only freshman allowed to have a car on campus. But I soon could detect that motive.

I let no one borrow my car. Even John—who was dating a girl from Penn State—wanted to use my car to take her back to Penn State in the middle of a snowstorm. I said, "No." That car wasn't going anywhere without me in it! It was a good lesson in responsibility.

I have always identified with the "least" and the "last." Seeing a disabled child throws me into such pain. I see me over and over again. I identify and, hard as I might try, I cannot deny it.

At the end of my life I understand so much more of how and why I think and react as I do. I don't deny or reject anything. As I struggle with my downward spiral, I have every right to say, "I've done this once, why do I have to do it again?" But it's just my reality.

John's brother gave me a plaque last Christmas that read, "You are an odd combination of 'sweetness' and 'don't mess with me.'" I think he may be on to something!

I love, and I need to be loved. I laugh, and I need to do that also. I enjoy my solitude, and I enjoy being with friends from time to time.

When I reach those Pearly Gates and am asked for my identity, I plan to reply—as the African American in "Green Pastures," "It is I, Lord, and I is all I got!"

Spirit Versus the Body

WRITTEN SEPTEMBER 15, 2017

THESE PAST FEW WEEKS HAVE BEEN RATHER STRESSFUL. And since I am definitely not a passive personality, it brings out the worst of me. In my head, I know that the key to good mental health is acceptance of what is. Unfortunately, I don't like "what is"!

My polio ravaged body is once again complaining—big time. The muscles in my neck are pinching some nerves. The curvature of my spine is now pressing on my liver and pancreas as my strength ebbs away. My T.I.A. has just about murdered my short term memory (no pun intended)! Still, my humor bone is still intact, leading me to say to Mark, "Polio took my body, and now my brain is diminished!"

There really are no fixes. Sometimes I think, "Oh, just give up." But I can't, I can't give in, there's too much fight left in me.

This leads me to another topic—work, physical work. So many have said to me, "Let things go." I can't. At our last home in Maryland, I did a lot of yard work. I loved it. Yes, my muscles twitched afterwards and I was bone tired. But it was a good tired. Our lawn was manicured and I felt a sense of accomplishment.

Inside the house, it was the same "modus operandi." Clean base boards? No problem. Cloth in one hand, the other driving my scooter. Our house was large enough that I could get around in every room; thus, dusting was easy. Pushing a vacuum cleaner was another story. Of course, I tried, but it just wasn't in the cards. I found out my limits somewhat grudgingly.

All of this is to say work is good—I loved it! Why does the able bodied population try so often to limit their physical labor? Yet, after their work, where do they go? To the gym, of course.

I have had aides say, "Oh, the trash is too heavy."

I am dumbfounded! My reply was, "Can't you pull the trash bag? And if you can't, I can." The pure freedom to move is such a blessing, but somehow they miss that fact completely.

Now, in all fairness, not everyone is super strong, and I would never ask anyone to do something detrimental to their physical well-being. But if this poor specimen can do it, then I think most able bodied people can also. After all, when they are hired, they are asked to be my arms and legs—not a babysitter!

The M.R.I is always interesting—I've had a few. John was sure my claustrophobia would kick in, but I knew better. "Use your imagination, Mary Ann." And I did. First, it didn't sound like Kabuki dancers as my other M.R.I.'s had, but I did hear the ship horns, and I immediately thought of the Titanic and Carpathian.

Funny enough, I didn't hear any church bells, though some were like diesel truck horns. Sometimes having an imagination is quite beneficial!

So begins another phase of my life journey. In my adult life, my philosophy has been "if it ain't broke, don't change it!" So I am somewhat of a stranger to our doctor, who readily points out that fact. But, be assured, the Spirit is still willing even if the body isn't.

P.E.O. Program

WRITTEN SEPTEMBER 13, 2021

I NEVER THOUGHT THAT I WOULD WRITE ABOUT MY LIFE—let alone share it with others. My husband John said many times, "You have a story to tell." So, in a weak moment, I began to recount stories from my past. All of a sudden, I began to see how my life evolved, and understood my motivations for the choices I made.

All of those psychology courses in college really paid off. For sure, it was cheaper than visits to a professional psychologist!

Born to a young, prosperous couple, I was destined to be an only child—not by choice, but due to medical complications.

My early years were quite normal. I loved to run, jump a ditch, and try to climb a tree. I was the one who pushed the merry-go-round on the playground—for the older kids! But underneath was a timid little girl.

My cousin, known as my sister of the heart, swore that she didn't think I would have ever learned to ride a bicycle. She tried so hard, and I was fine until she removed her hand from the fender, and over I would go!

It was the second month of my first grade in school when I was stricken with polio. It started with a high fever, eventually going to a hundred and six degrees, and terrible muscle pain. Our little village doctor diagnosed it as either polio or spinal meningitis.

We drove to Baltimore and were directed to the contagious disease hospital.

I remember little of this, and I could not understand why my parents couldn't come into my room. They had to stand outside my window and could only gaze at me.

Hot packs were the number one treatment. The steamer was rolled into my room and the scalding hot pieces of wool were wrapped around my legs. Why I wasn't burned, I'll never know—but I surely remember the burn!

At this point, my parents knew my life, and theirs, would never be the same. After two months, I was transferred to Children's Hospital in Baltimore and was there for a year. While at Children's Hospital, I was fitted for braces and corset, and learned to sit, then walk with crutches.

By the time I was discharged—a year and three months later—I had forgotten home. It came back to me slowly. I was home schooled for four months, then allowed to return to school full time.

When I returned to Baltimore for a three-month muscle check, I had gained so much strength that my doctor said, "Let her go full time." And I did.

In junior high school, there were three floors of classrooms and no elevators. But somehow I made it through with a football player as my elevator. Other girls laughingly said they were jealous. But I would have gladly changed places!

For my seventeenth birthday, my parents surprised me with a 1956 Mercury, red and white, fully equipped with hand controls. The world became my oyster. I was allowed to have it with me at college, which made life even better!

College posed a host of new challenges. My roommate was paid to change my bed and generally keep things clean. I ended up doing most of the work. But I thought of it as early housework training.

John was paid to carry me up and down the many steps. One day my roommate was pushing my wheelchair to take me from the dorm to the classroom building (where was my scooter when I needed it?) Carol did not see the medium-sized stone on the ground, and when the little wheels of the chair hit it, the chair tilted backward.

The result was I was still seated in the chair, but the back was on the ground as well as my head. I was horrified for anyone to see me. Just then the grounds crew drove by in a truck, stopped, and one man came over and asked, "Are you all right?"

I was furious to be in this position and answered, "No, I always sit this way." He returned to the truck and drove away. I deserved that. Thank heavens, within minutes students came and rescued me!

At the end of four years and dating John for two of them, I knew marriage was the next step. Thus, we were married five days later! I got a job with the State of Maryland Employment Service so that John could get his Masters degree.

Then along came Mark. The doctors all said that I would never carry a baby to term. That never crossed my mind. I wanted this baby with every fiber of my being. And I was so blessed when he was born.

You see, I may not be able to do all things in a normal way, but I can achieve the same results with a few adaptations. My dear parents' love gave me every opportunity to go and do as much as possible. And I like to think that I did!

October 7th, 1945

WRITTEN OCTOBER 3, 2019

IT'S THAT TIME OF YEAR AGAIN WHEN I ALLOW MYSELF to turn back time—OCTOBER 7, 1945. It started with a sore throat and fever that climbed to 106 degrees at least. The paralysis began when I stubbed my toe on the way to the bathroom. I was soon semi-conscious with the paralysis spreading. It was if that little body was being invaded by an enemy, taking over one body part at a time—first, the right leg, then the right arm, to the neck, and down the left side.

It wasn't finished even then. It was so virulent that the attack continued—bladder, digestive tract, lungs—compromising for a short time before surrendering.

I think my spirit was the only victor, yet it has carried through some perilous times.

Then came wheelchairs, braces, corsets, and crutches. Two summers were spent in hospital for muscle transplant surgeries to hopefully eliminate part of a brace. It didn't work. Now it was a matter of living with what was left.

But it didn't stop wishful thinking—if only I could dance, if only I could play volleyball, or roller skate, or water ski, or run—and ad nauseum.

Life called for constant adjustments, and it still does. The difference now is I crumble a lot more. As bleak as this might sound, I have been richly blessed by parents who never saw a situation that they couldn't make better as long as they lived. We were together on October 7th.

Wherever I lived, I was blessed with friendships. And with few exceptions, our friendships continue. Case in point, this weekend I will see a P.E.O. Sister and her husband from Maryland. They are driving to Lincoln to see me.

My whole life has been filled with such friendships. It has enriched my life beyond measure. So, this October 7th, I might seek a quiet place, grieve for what was lost, but rejoice for the good life I have had.

Thanksgiving and Christmas Dinners

WRITTEN NOVEMBER 20, 2019

I MISS THE THANKSGIVING OF OLD. Today, Thanksgiving has been just another holiday, a fully functioning holiday.

The Thanksgivings of childhood were filled with family—grandparents, parents, cousins, and perhaps a friend or two—sitting around a table laden with food.

Often, the cousins would have a table of their own. The air was filled with talk, laughter, and the sweet smell of food soon to be in our tummies. The menu was pretty much the same each year—turkey, stuffing, mashed potatoes, gravy, sweet potatoes, peas, cranberries, and corn pudding, followed by pumpkin pie or pecan pie. (It wasn't only the turkey that was stuffed!)

My paternal grandparents always took Thanksgiving dinner to a "shut in" neighbor. Her name was Lona. She never left her home. I never even knew why that was, so I'm sure there was a good story here. But, sadly, it was never shared with me—not for lack of trying on my part! I always was full of "why!"

Then, we always had two thanksgiving dinners, one at noon with my paternal grandparents, and another at 4:30 or 5:00 o'clock with my maternal grandparents. This timetable repeated at Christmas!

When the grandparents died, the younger generation took their place. Most all of my family got together at each Thanksgiving and Christmas—dear ones, each contributing to the fabric of my life.

By the time I got married, Thanksgiving and Christmas dinners were much smaller. Yet, it was still always special, the feeling of completeness.

We, for the second year, will have Thanksgiving with friends of Mark.

It was wonderful, and with lots of good conversation.

Then I once again think of the early Pilgrim settlers. Their lives had been so difficult, but they had survived. And they were grateful.

We, today, have so much for which to be thankful. We, too, have survived and should for a moment count our blessings, one by one.

Our Marvelous Coping Skills

WRITTEN FEBRUARY 20, 2020

I JUST FINISHED A BOOK THAT I THOROUGHLY ENJOYED. Maybe it touched my psychology nerve. Briefly, the story was about a young woman who had been severely abused as a child. She had gone through the equivalent of our public school education, then had found a reasonably good job.

She had an apartment, where everything had to be in its rightful place, and chores done on the appointed day. She heard from her mother some distance away, at the same time, same day, each week. It was a routine life. That's the best that could be said.

Then one day she saw an advertisement of a band coming to her area. She immediately was attracted to the picture of the lead singer. Here was her prince. Her mind led her to believe she had to get his attention at the local performance, and the rest would be history.

She knew she had to upgrade her dress style by at least seventy five percent! Of course, sales clerks were most willing to help in this endeavor. After spending over budget, her dream came to naught. In the meantime, she came to see that the men around her were quite nice also.

Where am I going with this? This woman knew that she was starting a relationship search with a big deficit. May I introduce the psychological term *defense mechanism*. We all have that ability.

Sometimes I laugh at my attempts to do normal things. Defense Mechanism! It's better than crying! I try to dress at least appropriately to defeat the old mentality of the poor cripple.

These aren't reasons always apparent to me at the time. Yet, looking back, I felt I had to try harder.

Probably no one could understand the monumental moment in my life when I was given my own car with hand controls. It was liberating.

I was the unstoppable Mary Ann. I could come and go on my own and I could decide where I wanted to go. It was my great leveler—the playing field was almost normal.

Being allowed to have my car on my college campus was a bit tricky. I soon realized who paid attention to me because of my car and those who didn't.

Maturation was a large part of my response to this situation, but I also had to be somewhat defensive. I realized if I lost this privilege, I would again be severely restricted, so I had to give the most pleasant refusal and smile all the while. Inwardly, I seethed!

After we were married, I realized that I wanted a child. Now, I always had said that I would willingly adopt a baby. But what agency would let us adopt a baby? They saw too many negatives with me.

So, we had our son; I thought it was a gift straight from heaven. Most everyone thought I would never carry a baby for nine months. I knew differently, though I carried him for only eight months.

Ordinarily there would have been baby showers. But friends, thinking they were being kind, never spoke in future terms. I was very aware of what they were thinking, and tried not to show my bewilderment.

My church circle, against all odds, gave me a baby shower. It restored my belief in myself and the innate goodness of people. Even if I had lost the baby, there were those who knew how important preparing for that little life was.

So many defense mechanisms during this time. Put on a happy face, accentuate the positive. I can do this! As I was wheeled into the O.R., I instructed the doctor, "Never mind me, just save this baby."

Moving to Nebraska was another gigantic decision. We were "wined and dined" for months. Yet, deep within me, I felt that I was leaving my security, my little world of friends, church, theatre and concerts, dinner parties, being involved in so much. I had spent all of my years trying to achieve this life. Yes, there were some negatives. Fear being the top one.

John had a life-threatening event and I panicked. I could call for help, but I couldn't go with him to the hospital. And we all know how communication with hospitals works. I couldn't call even my best friends and get a ride to the hospital.

I have to travel with a wheelchair. This immediately eliminates all small car owners. A lot of friends are reluctant to drive my car. In an emergency, it was daunting. So moving to Lincoln where our son lives seemed to be the answer. I guess events proved the truth of the matter.

Don't get rattled. Think, Mary Ann. Smile though you feel like you are dying inside. Then comes the calm assurance of faith. You can do this slowly, thoughtfully.

Yes, it is well with my soul.

One of My Very Favorite People or, Another Life Vignette

WRITTEN SEPTEMBER 26, 2019

AUNT MAXINE, ACTUALLY JOHN'S AUNT, was, from the first time I met her, my ideal woman. Like her sister, John's mother, she had a definite New England brogue.

She was a fairly small woman who made sure she stayed fit and trim. She wore clothes well and always was attractively dressed.

Aunt Maxine admitted she had a bit of ginger on her personality. But, to me, that made her even more interesting.

She was passionate about her husband, son and his family, parties and politics. She loved to laugh. She was an excellent cook, and entertained beautifully. Her dining room table was always a masterpiece.

Aunt Maxine was always fun to be with. Uncle Jack was a typical

New Englander. He was tall, dark, and handsome, a man of few words whose wit was endearing.

They made a beautiful couple. Uncle Jack was, in his words, "in the Bureau"—the F.B.I. He worked on a few notable cases, carried a gun, but never spoke a lot about his work.

In his late years, he worked as an insurance fraud investigator. If Uncle Jack had work in Washington, D.C., he would stay with us, much to our delight.

Then there were those fun times when they both would come for the weekend. John and I would find a time when we could see a Broadway play or a special artist in concert.

There was the time when we came out of the Kennedy Center only to find that we were in the midst of a severe ice storm. Everything was covered with two or three inches of ice.

John drove home very slowly—it took us three hours instead of the usual forty-five minutes to an hour. It was a white knuckle ride, and we laughed for many years about our "sleigh ride"!

When Mark was quite young, we visited Aunt Maxine and Uncle Jack in their home. Mark adored Aunt Maxine. At that time, Mark had a favorite blanket that he could not sleep without. I had packed this blanket when we left home. Mark did not want anyone to know about this, so we carefully were very discreet.

Unfortunately, he forgot to give it to me for the trip home. A few days later, Mark received a package and letter in the mail. Aunt Maxine expressed how sorry she was that this "special blanket" was left at her house, but it would always be their secret. She just knew how important this was to a little boy.

Uncle Jack died after a short illness. Aunt Maxine remained in their home for five or six years. During that time, she had to have hip replacement surgery. I was so frustrated that I couldn't be there to help her.

Then I got the idea, which I expressed to her. When she got at the point that she could stand the five-hour drive to our house, she could come to our house to recuperate. After all, we had no steps, and moving with her walker would be easy.

She agreed to come. I, then, could cook and do laundry for her. It made me so happy to do this. Then, Aunt Maxine decided she would try to get in the bathtub, which she did. I offered to wash her back, legs and feet. She gratefully, I think, accepted my offer.

Never will I forget her words "You are a good woman, Mary Ann." It was my privilege. Since then, I have thought the foot washing in some church services brings a humbleness to both participants. At least, that is what I felt.

Aunt Maxine met us on the train going through Philadelphia to New York City when Mark and Nicole played at Carnegie Hall. The train car was filled with all our friends who had been so dear to us throughout our married life. I called it "The Carnegie Hall Express"!

After the concert, we were walking to a restaurant to celebrate further this event. John said to Aunt Maxine, "What would Uncle Jack say about you walking the streets of New York City at 11:30 at night?" She replied, "Jack would say, 'Good Lawd, Maxine.'" We all laughed because it was true!

At seventy-six years of age, Aunt Maxine took a trip to Africa. She went skyward in a hot air balloon, spent the night in a forest where a bell would awaken you when some animal would appear.

Isn't she amazing? I loved her spirit—ready for anything. She loved to learn and never lost that edge. I'm so glad she was a part of my life.

Aunt Maxine was visiting us the weekend that Princess Diana was killed. We had been to church and we were having dinner when John says, "Let's go down to the British Embassy." We left everything and drove to D.C.

As you can imagine, cars were parked blocks away, but we found a spot and walked to the embassy. There were huge crowds, and flowers piled on flowers so that not a blade of grass could be seen.

There was a reverent silence—yet so many people.

We signed the Book of Condolences, stood with the crowd, and finally drifted away.

Bits and Pieces

WRITTEN JUNE 4, 2021

RECENTLY, I WAS READING ONE OF THREE POST POLIO NEWSLETTERS, when I saw an article by a polio survivor describing the first time she wore braces.

First, to a child they look like a piece of torture equipment—pieces of steel with leather strapping, at the end of which are monstrous high-top shoes. Ugh-ly! You are so overwhelmed by this sight that I'm sure they—like me—zoned out!

In a child's mind, you wonder how these ugly things will be able to make you walk. In that child's mind, you somehow think that one morning you will awaken and walk like normal.

And the shoes!!! Brown hightops! Babies wore hightops—though they were white!

Mother tried to encourage me. I tried to keep my disappointment to myself. But I left the hospital with these devices—and to this day wear the same devices. Going out into the world, you suddenly stick out like a sore thumb. And wearing those shoes around other normal children? Just how different you are!

Mother, always my number one advocate, asked my doctor if perhaps I could use an Oxford style shoe. The answer was yes as long as it held my feet in place. Before you knew it, I had black and white saddle shoes, and suede shoes for dress. Now I have shoes for each season.

I can't switch shoes by myself, so must orchestrate time and when. Oftentimes for evening, I would not wear braces. Then I used regular shoes. Of course, then I needed a dressy slip-on shoe.

Most all females can't wait to wear high heels. I was one of them. I found a store in Washington, D.C. that carried small sized shoes—even heels! I promptly ordered two pairs—one black and one white, and loved every minute of wearing them without braces.

It is not only disabled women to whom it is very important to present yourself as best as possible. Yet, I think we women have to try harder. Self image is important.

My roommate in college paid me the supreme compliment when, after pushing me to the quadrangle of class buildings, walked up the six steps, turned, and said to me, "Well, come on or we'll be late."

She immediately realized what she had said, and started to apologize. I interrupted, "No, you just paid me a supreme compliment—you saw me as me, not somebody in a wheelchair."

Stubborn, Determined, or Too Dumb to Give Up

WRITTEN NOVEMBER 10, 2017

Many of my friends caution me continually to not overdo things. And part of me recognizes the valor in this, but I find I am energized in doing things. My mind is functioning.

Case in point. I have a silver spoon collection of about 150 or so spoons. I have an international board, a family board, a vacation board, an island board, a fifty -spoon United States board and a miscellaneous group on the hutch. Before Nebraska, I polished these spoons every three or four months. That way, it was an easy buff and the job was done.

Since moving to Nebraska, I have suffered some kind of malaise in the polishing department. So, with much shame, I confess to not polishing spoons for a year!

My Jimminy Cricket conscience has been ragging me mightily. I wouldn't even look at them. But, still, I heard that voice, "Are you trying for black spoons?"

So last Sunday, I made the public pronouncement, "I am going to start polishing my spoons tomorrow." And I did, and I have, almost. I have another seventy-five or so to finish. But I smiled my way through it—so many beautiful reminders of family vacations and gifts from friends who traveled extensively.

After my mother died, I found a large box of spoons in a closet. I never knew she had them. There were more than enough for another board. I really had forgotten them until I did an under-the-bed inventory, and there they were—another forty or so spoons.

So, the marathon polishing began. When I got to Mother's collection, I was amazed that she, too, had spoons from many vacations. One spoon in particular caught my attention. It had a moose head with full rack of antlers on the top of the handle.

I thought, where on earth did she get this? I turned it over and there was nothing to indicate its origin. Then I looked at the bowl of the spoon and I saw it. I laughed so hard that there were tears running down my cheeks. In that bowl was written, "Mary Ann."

Somewhere Mother found a spoon with my name on it and that's all she cared about. She never showed it to me, which made it even more comical!

I think I was born with a stubborn streak as evidenced by my bunny attack. It was a beautiful stuffed bunny from my Easter basket. For some unknown reason, I decided to pull off his button eyes.

Mother discovered my attack as I was working on the second eye. She took the bunny from me and put him on the fireplace mantel. He would stay there until I was quite sure not to remove the other eye.

Not to be deterred, I said I could get it from the mantel. Mother asked just how I would do this? After all, I was only four. I was sure I had a foolproof plan. So, innocently, I told her all I had to do was pull a chair to the fireplace, climb on it to reach bunny. She made that impossible by moving the chair out of my reach.

This was just a taste of what was to come!

In high school, one of my history teachers would always announce, "Well, here is Kennerly at the last bell." I believed he thought I was totally defective.

I walked on crutches then and it was a campus type high school. I had to walk halls as long as twice the length of our current hallway. He would never give me any grade higher than a B Plus. When the next big test was given, I made sure that I knew everything in those chapters. When he returned the graded test, he just handed me my paper. When I saw that "A," I gave a most triumphant smile. I had proven my point!

My father had rules for me, and no deviation was accepted. After I got my car and drivers license, he cautioned me never to allow a certain young man in my car. I accepted this—until, as it happened so many times, our group of teens would congregate at the beach, at the gas station, wherever. This particular night, the unacceptable young man was in the group surrounding my car—not in my car—when, who should drive past but my father.

Returning home, he asked for my car keys and said, "Two weeks." I handed him the keys and said, "He wasn't in my car and I couldn't order someone to leave the group." That fell on deaf ears.

Mother tried to convince him that this wasn't right—to no avail. After a week, he said, "Okay, here's your keys to drive now." In a blaze of glory, I said, "No, I'll wait another week."

I knew I had done nothing wrong, but I guess I just threw the gauntlet down. "I can be as stubborn as you." Stubborn, determined, or just true grit? I could be remorseful when I did or said something wrong, but when I thought I was in the right, I stood my ground through thick or thin.

Oh, if you should phone me, you might be greeted with "Mary Ann Moose here"!

The Spirit of Community

WRITTEN MARCH 8, 2019

I AM A SMALL TOWN GIRL. My little village of two hundred and fifty residents insured you knew everybody and everybody knew you—which was not always a good thing! Yet, I have seen, time and time again, the beauty of community in so many ways.

The winter blizzard in the early '50's brought out the best in people. A former neighbor of ours had married and lived in a somewhat isolated area some fifty miles away. Her husband died at the height of the storm.

My father was one of the men who heard the news. Roads were impossible. Daddy remembered seeing a piece of road equipment that was being used for road repair. He and a group of men in a heavy truck drove to that heavy piece of equipment, jump started it, and drove to that remote home.

They took her to a friend's house who had heat. I believe on their return, they shoveled a few driveways of senior citizens. That was community at its best.

When I first had polio, the community surrounded my parents with such caring. If they saw their car in the driveway, they would come to the door, offering support in every way possible.

As I started to improve, I was inundated with get well cards—so many that mother put them in a scrap book so I could look at them over and over. I did not remember many names. My mind was like a chalk board that had been completely erased.

On a much grander scale, my parents and I happened to be in New York City when General MacArthur returned home from the war. A tremendous parade was held with numerous bands and marching military units.

The confetti thrown was so heavy that at times you could scarcely see. In their exuberance, some threw phone books out of the windows. But the spirit of the crowd was overwhelming. It was a good day to be an American. The pride and joy was most patriotic.

I can never forget that time—patriotism was alive and well. And it's for sure I looked at the American flag much differently.

That sense of patriotism was so evident after the Kennedy assassination. Americans came together. You could feel it. We are better than this hateful attack.

The 4th of July celebrations in Washington, D.C. are always inspiring. There was a nobleness in this celebration—family after family enjoying the celebration of our country. There is nothing wrong with patriotism on this night.

A young couple with twin girls lived on a farm just outside of the village. They had bought a farm with an old farmhouse that they lovingly and beautifully restored.

Early one morning, the house burned completely. Nothing was saved. The fire company gave them emergency funds to live in a rental home. The entire village supplied dishes, bedding, and clothes.

My mother went to her clothes closet and picked garments to give to the wife, who was more or less her size.

And food! They were given meals for weeks. They rebuilt the house, and the wife lives there today. As horrible as this fire was, there was such an outpouring of care.

My heart swells with pride as I think of this time. Out of ashes came the jewel of community! It brings out our best.

In a way, that spirit of community has been always-present in our history. May it continue down through the ages.

Confessions

WRITTEN SEPTEMBER 7, 2018

IT TROUBLES ME TO THINK OF THIS PARTICULAR POINT IN TIME, yet it very much is a part of who I am. Am I being disloyal? I don't think so. I felt then, as I feel today, that I did the right thing.

We were still living in Salisbury, Maryland, when John got a job teaching in political science at Radford University, Radford, Virginia. Mark was seven years old.

And for six of those years, Mark spent most Sundays with my father, his grandfather. After church, John and I would join Mark and my parents for dinner.

To say Daddy was "over the moon" when his grandson was born was putting it mildly. He had lists of things he wanted to share with him—plans for Mark that would have been out of the question for me.

I understand this. But when John accepted the Radford job, it meant we had to leave Salisbury. My father was angry, boiling angry. So he refused to speak to me. He knew how to be conveniently absent when I was around, and he definitely included John in the circle of silence.

After a few weeks, I somehow got him cornered and tried to explain that, like Ruth in the Bible, wither John went I went with him.

His reply was, "Let John go to Radford, and Mark and you could live with us or continue living in the house in Salisbury."

No way!

Mother organized a cookout for family and friends. Daddy cooked the meat, talked with everybody but me! That hurt. But my moral compass, or the voice inside, kept saying, "You have done nothing wrong." I don't think I could have lived with myself if that small voice within had not reinforced my decision.

Radford was a good ten-hour drive from Salisbury—a long way. We found a home, moved, Mark was enrolled in public school, John settled in his new job. I resumed my domestic engineering.

Oh, yes, Mark was enrolled at the University as a freshman studying music—at seven years of age! We made the newspaper!

We moved in August. It was October before Mother and Daddy came to visit. I finally heard the words I longed to hear. "Mary Ann, you did the right thing. You had to support your husband."

It was a lesson of love. You love someone for who they are, and sometimes you love them despite who they are. That still small voice within has carried me many times and has yet never guided me in the wrong direction.

After I got my drivers' license and a car, there were those in the community who delighted in reporting that I had been seen with this or that person of bad reputation. It was never true, as I could always prove that no such person was with me and I was somewhere else.

Except, the one time I was getting gas in my car, when there were a lot of teens around and I supposedly even talked with some of them.

When I returned home, my father was waiting. He told me to put the car keys on the table, and I would not be driving for a week. I had not done anything to deserve that, but I wordlessly followed directions and went to bed.

About four days into this sentence, my grandmother called me, asking me to take her to the cemetery. I told her I couldn't drive, but I would ask my Mother, and I was sure she would help. I made the request to Mother, who said, "Go ahead and take your grandmother where she wants to go."

"Oh, no," I replied, "Not until Sunday can I drive."

By Saturday, even my Father said I could drive, but I waited the full week. I knew I had done nothing wrong. But I am stubborn. If nothing else, I hoped to show that I always kept my part of the bargain.

I liked when Frank Sinatra singing *I did it my way* was played at John McCain's funeral. It certainly was true of his character.

I think Sinatra singing, "I gotta be me, who else could I be, I gotta be me, that's who I am," should be on the program for my funeral. Or, at the least, "To thine own self be true."

Current Events

WRITTEN FEBRUARY 23, 2018

I STILL REMEMBER MY NAME, my phone number, and my address right down to my zip code. I do not remember my Social Security number because I chose not to. I hated the thought of being reduced to a number.

Now, in my advanced years, I say every month, "Please don't forget my number." This has to be some sort of divine justice!

I do forget names. So many new faces. John, on the other hand, rarely forgot a name.

I have tried all kinds of ways to have a name stick in my mind. For a while, when first introduced, I would look for something significant in their appearance—a mole, a lisp, a hairdo, or in a man's case, no hair.

You can immediately see that this, in no way, was foolproof. So now I just smile, comment on some innocuous topic, and hope to hear someone else call out the appropriate name. Then you can end the conversation with "nice seeing you again."

But sometimes I just admit that "I remember your face, but not your name. Please forgive me."

Then I forget where I put an address or a piece of jewelry or an article of clothing. I had it earlier, so where is it now?

I try to be methodical in everything, but all it takes is a phone call or breaking news on CNN to interrupt my plan of action, then I grumble about weak-mindedness.

Yet a few weeks ago, the calf of my right leg burned as if it were on fire and the hematoma area throbbed just like it did originally seventy-two years ago. Why did I remember that?

Why is it that my first reaction was, "That's how it was in the beginning"? What else is locked there?

I remember every inch of our former home. But some of the streets in the area are vague to me. Really? After twenty-two years!

I think I will choose a friend's explanation of forgetting, which is, "I have so much information stored in my brain that I have to delete bits and pieces from time to time." It works for me!

And then there is clumsiness. Someone hands you a car key in the car, which you promptly drop. Since neither of us could see the key on the floor, I got out and emptied my purse (no small task!), only to discover that I didn't have the car keys!

Now, panic sets in. We look under the seat, from the front and back. No car key. I heard them hit something when they fell, so where were they? In the trash container? No such luck!

Then I heard, "Found them!" "Where"? you might ask. Well, of course, they were in the Kleenex box which I had removed from the floor to the dashboard!

A ten minute search for car keys! I was late for my appointment and I felt ridiculous. After it was all over, I decided it was worth a chortle, not a full laugh. Who knew that the foibles of advanced years could be so, well, exasperating!

Worst of Times and Best of Times

WRITTEN JUNE 13, 2019

I AM A PACK RAT. I UNASHAMEDLY ADMIT TO IT. My mother was a pack rat—to a superlative degree. In other words, I learned this trait from the best.

I laugh at all I save. Throw a plastic bag away? Heaven forbid! Surely, some day, I will desperately need this size of plastic bag!

Just this week I spied two suitcases that, try as I might, I couldn't recall what was tucked inside. Upon investigation, I discovered packed tightly inside were photographs—lots and lots of photographs—two suitcases full!

The first suitcase was my mother's. So, of course, I couldn't discard it. It was made of pure alligator skin, and originally was designed as a fitted night bag. And, wouldn't you know, the first photograph I picked up was mother and daddy's home showing a bed of Black Eyed Susans—the Maryland State flower! Now, you can't help but get dewy-eyed over this!

I haven't continued the investigation of all other pictures. I hope I can still identify the people, time, and place. But, for sure, it will be a walk down memory lane!

I guess I look at things that I have saved and realize it is my personal history. When I'm gone, no one will care, and I won't care if at last they will be discarded.

Yet, I have older photos of my parents as children and my grandparents and even my great grandparents. I love to look at their faces and see how much the younger generation resembles their ancestors and about the historical time in which they lived.

Those who lived through the Great Depression did not throw much away. I have a hazy recollection of my grandmother trying to get P&G soap from a black market source. And once you got it, you used every little sliver!

World War I and World War II took a lot of young men, and a good many never returned home. I remember the gold star displayed in many windows, particularly in Baltimore.

Streets were lined with what today are called townhouses, except all of them had the famous marble steps that were scrubbed every morning.

I guess it could be said and applied to all segments of history it was the worst of times and the best of times!

Soap Box Discourse

Written March 8, 2018

I have had numerous times in the last four or five months of people who, matter-of-factly, advocate a "we and them" way of thinking. To say it upsets me is to put it mildly. Haven't we learned anything from our history?

When I hear on the news that people blatantly state that the Nazi creed is their way of living and they aren't in the least afraid to espouse their viewpoint—oh, yes, I get the definition of free speech. But it doesn't mean inciting people to marginalize those who are the least bit different from themselves.

You see, I have a dog in this fight. Germany, in World War II, arrested all Jews and put them in concentration camps. They barely existed, and thousands and thousands died. They put anybody who might be homosexual in the camps and tortured them. They also collected any disabled people—in no way could they be judged whole or perfect—and did all sorts of brutal scientific experiments on them.

We like to think that we are much more enlightened now. This could never happen again! Really?

Watch the news, listen carefully, observe the swastika signs. We must not let such dogma destroy our democracy.

Dietrich Bonhoeffer wrote:

"First they came for the home, and I did nothing;

"Then they came for the crippled, and I tried to be more careful;

"Then they destroyed the churches;

"Then they came for me."

We mustn't be doomed by the past, or we will be doomed by repeating it.

1 - The Good
2 - The Bad & The Ugly

The Good

WRITTEN APRIL 5, 2018

IT WAS A SOMEWHAT NORMAL BUSY DAY. "Busy" meaning completing household tasks at the speed of "molasses running uphill"!

Hurry is no longer in my vocabulary, but I did accomplish a few things, deriving more satisfaction than I deserved.

Thankfully, the day ended on a very high note (pun intended)! The Prague Spring 50 Concert was marvelous. The first music played was by Karel Husa. The UNL Wind Ensemble did it justice and then some.

Many Americans cringe at any discordant sound, but this was a musical history lesson—the pounding boots of the Communists trying to take over the beautiful City of Prague and the breakthrough sweet moments reminding us of that beauty and the beauty of the human spirit as well. It was a musical documentary!

The second piece was written for a brass quintet. I wondered if the theme may have been from the Czech National Anthem, only to learn the theme was from a beloved hymn. The theme was translated into five different musical styles, which I found quite interesting.

The third piece was fairly short, only just written in 1996. Maybe my brain was tired, but this just did not speak to me.

The last musical moment was a Dvorak piano quintet. The audience loved it, and it was beautiful! Dvorak wrote about Prague in happy times.

I heard joy, poignancy, and sweetness. It spoke volumes of Czech love for Prague. It was masterfully presented.

I might be just a little prejudiced since I have a relationship with the piano player! But it was truly beautifully done. And, judging from the audience applause, they thought so, too!

The champagne reception was the perfect finale. It was a time to bask in the joy of a fine performance and enjoy high caloric delight.

The one and only negative, as I see it, is that too few people were there. It was a world class event, one of many venues throughout the week celebrating Prague Spring.

I do think this publicity could have been much better, but I will always regret that this jewel of the time wasn't shared by so many more music lovers.

The Bad & The Ugly

WHAT IS IT WITH LINCOLN and the "Americans With Disabilities Act"? Is this an exemption zone?

My first surprise came some five years ago when we first moved here. We had heard so many good things about the Sheldon Art Gallery that we decided to spend an afternoon there.

We arrived only to find numerous steps in order to enter the building. John climbed the steps to ask for directions to the handicapped entrance.

He was told there was no such entrance. Thank heavens it wasn't raining or bitterly cold, as I was left sitting at the bottom of the steps! I'm sure John gave a lecture on the process of conforming to the ADA and the benefits thereof.

He chaired the Maryland Governor's Committee on ADA. We were on the White House lawn the day the ADA bill was signed.

I wasn't privy to this conversation, but I'm pretty sure the people at the Sheldon blustered and finally offered a ride on the freight elevator which I agreed to do!

It was a lovely visit; however, in retelling the incident to fellow residents at The Landing, we got the feeling we were attacking something that was sacred. I had never gotten the feeling before that an art gallery was only for the able bodied.

We encountered other places in Lincoln that were off limits to us. The excuse was "so much would have to be changed" and "the cost might put them out of business."

Then this week I encountered more of this mentality. I had wanted to see the Czech photo exhibit and attend a lecture followed by a reception—except the reception was held on the basement level.

And Wednesday night, I was back at the Kimball Hall for the Prague Spring 50 Concert—but the reception was at the Sheldon. It was a hike to get there, never mind the broken concrete that seemed to suggest I would surely do a catapult before ever arriving at my destination.

And poor Mike pushing me must have felt that we were crossing the frozen tundra! We made it, but why should it be so difficult?

And what about senior citizens? A woman stumbled in the dark trying to climb the steps.

Now, one of the arguments often used is: "It is a historical building, and we can't modify it."

John and I have traveled to many, many historical sites; and they, most all, used ADA recommendations to accommodate the disabled community—and it was done well and did nothing to compromise the integrity of the building site.

It can be done. And isn't it better that these places be seen and enjoyed by all interested citizens?

Musings

WRITTEN MARCH 15, 2018

Some days I feel as old as Methuselah. The old body just will not cooperate. But then I worry, will my mind go down that same path? Will I get to the point that I am not interested in seeing or hearing anything new? Will I become a stereotypical old person who sees things in just one way?

Music is often the subject of much dispute. I heard rap music being done on TV the other day and suddenly realized the meter was great but I would have to hear the words five or six times to understand them.

Dress. Or lack of dress. That's a topic that gets us fired up. I'm right there, front and center. More often in my advanced years, the phrase will come to mind, "This, too, shall pass away."

Have you noticed how much health matters are discussed? I guess this is so, because lack of good health is frightening for us all. I have come to realize we can't change what will be, so it is best to deal with it one day at a time. I would never have thought this ten years ago!

My "to do" list is as long as ever. But my attitude is a complete reversal from that of years ago. If the coffee pot isn't washed until after dinner, well, it waits for me!

I have to make myself make phone calls. I never did like talking on the telephone, but now I'm even worse. Am I isolating myself from the outside world?

I love my friends, and am interested in them. But after four or five long phone conversations, I'm almost a babbling idiot! Is my brain weary, too? Yet, when I am involved in political conversations, or anything historical or in the arts, my brain wakes up. I'm rejuvenated.

Maybe in senior years, the brain becomes more selective? Or do I have so much stored in that brain that it can't take in anymore?

I have thoroughly enjoyed CNN's presentation of the Kennedys and also the Pope. I thought I was quite familiar with the Kennedy history, but I heard a lot of new material.

The history of the Popes could have gone on for two more hours. The old brain was alive and well—meeting that early history of the church like an old friend.

Senioritis can be good or bad. A sense of humor is really quite necessary for this time of life. And our sense of what really is important to us is also quite necessary.

Nostalgia

WRITTEN AUGUST 30, 2018

I DON'T THINK YOU EVER GET OVER the death of a spouse. John filled my life for some sixty years. Everywhere I go, I am reminded of him. And that's not a bad thing at all. But sometimes it catches me by surprise as it did a few Sundays ago.

Mark and I attended what was billed as a Distinguished Artist Event for the Friends of Lied. Steven Rich was the Distinguished Artist, a singer, and was he ever!

He sang songs that told stories so very beautifully, and I was transported back to the numerous times John and I attended Barbara Cook concerts. She was a master at singing musical stories.

Hearing many of the same songs made me just tearful, tears that flowed uncontrollably, and I cried my way through the concert.

Number after number brought back memories of so many good times, each one a gem in the tapestry of my life. I am forever grateful for each one.

Signs of fall and winter are more and more evident from my balcony. I can't say that I eagerly anticipate those changes. Have you noticed how early it gets dark? For me, that means less balcony time. Not a pleasant thought at all.

I like watching the geese and ducks. I know they are messy, but they are a living panorama. My imagination ascribes each scene with human tendencies. They have become a wonderful source of entertainment. It takes so little!

Snow is pretty until you have to go out in it. But there is nothing redeeming about the cold! I still can't understand why South Point is an open mall. Did the powers that be forget how cold it gets here?

Just thinking of these changes makes me sad. I like changes that are positive. But it is harder to be positive each and every day. My body will less and less respond to my spirit.

Tuesday was a good example. I saw some plants on the balcony needing water, so out I go to take care of it. Trying to switch arms in order to carry the full watering can, I spilled half the water in my lap. Not deterred, just supremely aggravated with my task.

When I returned to the kitchen, I realized that I was totally soaked from underwear out to my slacks and down the legs. I changed underwear and put slacks in the dryer.

I had been dressed for a one o'clock appointment, which I was able to keep. However, when I returned, I remembered I desperately needed to run the dishwasher. So I twirled the corner cabinet to get a cup to use for dishwashing detergent.

As I reached for said cup, my hands lowered a little too much and I knocked a bottle of rosemary to the floor. Most of my bottles of spices are plastic. But, no, not the one I hit.

So, of course, I not only had rosemary over the floor, I had a zillion pieces of glass everywhere. Now, this was war! I got one of two hand vacs to take care of the situation. And, wouldn't you know it, it would come on and then quickly off.

I couldn't get the second one unplugged. By now I am in full battle mode. The electric broom should do it, except it was behind an untold number of other pieces of equipment. No matter if I could get hold of it, I would pull it over or through any obstacle. And I did!

I got most of the glass from the floor and just prayed I did not have a shard in my tires! Mission accomplished. Thank goodness the worst was over.

I continued to drop most everything I touched, but that has become normal for me. Needless to say, I was glad when it was time to go to bed and the Day from Hell was finally over.

Through all of these escapades, I couldn't help from thinking of the old refrain:

Open the door, and the flies swarm in,
Shut the door, and you are sweatin' agin!
Life gets tedious, don't it?

I Remember Mama

Irene Dunne

WRITTEN NOVEMBER 16, 2021

THERE IS SOMETHING ABOUT HOLIDAYS that always triggers my memories of days gone by.

Thanksgiving was always celebrated with two dinners—one at each set of grandparents. It wasn't only the turkey that was stuffed!

The first dinner at my paternal grandparents was always at 12:00 noon. My father was an only child, so there were only five of us.

But, after dinner, Gram fixed plates of food to send to a lady that never left her home. As far as I know, she was never married and seldom or never seen.

There is more to this story, I'm sure, but the excuse was always "your ears are too young"!

The second Thanksgiving dinner was at my maternal grandparents. Here there were eleven or twelve of us. Mother had two sisters, both with husbands and children. Conversation flowed like water. I can still hear the many conversations punctuated by laughter.

One year, probably 1944, the Thanksgiving dinner was held at our house (in earlier weeks). The cousins always ate in the kitchen.

Mother had made three or four pumpkin pies. They sat in the little pantry. Interesting, I thought. Then, when no one was around, I sampled each pie by placing one finger in each pie. Right away, I knew I loved pumpkin pie—until my deed was discovered.

Fortunately for me, Mother was too busy to dwell on this minor catastrophe, but she, in no uncertain terms, let me know my deed was not appreciated! Many years later, I was invited to put my signature on each pumpkin pie.

In 1948, I saw my very first television. We were traveling in Canada, and in the bar of the hotel where we were staying was a television set showing a boxing match. Daddy asked if they would allow me in the bar to see this television.

What an amazing device! I was impressed—and I wasn't. Why would anyone want to watch a boxing match? In my eight-years-old brain, I concluded that this strange device only showed boxing matches. How weird was that?!

My parents were always eager to show me the world. This says volumes about them. Traveling with me was no easy task. I had a collapsible wheelchair for travel, which today is archaic.

I think my first big trip was to New York City. We went to Radio City Hall to see the movie *I Remember Mama*. This may have been one of the first movies I ever saw and I didn't see all of it, for when Mama (Irene Dunne) died, I, too, was grief stricken.

And I not only cried but I sobbed! My father had to remove me from the theater. I just couldn't stop crying.

Why was this so personal to me? Did I somehow see myself or maybe my mother dying? I was traumatized like never before.

It is from my father, I think, that I get my great love of all creation. I remember him leaving work after a snow storm to drive me around the countryside to see the winter landscape.

As I started to cry, I told him the world had turned white, so clean, trees dressed in white, houses completely outlined, roads had disappeared.

It was one of those moments in which the bonds of father and daughter were forged forever. These are just a few gifts from heaven that are forever in my heart.

Spring

WRITTEN APRIL 29, 2021

THE SAP IS RISING—A SURE SIGN OF SPRING. Every year I respond in kind. It is rather like an internal time clock. I get this urge to bring out spring and summer clothes and put all signs of winter away. Winter coats—Off to the dry cleaners. This is just the beginning. Go through all drawers, remove items, wipe out with a damp cloth, then rearrange.

Occasionally I even dispose of an item or two. But you can't really tell much has changed. I believe all drawers must be filled, and if I have any talent at all, it is the ability to fill each drawer to full capacity.

Some say I have too many clothes. And it's probably true. However, I take good care of them, hence, many items are twenty years old.

Then there are desk drawers, kitchen cupboards, files and entire closets to inventory. No stone unturned. Balcony furniture is returned to its space. And in another month plants will fill any empty spaces. I need all the sap I can get to accomplish this.

But it's not just me that feels this compulsion. Animals show like traits. Just this morning I watched Rosie the robin try to pull some nylon string from the railing. She is building, or in some way is fortifying, her nest. She worked so hard, to only fail. But I am sure she will return for a second or third attempt. I identify with her stubbornness.

And throughout all of this, I discover so many past treasured times. The metal bookends my father had in college. A stocking hat that my grandmother wore because it belonged to a much-loved, deceased family member. A baseball hat that my other grandmother wore because she was such an avid Orioles fan. A stack of "love you" cards in John's desk that would be at my place at the kitchen table in the morning.

And pictures! Suitcases of pictures! Faces that I can no longer identify by names, yet I recognize them. They were all part of the fabric of my life. Sunday school class parties, birthday parties, receptions for our guests from India, Great Britain, and Germany. And I loved each and every minute of it all!

My mother was a pack rat and I am her daughter. In a small hat box I find a darling pink hat with a note: "Mary Ann's bonnet worn home from the hospital," with my birth date.

These things are the real treasures of life. They represent so much love. Am I lucky or what? Lead on, my sap-filled days!

The Age of Negativity

WRITTEN APRIL 13, 2018

WE SEEM TO BE LIVING IN A VERY NEGATIVE AGE. We turn on television and see the turmoil of the day, be it political, violent, or prejudicial. It happens every day.

I am certainly no Pollyanna, but I do think there are good things still going on. And we need to see/hear them.

I am told that the Journal Star has a policy of not reporting University events. Why? The University has a myriad of different events going on at all times.

Now, there is one exception to this rule. SPORTS!!! Television and printed news is all over these.

Is it because of the money that is generated on each event? I'm not naive, but surely the news could be a little more diverse.

Case in point. Last week the local newspaper printed a mug shot and article of the charge against a music professor. But, somehow, they completely ignored the *Prague 50 Spring* event.

Now, this seems strange to me since Nebraska has a large Czech population. The Czech ambassador was here and Vac Havel's press secretary spoke and had an exhibit of photographs from the *'68 Prague Spring*.

There were programs every day and evening. Why would such an event be largely ignored? It would seem this is *modus operandi* for the Lincoln Journal Star.

A few years ago, another professor was charged with drug dealing. That made front page news, plus several follow up articles.

Movies are no longer listed in the newspaper. I was told it was a cost-cutting issue.

Lincoln has varied and marvelous music and art programs as well as very supportive audiences. The line-up of coming events is the envy of many east coast areas. So, why don't we see more about them?

It is a tragic picture—positive, stimulating events go unseen, but you can bet the next big car crash will make it into tomorrow's news.

Rambling

WRITTEN AUGUST 10, 2018

I RECENTLY READ AN ARTICLE IN NEW MOBILITY MAGAZINE that at first startled me, then made me smile. It affirmed much of what I've been writing.

A "young" sort of man with multiple sclerosis wanted to be a comedian—a rather lofty goal for one in his condition. He did his routine in a number of venues. Then he entered a contest for comedic acts, and he won.

Now he had an entrée into a larger world of comedy. However, he discovered that just being funny was not enough. From the very first moment on stage, he—from his wheelchair—had to convince the audience that he could really make them laugh.

He had to overcome that gasp from the audience, be it pity or surprise, when he first rolled onstage. He had to show them that for most of the disabled, there are often a lot of peculiar and humorous times, and it is okay to laugh. And he has to do it over and over each night on stage. It verifies the adage of the disabled, "I can do it and I can do it better."

On the other hand, John and I knew and tried to support a struggling comedian back in Maryland. Michael trembled, his whole body trembled, and his speech was somewhat garbled. He would hold the microphone in his hand and walk the stage as he delivered his monologue.

I could not understand him. Try as I might, I just could not make sense of what he was saying. And his walk was such a stumbling gait that I feared he would fall at any minute. The humor didn't come across to me, even though I desperately wanted it to do so.

It was a Catch 22—I wanted Michael to succeed, but how could he connect with an audience if they couldn't understand him? He really did have a comedic mind, but perhaps he could write or put his thoughts in cartoon form. For sure, they would bring laughs then. But God bless him for trying.

Maybe it boils down to a matter of perception. I pretty much know who I am and what makes me tick. I never thought I could do anything on stage. But we had one brief shining moment. John convinced me to do A.R. Gurney's "Love Letters" with him as a money-making event for our church in Severna Park. We did, and we packed the church.

Then the phone began ringing, and we ended up doing it another six or seven times! It was fun to do, and really a quite beautiful story. Who knew? I certainly never believed I would do such a thing. Yet, it was such an affirmation of love.

I saw another affirmation of love of country, integrity, what is noble, and what is true, when we visited the Eisenhower shrine in Abilene, Kansas, this week. Where are these values now? Do they even exist? Would we even recognize a man of character today?

Reading Eisenhower's speeches, I wondered if a like man could ever be found in today's world. He was the embodiment of a true American patriot. Let's hope that these virtues are not a thing of the past.

Like Demosthenes, we need to hold the light high and look for an honest man.

Friend by Fate

WRITTEN OCTOBER 28, 2020

I MET PAMELA IN LATE 1945 OR EARLY 1946. She was in a white iron bed next to mine in the children's ward of Children's Hospital School in Baltimore, Maryland. She, too, had polio and was paralyzed much like I was.

Her parents were British citizens who lived in Bombay, India. Her father worked for Gulf Oil there. At the time, Great Britain controlled India. When Pam contracted polio, Gulf Oil flew her and her mother to Baltimore.

Eventually, my bed was next to hers. Even though she was six years older than I, we became friends. She would write notes to my mother, and I still have several. One such note reads: "Dear Mrs. Kennerly, Mary Ann drank all of her orange juice." Mother would buy oranges and bring me fresh orange juice each visiting day. Mother never stopped trying to make my life better.

Pam's mother stayed in a rented room close to the hospital and never missed a visiting day—there were only two. She always called Pam "my darling."

After a few months, Pam was measured for a corset and brace, as I was. Pam was never to go without her corset. And though she learned to walk with her braces, she seldom used them. I am not sure if that was a vanity call or not, but she definitely preferred no braces and loved many different kinds of shoes.

Pam had a gorgeous singing voice. Her father and brother had a band in Bombay that performed every weekend. Pam was soon singing with that band, and it was heard in many cities of India.

Of course, she was on display (she was already quite beautiful) and required formal attire. So mother was asked to find suitable evening gowns, which she did, and sent them to Bombay. Pam had a friend who was an airline stewardess; and if the timing was right, the stewardess would take the package to Bombay, India.

In the mid '60's, the McCarthys moved to Australia. Living was easier, but you no longer had a large staff of servants. In India, Pam had a servant to carry her down some serious steps at any time of the day or night, someone to help her bathe and dress, to assist her in any way in the bathroom.

This couldn't be duplicated in Australia; yet, I think she was happy there. Her parents had passed away, but she proved to be quite capable of carrying on. In Australia, she learned to drive with hand controls; she also participated in the Para Olympics at the swim meet. And she kept singing.

Pam and her parents came to the states in the '50's. The motivating reason was to get new corsets. Apparently they, try as they might, could not get a corset made like the one she was used to. In Pam's case, without the corset, she would fold like an accordion. The impact on breathing would have been monumental. So, Children's Hospital made her two new corsets.

The six year difference in our ages faded the older we got. On her first visit back to the states, I was only eight or nine. Her parents were with her. I can't recall what we did, but there was a lot of conversation. Pam definitely was more limited than I. She could not believe how I could maneuver my "old Franklin," as I called my wheelchair. My chair was like what we saw F.D.R. use. I knew exactly how to tour our yard, having figured out which was most level and which was not!

Pam and her family went on many cruises. During one such cruise, she met a young man and they fell in love. I think it was quite serious. But her parents ended any and every contact with the young man. To my knowledge, there was never any other romantic interest.

To me, this was so sad. When her parents died, she had no one to fill her life. This valiant soul soldiered on until July 2013. When her aunt called to tell me of her death, I was grief stricken. And I was even more distressed when Jean told me she died a terrible death.

The words her mother said to her each night is the perfect closure for Pamela's life: "Goodnight, my darling. God bless."

In the late '90's, Pam and a companion, Betty, came to Maryland one last time. New corsets were the top agenda. Of course, our home was perfect for her—no steps, extra wide doors, and fully accessible bathrooms.

My parents were still living and were so delighted to see her. And, of course, we had a little (30 or so!) people meet and greet event. Pam was a real charmer.

In one of our conversations, I asked Pam how she managed using the bathroom on airplanes. Remember, she could not stand at all—she didn't use braces. She giggled and said, "Oh, Mary Ann, first you look for a cleric collar; if that doesn't work, find a strong, handsome man!"

A Pack Rat's Treasure

WRITTEN APRIL 20, 2018

EVERY SPRING OR FALL, SOMETHING RISES WITHIN ME. I described this to my father as "sap rising in the trees."

It is a compunction—in this case, all things winter must be washed, ironed, folded, and put away. Shelves need to be emptied, materials sorted as to which ones need to be kept or put in File Thirteen.

So, true to form, I began this process on Wednesday even though I had targeted next Monday as the start. One can't deny the sap rising!

The first day, I decided to check all the books under the television stand in the bedroom. To my amazement, far back on two shelves were an assortment of Bibles.

I recognized them as ones I used at different times of my life. And even more important were the notes tucked throughout the Bibles. Suddenly, I was back to the early years of my life!

The first Bible was white, with my name in gold on the front. It was left at home when I married.

My mother then used my Bible within which she had tucked items that were near and dear to her—the funeral program of Daddy's aunt, who was much loved by all who knew her; numerous notes and cards from me. She had recorded inspirational quotes such as "everything comes in God's own good time."

There are programs from memorial services of friends. She even had emergency telephone numbers in the Bible which resided on her night stand! There was a note from her Mother thanking us for a Thanksgiving dinner. There was Mark's baptism record from March 1964. No wonder we couldn't find this record!

A Christmas gift tag in my paternal grandmother's own handwriting saying, "to my darling granddaughter." This was followed by postpartum instructions!

A pressed flower was there, but no identifying tag.

Then came a business envelope from my father's business. Inside, the note was addressed to "my love." My Christmas bonus when I worked for him.

Then a note that said, "Remind me to tell you of tax implications," signed "H.B. Kennerly, Jr." I laughed and laughed. It was so Daddy.

Mother had church programs from churches where John had given the sermon.

A beautiful note from my Mother to me on my first Mother's Day.

Another note from my aunt who held a beautiful reception in her home after one of Mark's performances.

And obituaries and obituaries!

Another quote that Mother had recorded was "God gave her wings." And she earned them!

What treasures I found! To revisit various times of the past brings a sense of clarity. They all became a part of the fabric of my life.

To be so treasured and loved is a gift straight from heaven. Just bits of papers, really. Some would toss them in the trash. But, to me, they are more valuable than any diamond, gold or silver.

Problems, Great & Small or, The Dark Side

WRITTEN APRIL 26, 2018

PROBLEMS! WE, ALL, HAVE THEM! BIG AND SMALL! They can define you or recline you. Or they can bring out the worst or best of you.

For most of my life (minus my first six years), I have had to learn how to manage living with a disability so that I could blend in with the population of the time. Fortunately, I had parents who smoothed the path in every way they could.

College was really the beginning of my actual independence. I didn't have mother to help take braces off or lay out clothes that I had selected to wear.

Meals were provided. I did dry dishes growing up. I thought it was a great treat, because all my girlfriends had to dry dishes.

You don't miss something until you don't have it. Not being able to dance was gut wrenching. But I was able to attend parties. And some dances (why, I don't know). They really did not help my state of mind.

College and maturation helped me develop a sense of self.

As a married woman, it was learning a whole new lifestyle. I had never cooked, but I could read and follow a cookbook.

I learned not to dry a wet sheet by ironing it! Then Mark was born, and a whole new skill set had to be developed and refined.

I had enjoyed working outside of the home when we were first married. But I instinctively knew I could not work outside of the home and care for a child. That hurt my sense of worth.

Throughout my life, John was there supporting me in every way possible. Steps never presented a problem to him. He just looked around, asked a complete stranger to help him get me up the stairs.

There were times, I didn't remember, that I was quite different from eighty percent of the population.

My only requirement for coming to Lincoln was to live in a place that I could get into and around in each room. It has been a major adjustment.

And now, without John, problems arise increasingly by the day. I am getting weaker and weaker. I feel as if my body is dying, one piece at a time.

My hands have trouble with buttons, zippers, earrings you name it. I have spent twenty minutes just trying to get myself off the toilet.

My shoulder and arm muscles remind me constantly that they are overworked. Some would say, "Just slow down." But the truth is, if I did this, I would be completely immobile.

A big blessing is that the seat of my chair can go up and down. But the kicker here is—they are no longer making chairs that go up and down! Dear God, if I didn't have that, I would be restricted even more.

I am using various pillows to help sitting easier. But the fact remains that there is no movement on the right leg to the pelvis. The muscle in the right buttock is dead, so the bone just grinds on tissue leading to pretty much constant pain.

My severe scoliosis has pulled my ribcage so it rests on organs that it shouldn't. To sit halfway straight is a big problem. My poor body is tired of all the constant attacks.

My brain is showing signs of aging, too, and I hate this most of all. I don't remember names or dates. My thinking process is slow. I forget anything! It's like "out of sight, out of mind."

But then I remind myself how this old body has waged war on so many fronts. It has a right to be tired of fighting. Now if I could get my brain to accept this, life would be less problematic.

Problems
Part 2

WRITTEN MAY 3, 2018

I AM SO GLAD I CAN'T READ WHAT THE FUTURE HOLDS. If I could, I probably wouldn't get out of bed in the morning. I certainly would have remained in bed last Thursday.

The day went reasonably well and was topped off by dinner out with Mark. When I returned, I began my nightly ritual—preparing for my bath. Somehow, my left foot slipped from under me, and down I went, face slamming into the tub.

I knew I had broken no bones, but my face felt strange. I couldn't see down from my left eye. Assisted Living was called. I asked for help, and reminded her that my front door was locked.

Then I called Mark. By then, I was swollen and starting to turn black. I tried to stay out of sight for three or four days.

Why? Why? Why? It just happens.

As I tell Mark, I refuse to be intimidated by what might happen. I try to be ever so careful, and that's all I can do.

Then I remember, from Winston Churchill, the refrain "never, never give up."

I think there is a lot of fight still left in me. It's a way of life!

A Somewhat Tortured Soul

WRITTEN JULY 27, 2018

WHEN IS IT TIME TO GIVE IN OR GIVE UP? It certainly is a judgment call either way. Do I make a decision that will give my son peace of mind? Or do I hold on to whatever freedom I still have?

I am such a rebel at heart. I think the phrase "I can do it" is imprinted on my brain. There is something deep within me that fights against any more limitations.

Falling is definitely *Enemy Number One*. But I can fall any time, any place. And unless someone is glued to my side, it is not preventable. True that someone can call for help, but so can I. I have my phone and call button with me at all times.

It is startling when I realize that this is the first time in my life that I am living alone, unless you count my senior year in college when I chose to live alone.

After dinner, which may be six or seven o'clock, I do minimal kitchen clean up. Then I may read for a few hours or just watch the sun set.

After a nice hot bath, I finally get motivated to put things away—like clothes freshly laundered, or all types of reading material. The evidence of success is an empty top of a cedar chest. All kinds of things find their way there.

Like "Br'er Rabbit," this is my "thinking" time. I review what I have done and what needs to be done. And I can take all the time I like. My state of mind is completely relaxed.

The other side of that coin is that with someone with me, I can't look at a complete television program, read, or get into bed until that person leaves because I lock my door.

Conversation, at that time, is more of a stimulant than I need. It is a real dilemma, and it is nothing against the care givers. They are more than willing to help in any way. I just don't require any help at that time of night.

I fully realize that I will, indeed, need more care at some point. I just don't think I'm there yet. I'm holding on with my fingernails.

But, then, there is always something positive. My dear friend from Maryland will be here for the week starting Sunday. So if we get a little noisy, you are more than welcome to join in the laughter!

From My Corner of the World

WRITTEN SEPTEMBER 21, 2018

WE ARE OFTEN SEEN AS A SOCIETY THAT IS DEFINED BY "problem identified + trial period = a solution" in whatever time we, as citizens, believe that there are answers for everything.

But there is one area in which we have barely begun to find answers. That is the area of "mental health." No wonder it is so, when you think of all the ways that each of us respond to love, anger, deprivation. The list goes on to infinity.

But there has to be a way of preventing these mass shootings. We must be able to identify traits that could set someone to shooting or molesting.

Parents and teachers have awesome responsibilities. Just as medical doctors are trained to recognize symptoms which lead to a diagnosis, we need psychologists to be able to recognize traits that could lead to violence. It is easier said than done.

Yet, if you notice, after a crime has been committed, authorities seem to discover things in the perpetrator's background that may have contributed to his actions.

Psychology is not an exact science, but it can be a very useful tool in the prevention of some of these horrific crimes.

Perhaps one day we'll have school psychologists in each school. That won't eliminate all problems, but it could reduce some of these terrible crimes.

I have known children who, from the very beginning, evidenced traits that could only plague them throughout their life. Beautiful children. But their parents would see it as "a phase," something that they would grow out of.

Or a child who became injured while playing a much loved sport and would never play again. His or her sense of identity wiped away in a matter of minutes. The stock answer would be, "Oh, you can do something else."

No, it's not that easy. And for some it remains a stumbling block. Left unrecognized, it can fester and fester, until one day it explodes either in suicide or damage to others.

It's a tough old world. Our psyches are bombarded with a lot of stimuli. But we can manage, even flourish, with proper attention to our mental health.

This leads me to my mental health. My frustration with my body losing strength almost daily. This week, it's my hands. Trying to unscrew the cap on a bottle of milk becomes a battle royale. I twist and twist, with no results. After five minutes of that, I think *needle nose pliers.* Nope, they are too small. *Regular pliers then.* Yes, they'll do.

Try to button or unbutton a shirt. That can take another ten minutes. Adjust the A.C. temperature. You'd would swear I was drunk. I can't aim the baking probe to that tiny button.

Then I drop everything—papers, food, pens, soap, you name it. My writing is more like hen scratching.

Hands that used to pat, to hold, to wave or caress, now seem to claw, scratch, unable to undress. What can I do to change the scene from gray to fair? I can still fold my hands in prayer!

Time

WRITTEN APRIL 22, 2021

WE ALL HAVE TIME. IT IS HOW WE USE IT that becomes so interesting. As a child, your time is directed by a parent. There is time for sleep, naps, eating, and play. Child care experts say children do better with a schedule. There is some truth in that, but I think each person needs time to just be, to think, to create.

My childhood was pretty much shaped by hospital routine. So much so that I carried that same routine home. When I was fed a meal, it went like this: First, eat all your vegetables; then all of your potatoes; and then the meat. It was then, and only then, that you could have dessert. Your food tray had to be empty.

Imagine—particularly foreign children, of which there were many—being told you had to eat all of your lima beans, and if you didn't, your bed would be moved under the red exit light for a few nights. That was punishment worse than death! Mary Ann to the rescue! I would eat the rejected twelve or so servings for the good of the order.

Dear reader, I ballooned to a great size that puzzled the staff, but not my cohorts in crime. My philosophy was all for the good of the order! And the meals came at the same exact times for fifteen months. Is it any wonder that I was so regimented?

As for play time? I don't remember any. Children, being so creative as they are, devised a game that by holding a hand mirror while reflecting it on the ceiling, you could have a game of Tag or War. Looking back, that was pretty clever.

Returning home was a momentous occasion. I had forgotten so much. And what was monumental was that there were no others in wheelchairs. I was definitely "odd man out"! And we didn't have a rigid schedule.

Time is really the essence of life. I absorbed the hospital schedule so that, when I returned home, I needed that schedule in order to relate to my new life. It took a while to adjust. I would no longer run, jump ditches, play hide and seek with my friends. Now I was introduced to board games, and many of my little friends soon joined in this new activity. But there always came a time when youthful energy had to be exercised while I could only sit and wait.

Through my teen and college years, I learned how best to pace myself, do the difficult tasks when I had high energy. As a wife and mother, it was a bit more difficult, but I always had tremendous support from my husband and parents.

One unusual time, a rather strange event happened when our son was a new born. Talk about change. It was another lifetime! A high school friend called to say she and her husband were in town and wanted to visit us—that very day! I replied, "I have an appointment to take our cat to the vet to be spayed." She said, "Don't waste your money, we'll come over and Hans will do the surgery." Hans was an obstetrician.

They soon arrived at the front door. Hans had his little black bag and quickly disappeared into the bathroom with our cat, "Miss Sniff." Ten minutes later, Hans reappeared with Miss Sniff who never knew what had happened. This is what I call perfect timing!

Then there are the trying times. Living with a teenage son was a whole new experience. His piano teacher took all of his students in his studio out to dinner, downtown Washington, D.C. We were told they would return by 11:00 p.m.

Eleven p.m. came and went. John went to bed. Mary Ann was on watchman's duty. Twelve o'clock came and went. Now, I'm getting a little nervous, so much so that I pulled myself to the arm of my old Franklin and then scooted over to the kitchen counter in front of the window overlooking our driveway. At 1:30 a.m., headlights appeared, followed by Mark. I didn't know if it was time to laugh or cry! I'm sure I lost ten years of my life that night.

Time for this senior citizen is, well, different. I don't have as many "I have to's" anymore. And those that remain are often put on the calendar for another day—or whenever I'm so motivated! Yet, I always hope that I've put a smile on someone's face or brought comfort to someone who needs it. Now, that is timely!

It Takes a Long Time for Change to Happen

WRITTEN FEBRUARY 8, 2019

THE NEWS THIS WEEK HAS STIRRED MY MEMORIES OF LONG AGO. Politicians in black face seems so out of place in our culture now.

The pictures were so startling, I was jolted to the past. I remember "Black Faces" in the yearly minstrel shows in the late '40's and early '50's sponsored by the Lions Club. They had Standing Room Only crowds.

There was always black faces—Rufus and Rastus leading to the lines "Rufus Rastus Johnson Brown, what will you do when the rent comes 'round"?

The music and singing were really good. Even the dancing—mostly tap dancing—was outstanding. But, as I sat in the audience, I never thought beyond what I saw.

Was I brain dead? It never occurred to me that it was insulting to the Black population. It was just the way it was. I never thought much about the difference.

Schools were segregated, but the county commissioners made sure the "Black schools were well taken care of." They saw the writing on the wall, I guess! I, on the other hand, was so insulated from the dynamics of the situation I never questioned any of it.

That all changed in college. We had two black students in my freshman class—a young black woman and a black man. When I instructed my roommate "never to ask the young black man to carry me up the steps," she looked puzzled and asked, "Why"?

My response was quick and simple, "I will be too close."

Where was the logic here? I had been carried by black men ever since I had polio. As fate would have it, I had to swallow my shallow belief when that young black man was the only way I would get to my class. Divine justice, I think!

John and I saw Tony at a class reunion some ten years ago. What an amazing man! Tony became a United Methodist minister in Detroit—the bad part of Detroit.

He has worked tirelessly serving the mostly black populations. He has provided all kinds of services to get education at the highest level, to get medical care for the sick and needy, job training—the list goes on and on.

How fortunate I am to know this man. Why couldn't I see this before? How many times have I heard the phrase "It's just the way it was then." But just think how diversity has already enriched the world!

Racism was certainly a part of our history, but, hopefully, we have moved past that mentality. Yet, I still wonder why I never saw the discrepancies growing up. It was only as an adult that my eyes saw the blight of racism.

I can only explain it in this way. When I was a child, I spoke as a child and acted as a child. When I was grown, I put away childish things.

It's Never Too Late to Change, or, Maybe You Can Teach an Old Dog New Tricks

WRITTEN FEBRUARY 22, 2019

I CAN SCARCELY BELIEVE IT—I'M LEARNING TO USE A COMPUTER! Maybe in a few years, I will even become somewhat competent. But what fun it is to explore this new dimension! I love the fact that I can have my continual questions answered.

Did you know squirrels see more colors than humans? And hear more pitches of sound than a dog? I'm fascinated by this!

The real clincher came yesterday. Last week my daily devotions had a theme of "The Bible on one hand and Ojibwa faction on the other."

All week I wrestled with the writings. I just couldn't seem to relate to the writings, try as I might! My encyclopedias have long since gone the way of the dodo bird.

A new week came and a different writer. But, still, it bugged me that I couldn't understand the writer from the week before. Viola! Ask Google!

In the back of my mind, I thought that this was so obscure there wouldn't be an answer; or, "dummy, you are making a mountain out of a mole hill."

But there was an answer—a good answer. I asked Google to tell me about the Ojibwa faction by Richard Wagamire. Much to my surprise, Google said that the Ojibwa is of the Chippewa tribe, and the puzzle pieces fell into place.

I had been reading about the Indian belief in the Resurrection, similar to the Christian belief of Resurrection! It was so beautifully done and so amazing to understand.

So, thanks to Sally, I am beginning what promises to be a glorious journey. I just hope Google can keep up with all my questions!

Fifty-Six Years!!!

WRITTEN JUNE 10, 2021

June Tenth. June Tenth sixty years ago I was married on a day just as hot as this one (in 2021). All of the windows in the little church were open. No air conditioning! The church was packed (I don't know how people did it), and outside of the windows were another fifty or so people looking in.

I was not even aware of the heat. I was too busy enjoying my special day. The tears that came to my eyes were for all the people who came to see me get married. What a tribute that was! The two hundred or so thank you notes I had written faded into insignificance. Happiness just bubbled within.

John and I had fifty-six years together. We had our challenges, but we always found a way to master the problem. My disability, as always, presented the most problems. First, and the most foremost, was finding an apartment on one floor in the Washington, D.C. area.

Remember, this was the age of split level—in housing and apartments. It took some doing, but we finally found an apartment with only four steps down, which John carried me. Not ideal, but we managed.

When I stop and think about it, my John carried me many, many miles. To him, steps were no problem. He would scoop me up and off we would go.

One year John and I went to Salzburg, Austria to travel with Mark after he completed his three weeks at the Mozarteum. John was a good researcher and planner. Having the benefit of studying German in college, John taught himself the phrase "Meine Frau sitzt im Rollstuhl." That got us in at numerous places—no waiting required.

John was a patriot. He loved this country and its flag. He would have Mark stand any time the National Anthem was played—even as a toddler.

John taught school and college throughout most of our marriage. And, without fail, his students adored him; hence, our home became the meeting place on Friday nights. Thank heavens for Coca Cola and Charles Chips.

John was with me for fifty-six years. What a blessing that was given to me. My disability was never an issue. He saw me as "plain old Mary Ann." Who could ever ask for more?!

Autumn

WRITTEN SEPTEMBER 27, 2018

IT'S THAT TIME AGAIN TO PREPARE FOR COLDER WEATHER and less sunlight. Soon I'll return the balcony furniture to storage and start to retrieve winter coats, long-sleeved garments, gloves, and whatever else is needed to keep me warm. At this point, I have enough laundry of summer apparel to keep my washing machine churning until December.

I am constantly reminded that I went through this process for two people for over fifty years. But it's not really easier. The pain of John's death is only sharpened by the absence of his clothes.

I have always taken great pleasure in washing, ironing, and folding clothes of one season to be packed away for the next six months. It's an awesome task which seems to be more daunting each season.

The autumn skies are beautiful and the setting sun goes down in a blaze of glory. And the moon this week has been spectacular. A lazy, hazy cloud would cover the moon, yet it only enhanced that somehow ethereal beauty.

It becomes another reminder of my loss. Sharing these moments with your life partner was automatic, and now I can't help but feel deprived. Then I remind myself to rejoice in all the times I could share such moments. Still, the loss invades my every minute. Maybe it is the season itself.

Fall is the time to reap the harvest and let the land rest until spring brings a great awakening once again. I don't really expect to experience any great awakening, but I will forever be amazed at the beauty of this earth.

As if I needed to be reminded of this beauty, a red tailed hawk perched on my balcony railing for fifteen minutes on Monday. Beautiful doesn't do him justice. His clawed feet gripped the railing, showing his ability to rip his prey into pieces.

His head of dark brown feathers—with a circle of shorter feathers in the center of his head—turned 180 degrees one way, then 180 degrees the other way. His back was a mosaic of color so wonderfully patterned.

His breast was cream colored, not a ripple showing. You just wanted to stroke this awesome bird. I just hope he will return.

So I suppose this is all to say that, in the autumn of my life, there is still a joy to be found in the earth and all creatures great and small.

Covid Brain

WRITTEN NOVEMBER 4, 2020

I AM THINKING THAT HISTORY WILL SHOW that Covid 19 has impacted most every aspect of our lives. The most obvious, of course, are the physical affects which more and more increase to the point of long-lasting symptoms.

But just as important is the mental effect that many here at The Landing are experiencing. We forget we are social beings. We learn and we grow from interactions with other humans. The difference is a matter of degree. Some seek constant interaction with others, while there are those who have less need to be with others. The bottom line is we all need each other to varying degrees.

Lying in bed one night, I was in a negative mode. I am not ready for another day of routine, nor am I ready to stare at the television. I already know all the words in most commercials. Now that cold weather has arrived, I can't go on the balcony and commune with nature or spy on residents!

The words of J.F.K. came to mind: "Ask not what your country can do for you, but what you can do for your country." VIOLA! My personal shopper was willing to indulge me. Some sixty or so Halloween treat bags later, I donned a costume reflecting my authentic self—black cape covered with spider webs and a witch's hat with long, scraggly gray hair. The halls were quiet, so delivery was quick. What a joy it was to do this! I was like a kid again. It truly is more blessed to give than to receive!

Then there are the elections. Normally, I like watching the process. My political science professor, John, was always glued to the television and kept up a non-stop narrative. But this year has been different. There is so much vitriol and negativity. I find myself turning the television off.

Covid brain? I am quite overwhelmed. This morning I was sure that the votes would have been counted and we would know who the next president would be. Wrong!! So, I still am in a state of turmoil. I tell myself you are just too old for this—then, not at all. It's covid brain!

Covid Relief

WRITTEN FEBRUARY 26, 2021

I THINK WE CAN ALL AGREE THAT COVID ISOLATION, though completely necessary, takes its toll. I know that this is true in my case. I also believe that we all need something to love—it can be a weekly card game, or watching a sports event, or working out in the gym together.

For me, in my sedentary life, it is the joy I receive when my Sammy squirrel comes to the sliding glass door, stands erect, folding his front paws (as if to pray!) and gives me a look, saying, "Feed me."

I first have to tell him how beautiful he is, how perfectly he is made. Those little ears seem to hear the least sound. The sound of my chair no longer frightens him, and his attitude towards me is total acceptance. I am certain, quite frankly, that he knows I love him!

One day, after he devoured all the peanuts and came to the door, it was clear the question was "more"! At that point my internal dialogue was: No way am I going to open the door because he will come in.

So, I took a single peanut. We continued this for a while until his hunger was satisfied.

What a blessing to be able to see this, animals just trying to stay alive. A squirrel's life span is only about three years. I guess Sammy is middle age. I had thought that a squirrel's tail was made for balance, but it also provides extra insulation for him when he brings it up and over his back.

I brought the bowl from my bird bath back in Maryland to Lincoln. And, with the help of a warming ring, fresh water is always available, and he promotes good mental health. Sammy—and he knows his name—brought me such pleasure. It is a diversion of the every day monotony.

I have always loved wildlife. Just last week, I heard a crow cawing. I would answer him with the same, and we "talked" about five minutes. The Bob White birds in Maryland would respond to me until my whistle dissolved. This connection to nature is so fulfilling.

Coping

WRITTEN MARCH 5, 2021

WITH THE COVID ISOLATION, I HAVE THOUGHT A LOT about my coping skills as a child, dealing with polio. I realize that so many times I floated above any situation. At first I was too sick to think. I cried because I hurt and Mother and Daddy couldn't be in the room to comfort me.

Then, I mentally withdrew; I just *was*. The only thing I reacted to was the Sister Kenny Hotpacks. Those hot wool strips of fabric were so hot they could and did cause blisters. The technicians used tongs to pick them up from the machine and put on my legs. For years I blocked that memory.

Mother never missed a Thursday visiting day for the fifteen months I was hospitalized. Daddy somehow convinced the powers that were to allow him to visit on Sundays. It was important for me to relate to them. Yet, I had forgotten so much. Still, we had few points of reference.

The one thing I remembered when they talked with me was Snowball the cat who belonged to my grandparents. Sometimes these visiting hours just stirred too many emotions, and it would take another 24 hours to find that neutral zone.

Some children forgot who their parents were. One little girl stood at the end of her crib and would ask, "Are you my mommy?" to each woman who came into the ward. Can you imagine the bombardment of stimuli when I finally went home? I didn't remember so many people. Home was strange. Yet, given a few months, home was really home.

This ability to "zone out" during difficult times is a true dimension given us all. The first time I returned to the hospital for a checkup, I was so frightened. The dread of that place was almost overpowering. I couldn't sleep the night before, couldn't eat breakfast. I just knew they wouldn't let me return home.

After a muscle test and a consultation with the doctor, we were on our way home again. Yet, this fear of being hospitalized again always stayed with me. When the car reached the Chesapeake Bay ferry, I could begin to relax. Never let it be said that fear doesn't wrap itself around you, and the angst is never far away.

That neutral zone sort of a suspended animation has carried me through numerous times of stress. Two muscle transplant surgeries a year apart activated that defense mechanism. By then, I was thirteen and fourteen years old. All I could think of was a back-to-school writing paper of what I did those summers. Boring!

Do I still use my "zone out" valve? I do. At my advanced age, I see faith as my security blanket. We aren't promised a rose garden, but we are promised that we are not alone and will be given strength to endure. Too often we forget how wonderfully we are made, and our ability to make mental adjustments is part of the package.

Least or Last

WRITTEN JANUARY 29, 2020

IT HAS ALWAYS BEEN MY FIRM BELIEF THAT GOD put me here to be neither judge nor jury. Even as a young school girl, I did not like the THEM versus US mentality.

I always chose the "least or last" to be a part of my team or who would assist me on the playground.

And guess what? They always proved to be more than worthy.

Recently, I had two young women visit. They had phoned to ask if I would be available! Shortly thereafter, I heard the doorbell ring and, upon opening the door, I saw the two young women—one was a normal, attractive woman; the other had purple hair standing straight out from her head. I invited them in, and they said they just needed to briefly speak to me.

Ms. Normal Attractive hastened to apologize, and said she was sorry not to have warned me of the purple-haired one. I immediately looked at the purple hair, and said, "Oh, honey, purple hair doesn't bother me in the least." The look she gave me was amazement followed by a look of pure gratitude.

Maybe because of my disability, I am more aware of the stigma of being different. To be less than is never an enviable position.

That is probably why I never wanted handicapped license plates. They could make me more vulnerable. After I married, I didn't think it was much of a problem.

When actually it happened anyway, John had gone into a store to get ice cream after parking in a handicapped parking space. As he walked from the store, two ice cream cones in his hand, a middle aged man glared at him and shouted, "You sure don't look handicapped."

"Actually," John said," she is" pointing to me waiting in the car. Not believing John at all, he shouted an obscenity and entered the store.

Of course, I became just as angry when a carload of young people park in the handicapped parking places. And John had flyers printed with "Stupidity doesn't count as a disability." One night a car owner read it and wanted to fight John who very rationally tried to explain the reason for such papers.

You can talk, talk, talk, or bicker, bicker, bicker, but the bottom line will still be right versus wrong. And, generally speaking, most people know this. Let's hope our legislators do.

Over the Christmas holidays I received a note with a return address that was familiar, but I didn't recognize the name on the return address. Upon opening the note, I read that my friend had died, but her relative wanted to let me know. I had sent her a Christmas card.

Ellen was at college with me and I always felt a special bond with her. Maybe because she had health problems. The glasses she wore were thick as coke bottles. We always kept in touch.

Ellen's relative said she spoke of me often and loved my notes, and she knew that I would want to know. What I didn't know was that Ellen suffered from a birth defect all of her life.

Friendship is such a strong bond and enriches our lives beyond all measure.

God Incidences

WRITTEN MARCH 12, 2020

WELL, ANOTHER WEEK OF ISOLATION HAS PASSED. More and more people speak of the feeling of being so alone. I am convinced that in any form of deprivation, we can find joy. Even more, it is to our benefit to do so.

I experienced such a reminder, what I call a "God Incidence," just this week. One morning, sitting at the breakfast table, drinking my coffee, I looked on the balcony and saw a robin sitting on the railing, staring at me. Immediately, I exclaimed, "Rosie, you are back."

With that, she hopped down and came closer to the door. I rushed to get the raisins. She backed away as I put the raisins on the floor, and before I could get in the door, a grateful Rosie was enjoying her raisins. She remembered me and knew where to come.

I am blown away. Never did I think a robin would or could remember such. How much we still have to learn about all living creatures.

Now, why am I so surprised at this most recent "God Incidence"? It's for sure it isn't my first one. Many years ago, John and I struggled with the demands that came with our son's musical talent. By then, Mark was twelve years old, not yet able to drive, and was invited to perform all over the country. It was impossible to send him off by himself.

He had been invited to perform in San Francisco. Obviously, I couldn't accompany him alone. It was a real dilemma. My role as a mother was my greatest privilege. To be locked out would have been absolutely devastating.

The phone rang. It was my father. He said, "You three must be together. Go ahead with reservations. They will be covered."

How did he know? Another "God Incident."

I have fairly often been in situations where, confronted with steps, my destination became impossible. Without fail, someone would come along and offer the help I needed. God incidence?

And sometimes I am quite sure God has a marvelous sense of humor. Case in point: John and I were visiting Robert E. Lee's birthplace, only to find that there were a series of steps that led up to the house. A young black man offered to help. And when we finished the steps, we thanked him profusely.

Minutes later, John said, "I believe we just saw divine justice—a black man helping a white couple up the steps at the home of a leader in the Confederacy."

So, maybe I'm a cock-eyed optimist. But it surely beats doom and gloom!

Joy Unbounded

WRITTEN AUGUST 3, 2018

IT HAS BEEN A JOYOUS WEEK. My dear friend Marge has spent the week with me. As my former neighbor in Maryland, we know each other very well. And we laugh a lot. Our wacky senses of humor blend, and even encourage both of us to get even more wacky.

We also share the more serious side of life—our health issues, what we will do if and when. Of course, it almost goes without saying we talk about our children and grandchildren.

We watched the sunset last night, and both of us got somewhat contemplative—something you can only do with a friend.

Then there was the party. I loved seeing so many special friends gather to meet "my" Marge. Yes, I'm rather possessive!

Everyone chatting, friendly voices creating a happy atmosphere. I'll feed on that time a long while.

As I began planning for this week, I was on such a high. The old adrenaline flowed, and is still flowing. I love these times. They are like gold nuggets you cherish always.

On Monday, Mark drove us to Henderson where we toured the recreated Mennonite Village. The tour guide was magnificent. We all learned so much.

Did you know that Wilbur Hershey was a Mennonite? As was the founder of Kraft Foods? John Denver's family? And Dwight Eisenhower's mother?

The railroad was instrumental in bringing the Mennonites to Nebraska. They bought land, not from the government, but the railroad. I learned that "zwieback" given to teething babies originated from the Mennonites.

We had lunch at a little cafe where many of the "good ole' boys" had gathered. Proof that the food was good. And it was!

It is Restaurant Week in Lincoln, and we have enjoyed quite a few, with good conversation always.

How blessed I am. I had a gift on the guest room bed for Marge. It captures my feelings exactly. The little pillow reads, "You are the friend everyone wishes they had."

I couldn't have said it better myself.

The Lost Emotion

WRITTEN AUGUST 17, 2018

I REMEMBER MY FATHER TELLING ME THAT HE WAS READY to leave this world. Too much had changed. There was no real sense of right and wrong. I find myself in the very same position. There is something definitely missing, not only in politicians, but to a great extent in too many of our population.

Case in point. I have a distant relative (actually, John's relative) who has cancer. The type of cancer has not been determined, and won't be for another six weeks. Why? Because the diagnostic doctors don't have any open appointment until then!

Six weeks for this cancer to grow, and it grows quickly. The band-aid approach is offered—they will give all the pain pills needed. Maybe this salves the medical conscience. But in all likelihood the patient will die before six weeks.

What kind of medical system is this? How many others in this U.S.A. are in the same situation? We are told we have the best medical care in the world. Really?

Several years ago, I needed to have my braces re-covered. Calve's leather has always been used because it is so soft to the skin. I had started to make some contacts through Johns Hopkins Hospital in Baltimore. There was a choice of one, and it was doubtful that he could do the work due to frailty and age.

Then we learned that The Landing had an apartment for us. Brace work postponed! After settling in somewhat, we started our inquiry. There was one man in Lincoln who, years and years ago, had worked on caliper braces. God is good! He re-covered my braces, and then retired.

But what about someone else who might need brace work done? Do we just fall through the cracks? With today's Internet, you would think a specialist of this sort could be located. The one such polio specialist at Mayo Clinic is in Dubai for a year!

Some years ago, I had a breast cancer scare. I went to Johns Hopkins for an exam. The doctor said, "I will need to put you under anesthesia to do this biopsy." He rolled me into the operating room and asked if I could get on the table. I had had enough tranquilizers that I turned to him and said, "If you want me up there, you'll have to put me there." And he did.

When I awoke a few hours later, he was sitting by my side. At the follow-up appointment, I was given an all clear. I was overjoyed with the news. But, even more, I was grateful for the care.

The missing emotion is compassion—the relative with cancer told to come back in six weeks. You are talking life and death here. Where is the compassion here?

The gentleman who did the brace work for me had compassion in spades. And the doctor who took such good care of me after the biopsy made such a difference.

Care and compassion are what makes us human. Without these qualities, life is so very diminished.

There is a beautiful statue of Christ in the rotunda of Johns Hopkins Hospital. People from all over the world come here. And often, as they pray at the statue, they rub the big toe of Christ. Over the years, the big toe has become completely smooth—evidence of care and compassion for all to see.

A Junkie, Perhaps

WRITTEN OCTOBER 19, 2018

Once again I'm a captive of the news. I'm beginning to think that I am a news junkie. On second thought, I AM A NEWS JUNKIE!

The psychology in me loves to analyze leaders and cultures. This "big ole" world can be quite entertaining and, at present, terribly distressing.

Most distressing for me at this time is the surprising occurrence of a virus which attacks the spinal cord of young children.

My heart races when I see a child crying in pain and sobbing. I can't move my leg. I can't move my arm. That child's fear is almost tangible. I know that pain and I know that fear.

I had come to believe that any viral attacks on the spinal cord were pretty much under control. Then came the nightmarish news that children were becoming paralyzed much like the polio virus did in the '30's, '40's, and '50's.

How could it be? No one is quite sure what is happening or why. What comes to my mind is: "Could that polio virus have mutated?"

Reporters are saying that some have fully recovered from this miserable virus, but there are others left with some degree of reduced use of parts of their body.

I think, of the reports I have read, that many people who are now diagnosed with Post Polio Syndrome did not even know they ever had polio! As a child, they remembered being very sick and being left with some body weakness, yet eventually they became fully functional again.

My fervent prayer is that medical science is hard at work to identify this virus and find how to be safe from its poison.

I don't think I can look at any more cases of this disease. I never thought that I was a coward. However, in this case, I know too much.

Character

WRITTEN APRIL 1, 2021

WHAT DETERMINES CHARACTER? In the simplest terms, an honest answer would be "life." But I think it is so much more. Certainly the gene pool dictates a good amount of character; yet, time and circumstances are part of the equation also. As a young child, my approach to anything was: Why? It drove my family crazy and the response was, often, because I said so. Yet, there was still a lot of curiosity.

I loved riding my tricycle, especially if Mother was riding her bicycle. But, I didn't want her to be too far ahead of me. Consequently, I pedaled straight into her back wheel. I didn't just do this once, I did it every time we rode together. To my knowledge, it was the only time she ever gave up on me. That bond lasted until the day she died.

Daddy would read to me each night when I got into bed. I loved the stories (peppered with my proverbial "Whys"!) Years later, Daddy told me that one night as he started to read, he was so very tired, that he kept falling asleep, so he asked me to tell him a story. I began to elaborate on the story of "The Three Bears." As he told me years later, my imagination took off. He could not believe the elaborate tale I was telling him, as he was fully awake and somewhat mesmerized.

By then, we always had two phones: the house phone and an office phone. One day the office phone rang, and even though I was not supposed to answer it, I did. The caller asked for Mr. Kennerly, and feeling so very important, I replied, "I'll see if I can *rocate* him." The man was still laughing when Daddy picked up the phone. I liked words even then!

The advent of polio caused a lot of character building. First, my self image was completely changed. Somehow, I knew I was still Mary Ann, but it was so hard to hear: "Why are you so different?" "What happened to your legs?" "Why do you have that 'funny' chair?" And all the whispering about my condition. All I wanted was to be like everyone else. So, in today's parlance, I internalized the hurt.

Dear readers, there were some perks. When Richard Nixon made a campaign stop at my high school, someone in the crowd pointed to me standing in the front row on crutches, and he said, "Nice to see you, sweetheart."

A lot of years later, my husband John and I had been on vacation in Florida. When driving through Georgia, I saw signs to Warm Springs. It is almost "a given" that we were the first visitors of the day. I waited in my chair as John gave her money for two tickets. This dear little Southern lady gave the money back to John, and he said, "But I need two tickets." At which point the ticket agent said, "Oh, no, the lady is our guest."

It was such a dear response. And as she looked at me, her eyes locked on mine and she said, "I know." That said everything!!! As I got older, I became more and more feisty. As evidence: I was being examined for a muscle check up. The young doctor came in the room, looked at me in my chair, and said, "Let's get you on the table." There was no one else in the room, and he obviously wasn't going to help me. The words came out of my mouth before I could even think: "If you want me up there, you'll have to put me up there."

With my coaching, he got me on the examining table and started looking at my left ankle. He asked if I had had an accident, and I replied, "No. Triple Arthodesis." He gave up and hastily left the room. It must have been his first semester of Med school! I really didn't mean to embarrass him, but I figured if I knew these things, he certainly should. Or, he should have read my chart!

Now I'm even older and medical care for polio is just about nonexistent. I find myself over and over trying to educate the doctor at hand: "A dead muscle is a dead muscle, and no amount of exercise will change that." But, if nothing else, I am an antique, a certifiable one! I tried explaining my character to a friend. In doing so, I said maybe I was just too dumb to give up. So, we all have character, some more than others. I think the recipe is "Vim, Vigor and Vitality"!!

Inspirations

WRITTEN NOVEMBER 2, 2018

I THINK I'M EASILY INSPIRED. I'M JUST WIRED THAT WAY. The autumn foliage from our apartment has been exquisite, like a painting, really. It is there just for the looking.

The ducks in the pond form their own flotilla. How do they know to do that?

The moon last weekend was so very beautiful. And when a black cloud covered it only to reveal it again a short time later, it seemed to have enhanced both the brightness and the fullness of the moon itself.

For all of these things, I breathe a little thank you prayer.

So many people from time to time lift my spirits by a smile, a note, or just a pat as they go by. In all of our church homes, it just happened that when members would approach the altar for communion, many would pat my shoulder as they passed me, always on the front row. I felt so very blessed.

These acts of kindness are the very fabric of my life. My faith has always been a strong influence on my life. I don't think I could have survived without it.

I shall never forget when Mark completed work for his Masters at Peabody Conservatory, he applied to Rice University to begin his doctoral degree.

I knew how much he wanted this, yet for Mama Bear it was a drastic step. The fledgling would leave the nest. I wasn't ready for this.

John and I had planned an anniversary trip to Nashville, and I reluctantly left home. A few days into the trip, we were touring city sites and waiting for a call from Mark about his acceptance or his nonacceptance to Rice.

We happened by the Upper Room Chapel. I told John I would like to go there and pray.

So at 2:00 o'clock we entered the chapel where I asked God to do what was best for Mark, not me. And the greatest sense of peace came over me. It is difficult to explain, yet John could see that something happened.

Thirty minutes later, Mark called to say the phone rang at 2:00 o'clock inviting him to come to Rice for his doctoral work.

I was at last at peace with the move, and never looked back. Yet I must admit that I set the dinner table for three people for months!

Another inspirational moment was when the little five-year-old girl gave me her flower that her Sunday School teacher had given to each child to brighten someone's day.

She could have given it to anyone, but she deliberately chose me. What a treasured moment in time!

The same is true at the ticket office at F.D.R.'s Warm Springs, Georgia home. The ticket agent, when seeing me in my chair, returned my ticket money, saying, "Oh, no, the lady is our guest!" Her eyes seemed to say, "I know the battles you have fought."

Being recognized for having polio was something quite unexpected, yet I was grateful.

Music is one of life's finest gifts. It often transports me into a whole other sphere. When at sixteen years of age Mark played Rachmaninoff III concerts with the Washington Symphony at the Kennedy Center, I just knew that Angels in Heaven sat down to listen. It was magical.

And, yes, I'm sure I'm somewhat prejudiced!

So all of these moments are cherished. My grateful heart is overflowing with each and every blessing.

Limitations/Accommodations

WRITTEN JUNE 17, 2021

IS OLD AGE A CONDITION WHERE YOU BEGIN TO UNRAVEL? To return to a state of mind of being like that of a newborn? I am beginning to think so. I rant and rage at every diminution of strength and mental capacity.

There are those who will say, "Well, your case is different." I grant you that, but having gone through being a helpless infant, to being a helpless six-year-old, to becoming a helpless eighty-two-year-old leaves me in a very irritated state.

My motto was: *Accommodation. If I can't do it the so called "normal way," maybe I can achieve the desired result by some fine tuning with the desired results.* Not always perfect, but for seventy-six I made it work. Now I am running out of options. I couldn't walk with my braces and crutches across the floor any more than I could fly.

That leaves me with arms and shoulders to do all the work. You can guess what comes next? Well, shoulders can slip in the sockets and you fast lose all the remaining strength in the shoulders and arms.

Let's just say this doesn't improve my disposition. I am running out of options here.

Then I play Lucille Ball and become my own therapist. "Okay, Mary Ann, let's work with what you got."

Do I need to remind you my brain can get tangled easily? I remember some events, but the names of people at the event? Forget it. I have always loved history. But dates? I'd forget my own birthday!

This all sounds dismal, yet that's not all she wrote. There is a sustaining force here—it is faith. Early on, when I was very sick, I still said my prayers. I complained and begged for a miracle, but that was not the plan, and I came to terms with that, probably in my teen years.

Now, it is my desire that at the end of my life I would qualify to hear the words, “Well done, my good and faithful servant.”

My Sister—of the Heart

WRITTEN MAY 31, 2019

SHE HAS BEEN IN MY LIFE FROM THE VERY BEGINNING. She was four years old when I was born. From an early age, we spent time together —overnights at her house or at my house.

For the most part, we were compatible, but I’m sure at certain times she could have very well done without me. Loraine was a “steady as you go” child, while I was the “full steam ahead” child.

Loraine would access the situation and calmly proceed. I, on the other hand, considered only the goal and would rush pell mell ahead.

Just in our last years, she would tell me she really didn’t like that I would begin any playtime by taking all her dolls outside. She has told me I was rough and she was always the one to return all the dolls back into the house to the playroom.

Loraine was the one to try and teach me to ride a bike. I was fine until she removed her hand from the bicycle fender. Then down I would go on the street, knees scraped and bleeding. Her mother would put iodine on the cuts and a band-aid, and out we would go again.

In the last few years, Loraine has told me that she wondered if I would ever have ridden a bike. Like everything else, I’m sure I would not have given up.

The year before, I had taught myself how to ride a scooter. It was deluxe—with balloon tires, and I wore out a pair of shoes riding it. Mother kept those shoes for many years.

When I started eighth grade, Loraine and I were in the same high school, which secretly delighted me. She would check on me at first because I came from a class of three to one of one hundred twenty.

We were at very different stages of life—Loraine was full of life and laughter, ("Giggle Box" was her nickname), and was very much in the dating scene. I, on the other hand, was awkward and definitely not sure where I would ever fit in.

After completing high school, Loraine got a job and soon got a husband. I was in her wedding and, oh, how I loved that! The evening dress that I wore was a lush shade of blue—and I'm sure I wore it to dances years later.

When I was in college, we didn't have as much time together. On holidays, we would see each other, and soon John was a part of the group. John and I became Godparents to her second son, Jeff.

Loraine had her "Irma Bombeck" moments. I remember one in particular. Her boys had been playing in the front yard, riding tricycles up and down the sidewalks. On the grass was a wide assortment of toys. She had called the boys in for lunch and a short rest afterwords.

Then she realized the semi disaster area on the yard and sidewalk. Out she went to retrieve the tricycle two doors away and the array of toys. In a split second, she decided to ride the tricycle back to the house and pick up toys on the way. Think "adult woman on a child's tricycle, loaded with toys, heading home."

Unfortunately, she must have hit a bump, and Loraine, toys and tricycle were thrown to the street. She was injured; had to call her parents to take her to the emergency room. She had some severe cuts that needed stitches, but it could have been worse. I didn't help any when I asked her "where was her helmet?"

"Why did the moron drink a bottle of iodine? So he could dream in Technicolor!"

Loraine often went on vacation trips with me. One summer it was Boston; another it was northern New York state. We could get pretty rowdy at night, much to my parents' dismay. They were ready to sleep, but that was the fartherest thing from our young minds. We were too busy with Moron jokes!

Loraine was my matron of honor when I got married. She developed heart problems in her early forties and had to have open heart surgery. That was traumatizing to everyone in the family. But, thankfully, she survived, became a single parent, and raised three fine children.

In the last months, she started having breathing problems, was in and out of the hospital. It was determined that there was a hole in one of the arteries of the heart. She chose to undergo a procedure to patch that hole which, at this time, seems to have been successful.

I was on my "Hotline to Heaven" for two days! I can't lose her yet. She is my only link left to my early life. We have a relationship like no other. I, quite simply, love her.

A View in the Rear View Mirror

WRITTEN SEPTEMBER 17, 2021

LOOKING THROUGH MY WRITINGS, I detect a trait of personality, a way of expression. From whence it came, I don't know.

It started early in my life. I was four or five years old. The telephone rang and I ran to answer it. It just so happened that it was the business phone (Daddy, I believe, was home for lunch). And when I answered with my best professional voice, the caller asked to speak to Mr. Kennerly. I politely responded with, "I'll try to *rocate* him."

My father, fearing any more conversation from me, grabbed the phone. The caller was laughing so hard, he could scarcely talk.

In the same time frame I was following my mother as she was doing the weekly cleaning, when a car parked across the road, and I wanted to know who it was. She answered, "Ann."

I was puzzled. "Mary Ann, you mean?" Mother replied, "No, her name is just plain Ann."

Satisfied, I yelled out of the open window, "Hi, plain Ann." Mother was horrified, and later in the day called the family to apologize.

In the first month of my first grade, I got locked in the girls' bathroom when the wind blew the door closed and then locked. I pushed the screen from the window and jumped the six and a half feet to the ground. I seem to see evidence of determination here!

As a senior in high school, having a car made life even better. My girlfriend and I had been to the movies and were returning home. All of a sudden, I realized we were being followed. The car would come close, then back off on this dark wooded road.

Ellen said, "If we just had more people in the car, maybe they would go away."

I had my round pouch pocketbook which I rested on one of my crutches, and Ellen turned the pocketbook as if a head was turning. The car backed off, and we had the road to ourselves once again.

Fast forward a few years, and I was followed north on the Garden State Parkway on my way back to Drew University. I gave no turn signal, but got on the right street without them being able to follow.

If they had been halfway smart, they would have seen my Drew University sticker in the back window of my car and probably easily followed me.

Here again, my back was against the wall, but determination ruled the day. Or some might say, "you just are too dumb to give up."

A God Incident

WRITTEN AUGUST 8, 2019

IT HAS BEEN NO SECRET THAT I HAVE BEEN VERY CONFLICTED about my church attendance. When Westminster Presbyterian Church changed their times of worship, my attendance was severely impacted.

John and I visited many churches when we moved here, and we felt that Westminster was a great fit for us. Church has always been a top priority for us, and Westminster satisfied our souls and even challenged us.

Then the change of time was announced and there was no way I could get myself physically ready to leave for church at 9:00 a.m. Without John, it takes me longer to prepare myself for the day. I must not hurry because it increases the chance of falling.

I have been fortunate enough to find someone to drive me to church, but the early hour was problematic.

I have visited First Plymouth a number of times. Their accessibility is perfect—a long ramp into the church, and an elevator ramp into the church, and an elevator to take you to the sanctuary.

Still, I agonized. Several Sundays ago, it was decided that we would again visit First Plymouth. It was a beautiful summer day and we were running a little late. The parking lot was full except for one handicapped space.

Gerri got my wheelchair out of the car, and I planted myself and was ready to go. We were the only two people out there.

Suddenly, I found myself propelled out of the chair onto the concrete. The front wheels of my chair hit a tiny curb and I was airborne.

The (Carillon had finished playing, and everyone had gathered inside. Suddenly, five angels, disguised as normal people, appeared. "How can we help you?" they asked.

Somewhat dazed, I instructed them how best to get me on my feet, at which time I could sit back on my chair. I dusted myself off, thanked my angels profusely, and went into church.

I was most concerned about Gerri. As you can imagine, she felt terrible. I assured her that such incidents have been a part of my life for seventy-four years. No big deal.

Minutes later as we sat in the pew, the words came to mind, "You know you really are a stubborn old woman. It took falling at the curb of God's house to remind you God's people are everywhere."

How could I forget that? In that short period of time, a veil was lifted, the world seemed brighter, and my heart was filled with joy. Lesson learned.

Hallelujah!

Attempt to Accommodate

WRITTEN JUNE 24, 2021

HAVE YOU EVER SEEN SO MUCH HATE IN THE WORLD? Differences have become giant flaws. And the language on all media has become vile and in the gutter.

What is missing here? Has the church forgotten to spread the value of each person in God's sight? Yes, there will be some bad apples throughout the ages, but somehow we must learn differences are not all bad.

I recently read an article by a young man who has cerebral palsy. He stated, "First and foremost, my disability does not define me." He, like so many disabled people, knew there was more of him than the obvious disease.

I can't tell you how many times people would speak to me as if my brain was paralyzed, not just my muscles. John would always have a comeback, sometimes to the point that the person wanted to fight. Not me. That would have been easy. But John, who never believed in a physical fight, would declare a war of words.

Compare that to a question by a child, "Why are you in that chair?" Or, "What is wrong with your legs?" Parents are mortified. I see it differently. They recognize that I am different and want to know why!

If you can't explain, they will continue to spot the differences. But when I tell them that "When I was their age, there was no medicine to make me better; now there is. Aren't you lucky!"

History just seems to repeat itself. The white man comes to this new land and, from the beginning, saw the Indians "lesser than."

Yet, the Puritans left Britain because they were not able to follow their beliefs.

Today, we have migrants crossing our southern border; some just children, now living in warehouses—packed in those warehouses.

Those children, no doubt, will be scarred for life. This isn't new. There has to be a better solution.

Minds far better than mine should have a plan, not just warehousing people. At least attempt to accommodate. Who knows? We may discover a spectacular scientist, writer or even a leader! Viva la difference!

Escape Route

WRITTEN AUGUST 24, 2018

I HATE TO WRITE THIS, BUT sometimes my imagination works overtime. And it has been doing so quite a bit lately.

I sit on my balcony in good weather and watch other people going about their daily routines. I know very little, if any at all, about these people. So what I don't see, my fertile imagination fills in the blanks.

For instance, there is a car that rolls frequently into the parking lot across the pond at dusk. No one exits the car, which stays there for at least an hour. What is going on?

Occasionally, another car arrives, and the driver gets into the first car. Um hm! A tryst? Young people? Middle-aged people? A couple choosing to argue away from the children? My imagination goes wild. I chide myself and leave the balcony.

Some time later, the headlights of a car come on, and a car leaves. Shortly, the headlights of the second car appear, and the car drives away. How do I know these things? The headlights shine through my bedroom window!

To a more sinister thought, is this a drug transaction? My imagination is in overdrive. Then there are the visitors going into Harbor House, a memory care facility. You often see parents cautioning their young ones on proper behavior while visiting their loved one.

It seems probable that advice goes in one ear and out the other. Yet, when these little ones emerge from their visit, all the pent up energy has to erupt. Some children show sadness they expected to see the loved one in good health as before. Some young ones are angry. Maybe they misbehaved while visiting, or they can't quite comprehend the change that has occurred. It is a lot to understand.

I revealed my imagination at an early age. I do remember that Daddy read me a story just before bedtime every night. One night, as the story goes, he said he was so very sleepy that he could scarcely keep his eyes open, so he invited me to tell him a story.

Of course, I chose my favorite—The Three Bears. And I guess I embellished the story to the point he was no longer sleepy. He said he didn't know where I got all those thoughts, but my new story was utterly fascinating!

Why does my mind work this way? I think, because of my disability, I have done a lot of waiting. Waiting for a doctor, a therapist, waiting for someone to take me somewhere, waiting while a parent went into a store, or pick up meds from the pharmacy, do banking, etc.

If I didn't have a book, I think I made up my own story—self entertainment. Fortunately, my brain was always ready for the job and always, always there was a happy ever after ending. It couldn't get much better now, could it?

I suppose it could be said that, once again, it goes back to that little six-year-old girl whose entire life was turned upside down in a matter of forty-eight hours. She had to learn how to escape the pain and fear and the many hours of monotony.

Polio may have had an impact on my brain, but my imagination is alive and flourishing!

Dark Sides Revisited

WRITTEN APRIL 5, 2019

EVERYBODY HAS A "DARK SIDE." John certainly had his. It became more and more apparent the older he became. John always encouraged me to write. But when I did write, he wanted to change some sentences. And when he typed one week's writing, he changed much of the content.

That was the end of that, as far as I was concerned. I knew that what I wrote was me, that it was how I felt and saw things. My life experiences are mine—good, bad, or ugly. He never stopped trying to read what I wrote, but I never allowed that to happen again.

I would be remiss if I didn't acknowledge my own dark side. It revolves around my disability. I can't find a doctor who has a background with or knowledge of polio. If, perchance, a medic tried C.P.R. on me, it would kill me instantly.

My ribcage, riddled with osteoporosis, would collapse; and, since it is so twisted, many organs are no longer in place.

I keep telling myself: The good thing is that polio has been so reduced, most doctors are not familiar with the best approach to treat the thirty-eight-thousand remaining victims. The bad thing is, I am in that thirty-eight-thousand group, so I stew and fret.

I hate losing more strength. I have no compromising left. Then I accuse myself of malingering which, to me, is an abomination. It got so bad that I went to my polio bible—which opened to a random page. I could have written that paragraph myself, Bruno. "The Polio Paradox", Page 157, Chapter 11, Brain Brownout.

It is the not knowing what some of these symptoms mean that makes it so difficult. Unfortunately, I don't handle "wait and see" very well. As the song says, "I want it all and I want it now." The "it" being information!

On a lighter side, after reading the daily Peanuts strip comic, I was reminded of my sister of the heart's Beagle. Her son Jeff brought him home one day—just a puppy. There was no question, they would keep him. They had had dogs before. Their neighbor had a chain link fence dividing their property, so it was fairly easy to fence the remaining two sides.

I asked Loraine if the dog ever got out. "Oh, yes," she said, "He climbed the chain link fence."

Beagles are determined dogs. This one was given the name "Herman" after the mailman! Beagle Herman knew when the postman was three houses away, and would start howling. I wonder if the postman ever knew that the dog was named after him?

My life is so much more than a Polio Paradox. There is still wonder each and every day—just take time to look!

Fear

WRITTEN APRIL 19, 2019

I WOULD NEVER SAY MY LIFE IS RULED BY FEAR. But it would be fair to say fear has played, and plays, a big part in my life.

My first days or weeks in school were terrifying. I didn't know what was expected of me. It was all so confusing. I had never been with so many children. And when the teacher excused me to go to the bathroom, I knew she meant that I was excused for a very short time.

Imagine my fear when the door of the bathroom refused to open to allow me to go back to the classroom! I pulled, I tugged, I yelled, and nothing. What to do?

The only thing left was to exit from the window.

I don't even think I thought my plan was dangerous. To me, the thought that I would be chastised in front of everyone would be the worst thing ever. So, I jumped the five-foot drop from the bathroom window, went around the building, and entered via the front door.

I'm sure my heart was pounding loud enough to be heard as I finally re-entered the classroom. Of course, the teacher asked what took me so long, and I explained as best as I could. The teacher checked it out and, indeed, it was locked. But I remember the fear—I was so terribly afraid.

In the spring of 1945, I saw my first movie with my paternal grandmother and my mother. I have only since forgotten the movie. It is what followed that is so memorable. After seeing the movie, mother said she needed to use the restroom.

So, Gram and I waited in the lobby. When mother returned, we hastened to leave the theater, only to discover all the doors were locked and we were the only people there.

I was not comforted at all by my mother or grandmother. We knocked on the glass doors, hoping to attract some passersby. I was terrified. Suddenly, that lobby became a closet and I wanted out.

Somehow, mother was able to enter the office where there was a telephone. Years later, I wonder if she had to pick the lock on the office door. It seemed like days before someone came and unlocked the doors.

Needless to say, it was quite a while before I wanted to go to a movie again. It always seemed sinister to have to sit in the dark among strangers to watch a movie.

I was too sick for fear when I was stricken with polio. I don't remember much about the early weeks. I guess I was only partly conscious then. I do remember insisting that a chair be put by my bed for my mother. When the nurses couldn't calm me down, they brought a chair next to the bed. Obviously, psychology wasn't a part of their program.

By the time I was transferred to Children's Hospital, I was lethargic. I remember the leafless trees I saw on that ambulance ride. It was all so stark. My mind was a blank slate until mother and daddy entered my room at Children's Hospital. It was the first time they could touch me, kiss my cheek.

Probably in that moment, I was relieved and bewildered. After the brief visit, they had to leave again. I couldn't understand that. The fear returns—will they really come back? Another soggy pillow!

When I returned home fifteen months later, I was still a mental blank—not fearful, just passive. Fear came when I was around other children, when I saw myself through their eyes.

I couldn't change my physical self, but I fought a long battle for years to make myself a part of their lives. And, looking back, I think I succeeded.

Each change in life brought new fears. After going home again, I had to return to the hospital monthly for about four months. Then it was decided I would return for check-ups every three months.

This is when fear crept back again. I was home. I had a place in the family. At one of my check-ups, would the doctor want to put me back in the hospital?

That was a fear worse than death. I started to be fearful days before the check-up. At the hotel the night before, I could scarcely eat or sleep. And the day did come when they wanted me to come back for surgery. I tried not to think, but that didn't change a surgery date.

My parents did everything in their power to keep my mind otherwise occupied. Their solution was to have a private nurse with me throughout my stay in the hospital. It saved my sanity.

Yet, somewhere, I have proof that fear was still with me. In a crossword puzzle book the night before surgery, I wrote "completed by Mary Ann Kennerly, June 1953."

Fear is not always bad. It can cause us to look at alternatives or it can, and does, increase the adrenalin flow to enable us to escape or retreat. It's the old Fight or Flight rule. In my case, Flight was never an option!

TO BE CONTINUED!

Fear
Part 2

WRITTEN APRIL 26, 2019

FEAR IS A NORMAL RESPONSE TO DIFFICULT SITUATIONS. We all have fears and deal with them in our own individual ways.

Growing up, my parents could usually cushion my fears. Yet, there were still many adjustments that only I could deal with. I knew I was different from anyone else in school.

Yet, like everyone else, all I wanted was to be a part of my peer group. Girls usually were won over fairly easy. Boys were a whole other situation. Their curriculum was sports. Not much room for me there.

It was pretty pathetic to always be on the side lines. I would watch boys and girls play a sport, how their bodies could move, reach, run, until I just couldn't plaster a smile on my face anymore.

Beach parties were big growing up. I couldn't wear braces in the sand, so I saw myself as a lump—someone had to carry me to the beach and to the water. There wasn't much joy in Mudville!

Disability was, and would always be, my reality, and I was the only one who could manage it. Those teen years were rough, but something happened in the summer between high school and college. Maturation? Surely, that was a part of it.

But in my mind, I began to see that maybe there would be a place for me—not in a corner by a window, but where I could be a part of a community, a contributing part of a community.

College gave me that. Perhaps that is why I majored in psychology—I wanted to more understand the thinking pattern of a human and possibly be able to reduce their fears of the unknown challenges and point them to a meaningful life.

I will always regret not continuing my education, but I surely don't regret the path that I chose. John and Mark added untold joy to my life.

But fear was still my companion in that new life. I remember thinking, "Oh, God, what have I done?" when they put Mark in my arms. Somehow, maternal instinct kicked in and I seldom doubted myself.

But fear of the unknown is always there. Without John, I have to reconstruct so much of my life. Each step seems harder and harder. I must find someone to drive me to appointments, then I have to consider who can and cannot help me move from place to place.

Safety is always an issue and, for that reason, I must always be satisfied that the person to help fully understands how precarious any movement on my part is.

Falling is my biggest enemy and my biggest fear. On the other hand, I cannot and will not live a life dominated by fear. This is where faith comes in. It is the perfect antidote. This does not mean I won't ever fall. It means I will find the answer to accommodate whatever happens.

Is this "pie in the sky"? I don't think so. My track record so far shows that faith has been the one constant, and I'll stick with that.

Determination Versus Disability

WRITTEN MARCH 1, 2019

IT IS TRUE THAT MY DISABILITY COMPLETELY SHAPED my parents' life. That is such a beautiful truth. What I hadn't considered was how my disability had, in large part, controlled my thinking patterns.

And I was reminded of this when I saw the fire door at the stairwell closed. My heart raced. If there were a fire, the only escape for the third floor "A" wing is the stairs to the basement.

Fear equals panic and panic demands me to flee. Guess what? I would have to be the last to flee. I would never get in the way of others who are able to quickly walk down the stairs.

I see my best option as going on my balcony and bellowing! Who thinks of this? My fear of fire is almost irrational. Yet, I cannot deny that I am usually aware of escape routes wherever I am.

Put me in a room without windows and you might as well kill me. When I am a part of a group jaunt, I need to know if I will encounter any steps. How many times have I heard, "Don't worry, there are just three or four steps"! In most instances, I might as well try to climb Pike's Peak!

Then there is a bathroom situation. I have trained myself, if traveling, to limit my liquid intake. Good thing. When we were driving the autobahn from Germany to Austria, a seventeen-hour trip, there were no bathroom stops for me. Suffice it to say, the whites of my eyes had turned yellow!

Or the time John's mother and I had to use a public bathroom. She was sure she could help me. What we missed was that the floor was wet, so when I tried to stand, I slid from the floor under the stall door. John had to come pick me up.

Oh, yes, we had to station someone at the door to alert others that a man was there! I have always had to think out of the box—just proving, I think, that necessity is the mother of invention.

John was to return home to Maryland from a Convention of Disability Life in Florida the following day. I was fine alone, or I was until I slipped and fell on the kitchen floor.

I called my neighbor, explained my situation, and she promptly came with one of her boys who got me up and back in my chair.

I hurt, but dismissed it as, "Well, you fell on a hard floor, dummy." I did not sleep well that night either. I just couldn't get comfortable.

So, when John arrived home the following afternoon, I suggested a visit to the doctor. The x-rays showed I had a cracked pelvis. Not a lot you can do for this but let nature take its course. It would be best if I could lie down as much as possible.

"Oh, me," I said, "we fly to Houston, Texas tomorrow for Mark's graduation from Rice University."

There was no way I would miss seeing him get his doctoral degree. I went carefully. I made sure my legs never dangled, pulling on the crack. The doctor offered pain meds which I, typically, refused. All's well that ends well!

John and I were on the White House lawn when the A.D.A. bill was signed by the President. To the disabled community, it was a momentous occasion.

Unfortunately, there are still great holes in its application—the Sheldon Art Museum is one here in Lincoln—and it would be so easy to remedy.

Not all places can be made accessible, and I can accept that. But what many have done is take detailed pictures of each room and place them in a book for all who are interested. That attempt is much appreciated.

I have missed much in life, but I have done much. Far more than I expected. And I think God gave me an extra dose of determination.

My Birthday Bash

WRITTEN JULY 19, 2019

I HAVE CELEBRATED MOST OF THE MONTH OF JULY. Age has privileges, you know!

Paul, John's brother, and his wife, Doris, called early June to ask if they could come for the 4th of July. They love Lincoln's fireworks display and have visited here at that time for the last five years.

We have the tradition of a cookout at Mark's, then return to The Landing to see six or seven fireworks displays from my balcony, which continues to midnight.

Like the City of Lincoln, we started the party on the 3rd by watching the city's display from the Nebraska Club while having a champagne dinner. Mark brought a three layer chocolate cake with the appropriate candles.

Not only did my guests sing Happy Birthday, but most of the other patrons sang also. I was sure I had died and gone to heaven.

Then on my actual birthday, Mark had gotten tickets to the Meadow Lark concert at Prairie Pines Park. They had a Mediterranean buffet prior to the show, which was outstanding.

Mark played piano for Metropolitan Opera star Kitt Foss. She was wonderful and courageous! Before she sang, she had fainted but refused to cancel her performance.

Oh, yes, Mark had arranged for a group of my friends to carpool to Meadow Lark. And, my oh my, didn't the performers come back on stage and sing Happy Birthday to me. By this time, I'm flying high as a kite. It was all so wonderful.

What I didn't know was that there was still more. When I opened the door to my apartment, here was an accordion player and her three girls to sing Happy Birthday one last time.

This happy birthday time I'll treasure always. It was such fun, maybe I'll have another 80th birthday next year! I am so grateful for these years. When I think of what this old body has endured, I am amazed. In polio years, I am ten years older than my chronological age.

I have survived a virus that many did not. I was paralyzed from my neck to my toes, from my bladder to my lungs. I endured two major surgeries in hopes of getting rid of a leg brace, but it was not to be. I have had therapy from stem to stern.

Yet, with it all, I have been blessed. It has been a good life. And I am reminded how I started my writing with the phrase "INTO EACH LIFE SOME RAIN MUST FALL"!!!

Regrets & Dancing

WRITTEN JUNE 2, 2016

I HAVE REGRETS, QUITE A FEW, BUT SOMEHOW I had to play the cards that were dealt me. I regret not following my dream of attending Clark University in Worchester, Massachusetts, for a Master's Degree in social work. Many papers of Anna Freud's are archived there that I would have loved to see and read.

Instead, I married and worked to send John to school for his Master's Degree.

I loved working with people, hated paper pushing; so, I was glad to get the chance to work with people at the Maryland State Employment office. I saw a very diverse population from day laborers to secretaries from the offices of Congress.

One of my clients was a Union carpenter who could not be offered any job because he was Union. He asked me if I had a second pair of crutches, and I said I did. He said he would return the following day to pick up my current crutches and refinish them. If crutches can be beautiful, the pair he returned were. People constantly surprise me with their goodness.

There also was the client who completely surprised me. He gave me his resumé and I checked it over, then asked why was there a gap in his employment. He hung his head and mumbled, "I was in the hoose gaue." I was completely lost. "You were where?" He repeated his answer. So, I asked again. This time he spoke my language. "Ma'am, I was in jail." Next question, "Why were you in jail?" By this time, he must have thought I was the police because he simply said, "Joy riding in a stolen car."

It was obvious I didn't have a lot to work with, but when he said he had done some painting, I sent him out on a painter's helper's job. I don't think he worked too long, but I never saw him again. I had just gotten a nice promotion in the State system, when I realized I was pregnant, and that was that!

Regrets? My biggest regret is not being able to dance. Teen years were the most difficult. Teenagers are active—they dance, swim, bowl, golf—the list goes on. I had wanted to dance since I was five years old. I remember moving the rug from the floor between the dining and living rooms and practicing on the hardwood floor. I can still remember various pieces of music. Certain music makes my heart swell and I am in another world!

Not dancing was the reason for my one and only melt down. I was about eight, and my parents and I went to a dance recital of my little cousin. I was supposed to be up on that stage, I could do it so easily; every fiber of my being yearned to move with the music. On the drive home, I said not a word.

The next day I tried to put my feelings on paper—it was so painful. At some point, I hoisted myself to a standing position and felt the reality of those steel braces and threw myself to the floor. I wouldn't let anyone touch me. I could have seriously hurt myself, but I was past caring. Mother flew in the room, puzzled by my fall—until she read my note. She called my father and he came and sat on the floor with me, reasoning with me. And then he said, "Look at your mother, how upset she is. I know you don't want to hurt her."

Not the best psychology; however, he knew Mother's welfare would change my mind. It is only all these years later that I realize that the child needed validation of her pain. At that time, I doubt there was anyone who could have helped me face my grim reality in a manageable way.

Years later, John suggested I try wheelchair dancing, but I found it too garish for words.

But I will dance someday when I am called home. I'll be wearing six-inch heels and waltzing into heaven to Khachaturian's *Masquerade Suite*. No doubt about it!

My Philosophy of Old Age

WRITTEN FEBRUARY 1, 2019

No one ever told me it would be quite like this. It seems to me one diminishes in one way or another daily. At times it is comical, at others it is maddening, until you scarcely recognize yourself. I look into the mirror (that's my first mistake!) and ask myself: "Who is that old woman?" I have the double whammy of post polio syndrome!

It is in the last month or so I have lost major strength in my hands. I have trouble writing because I can't always control my hands. To pick up a small item becomes a major adventure. To unscrew a bottle top is a major event.

I am seriously thinking of getting a tool kit to carry with me. It would contain pliers, needle nose pliers, can opener and a small hammer!

Probably that would not have been so good last night when I couldn't open the pocket for the rinse agent in the dishwasher. Well, you know what would have happened. With any luck at all, I would have smashed the whole target area. Try explaining that to a repairman!

My tummy muscles are missing enabling me to slide right out of my chair. Add to that heavy winter clothing and I can scarcely move.

Please don't ask me to find anything in my pocketbook; or, if you do, be prepared for strange items tossed in the air and please have patience for this long endeavor.

The month of January always finds me reviewing old papers, looking at calendars and seeing what I have done or what I have attended in the past year. The trouble is, I had ten or twelve years of calendars, stuffed to the gills with invitations, programs from church and theatre plus any other paper that I just couldn't part with.

Why is this so important to me? It sort of defines who I am. I don't think that I'm a hoarder, but I think it's time to let it go. Yet, I feel bereft and, yes, diminished. It was hard to let that huge black trash bag be discarded. It is all so unsettling.

Then there is the mind. My brain seems to operate like a sieve. Put information in and, in all likelihood, it is lost. I try to write reminders to myself, but they get lost! And I lose things daily. I mumble a lot: "You would lose your head if it were not attached"!

And worst of all, I panic, and that helps no one. Pure Mary Ann—I've done something wrong or shameful. Why can't that diminish?

Somehow, I believe that essence of me is still alive and that it will be there in the days to come. Hope is eternal!

A Letter to God

WRITTEN OCTOBER 15, 2020

Dear God:

When my phone rang last week, with the great news that the writing group could resume meeting, I immediately went airborne, metaphorically speaking, of course. Yet, I'm pretty sure my scooter tires lifted from the floor.

Joyous does not adequately describe what I felt. Sharing our life experiences leads to compassion, understanding and appreciation of lives lived—"when you walk in someone else's shoes, you realize the inner connectivity of all humanity."

So, how has life been as we live under the shadow of the pandemic?

Isolation comes closest to describing life during this time. Isolation is foreign to most of the United States population. Today's society is all about togetherness.

Because of my disability, I have spent a good amount of time by myself. So, I found myself reading over twenty books. I'm not normally a phone person, but I received many calls from people I hadn't talked with in thirty years! It was fun to catch up.

I polished silver and brass, cleaned cabinets, and was even able to discard a fair amount of things. Yes, I qualify being a pack rat!

And, amazingly, I took the time to see the beauty in God's world. The little chickadee who came to feed, but due to some unknown injury her little wings never stopped fluttering. She sat just inches from the seed tray.

Wonder of wonders, another chickadee brought seeds and fed her. Who says that we humans have cornered the market on compassion?

It was an awesome sight to see the hawks perch on the balcony rail, heads turning 180 degrees in search of his prey. The red tailed hawk has a four foot wing span. And when he opened his wings to fly away, he was magnificent!

The second hawk, I can't identify. He was somewhat smaller than the red tailed hawk and maybe was younger, as their tail feathers don't turn red until they are two years old.

It doesn't seem so long ago that the earth slowly awoke from its winter sleep, and trees became a lush green and were often spotted with white and pink accents.

The splashes of color were like those a painter would have haphazardly used to clean his brush. From my balcony, it looked like a fairy land.

Now, we see the last hurrah of fall, the leaves turning vibrant colors and painting the landscape with beauty. It seems to me that there is a promise here—that after a rest, spring will come.

So, I have missed this group tremendously. Yet, I have seen such beauty in all creation. Look for it. It's all around us.

Thank you, God.

A Life of Accommodations

WRITTEN NOVEMBER 12, 2020

I DON'T THINK IT COULD EVER BE SAID that I am a very patient person. I want action now. And, yet, my life has been such that patience many times was a matter of survival.

Curiosity drove that little four-year-old to run away constantly. My mother, never at a loss for managing any situation, tied me to the clothesline with a long rope. After exploring that limited territory, I proceeded to twirl myself on the rope until I was completely bound.

Mother, checking on me, saw what I had accomplished, ran out and released me. Her greatest fear was that I would walk a short distance to the river and drown, but choking myself by hanging was a close second!

Polio changed everything. For most of a year, I was in a hospital bed, scared, not understanding what was happening. I learned to accept whatever came my way. If they moved my bed, they moved my bed. You ate whatever was put before you and, if you didn't, you were chastised loudly so everyone (other children) saw how bad you were. So at that point I became passive. It was all I could do as a child.

When physical therapy began, I just tried to do what they said. Looking back, it was like I lived in a bubble. You did everything they asked as best as you could. There was no thinking about today or all of the tomorrows. I call it accommodation at an elementary level.

Fifteen months later, I was released from the hospital. I had forgotten my home, my village, and people. It was like my mental slate had been wiped clean as well as my physical strength.

In the hospital, I had lived in a world of wheelchairs, crutches, and braces. It was my new normal. But when transplanted once again in the real world, I was different—odd man out.

Other children were somewhat frightened of me. Again, accommodation was necessary. Instinctively, I knew I had to find a way to relate. Board games became one of my connecting options. Kids loved games and the refreshments Mother always provided.

Still in a wheelchair when I returned to public school, I felt so out of place. I had forgotten my first grade classmates, and they had forgotten me. And, confronted with this girl in a wheelchair with odd looking leg braces, they didn't know what to think.

Even at play, it was difficult because there always came a time when kids wanted to play tag, run, jump rope, swing, and just be active. So, I made myself judge, scorekeeper, referee. Again, accommodation.

It only got worse as I entered my teens. The rules of the day were drastically different. Appearances became uppermost in teen minds. By this time, I was using crutches rather than a wheelchair. That helped my psyche, but the physical impact of walking two miles a day was grueling.

Dancing and sports were the paramount, extra curricular activities of teens, neither of which worked for me. This time was the most difficult of my life. There was no way I could measure up to any other girl in school. I was always invited to parties and had girlfriends. But I wasn't able to be a part of their world. Acceptance is the only way to face those ongoing challenges.

College life was somewhat easier. I think the key there was maturation. I pretty much knew who I was. I was fully aware of all the pluses and negatives. It was only at dances that I had to face my demons. Dear Lord, how I wanted to be on that dance floor! How difficult it was to insist that my date ask somebody else to dance. Particularly John! This dear man wanted me to stand on the top of his shoes and dance. It would have been too much of a spectacle, and I don't think I was physically able. But the offer was a beautiful gift!

Marriage was a piece of cake. I worked while John got his Masters degree. John did the cooking and I did the cleaning. Then Mark was born, blessing us all over once again.

At this point, my limitations once again reared their ugly heads. We cut the legs of the changing table to accommodate me in my chair. We did the same for the crib. I carried him in front of me, one arm holding him in place, the other arm propelling the wheels of my "old Franklin."

At an early age, I started teaching him that he must come when I called. Naturally, Mark felt the need to challenge that at some point. One day he grabbed something he wasn't supposed to have and ran behind the living room sofa. I could see those little wheels in his brain turning: "She can't reach me here."

Wrong! Oh, so wrong! I got the yard stick and tapped that little leg, all the while saying, "Ole Buddy, there will be a day you are smarter than I, but it's not today!"

This is all to say life presents us with many blessings and many challenges. It is how we deal with them that can make all the difference in the world. I would like to think, at my life's end, I would hear the words of a Cockney man shouting to Queen Victoria at her Jubilee Celebration:

"You dun it well ole girl, you dun it well."

Made in the USA
Middletown, DE
12 October 2022